STASILAND

Also by Anna Funder

All That I Am: A Novel

PRAISE FOR
ANNA FUNDER AND *STASILAND*

"The Stasi were the secret police of the former East Germany, infamous for their obsession with detail and for being, literally, everywhere. Some believe their network of collaborators and informants numbered one in every six people. Anna Funder went back to East Germany seven years after the fall of the Berlin Wall to interview those whose lives had been affected by the Stasi. Her portraits are by turns funny, heartbreaking, and stirring. She tells the story of the collapse of a way of life with wit, style, and sympathy."　　　　　　　*—Marie Claire*

"Impressive. . . . Funder's fully humanized portrait of the Stasi's tentacles reads like a warning of totalitarian futures to come."
　　　　　　　—Kirkus Reviews

"As well as the horror, Funder writes superbly of the absurdities of the Stasi, such as their practice of keeping the underpants or knickers of tens of thousands of GDR citizens in carefully labeled jars."　　　　　　　*—Evening Standard* (London)

"Written with rare literary flair. I can think of no better introduction to the brutal reality of East German repression."
　　　　　　　—The Telegraph (London)

"A highly readable and stylishly written account of the Stasi's forty-year reign of terror."
                                                                    —*Irish Times*

"To call the stories that she relates Orwellian is rather an understatement; the fact that they are true alone goes beyond Orwell: the mysterious death of a husband while in detention, the sudden 'nonexistence' of a rock star, a mother's separation from her critically ill infant. What the reader learns from these stories is that evil swings like a pendulum, from the banal to the surreal, but no matter where it is in the spectrum, it always leaves pain behind."
                                                                    —*Booklist*

"Funder moves through the former East Germany with a gimlet eye and a journalist's ear for the poignant, the perverse, and the absurd. . . . In clean striking prose she shifts with graceful ease from the telling blushes and tics, habits and souvenirs of her subjects to the concrete evidence of official documents to reveal the persistent effects of vast events."
                                                                    —*HQ*

About the Author

ANNA FUNDER was born in Melbourne, Australia, in 1966, and grew up there and in Paris. She has worked as an international lawyer and a radio and television producer. She is the author of *Stasiland*, winner of the prestigious Samuel Johnson Prize for Nonfiction in the United Kingdom (the world's biggest prize for nonfiction), the Index Freedom of Expression Award, and the W. H. Heinemann Award from the Royal Society of Literature. The book was also short-listed for the Guardian First Book Award. Anna Funder's debut novel, *All That I Am*, will be published in hardcover in February 2012 by HarperCollins. She lives in Brooklyn.

STASILAND

STORIES FROM BEHIND
THE BERLIN WALL

ANNA FUNDER

HARPER PERENNIAL

NEW YORK • LONDON • TORONTO • SYDNEY • NEW DELHI • AUCKLAND

HARPER ● PERENNIAL

A hardcover edition of this book was published in Australia by Text Publishing and in the United Kingdom by Granta Books, both in 2003.

HarperCollins books may be purchased for educational, business, or sales promotional use. For information please write: Special Markets Department, HarperCollins Publishers, 195 Broadway, New York, NY 10007.

FIRST U.S. EDITION

Library of Congress Cataloging-in-Publication Data is available upon request.

ISBN 978-0-06-207732-5

24 25 26 27 28 LBC 20 19 18 17 16

For Craig Allchin

CONTENTS

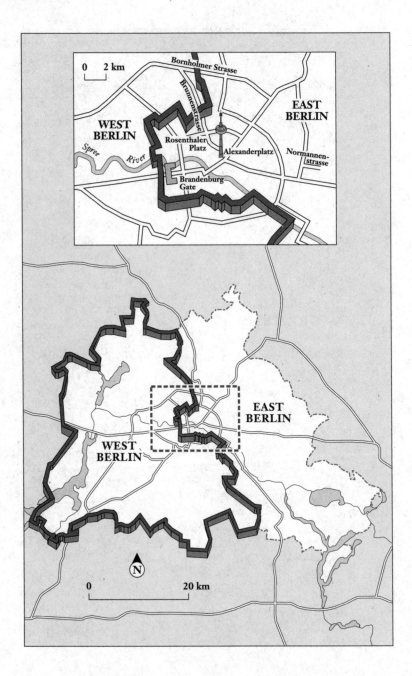

'…a silent crazy jungle under glass.'
The Member of the Wedding,
Carson McCullers

'The two of you, violator and victim (collaborator! violin!), are linked,
forever perhaps, by the obscenity of what has been revealed to you, by
the sad knowledge of what people are capable of. We are all guilty.'
The True Confessions of an Albino Terrorist,
Breyten Breytenbach

'Let the jury consider their verdict,' the King said,
for about the twentieth time that day.
'No, no!' said the Queen. 'Sentence first—verdict afterwards.'
Alice's Adventures in Wonderland,
Lewis Carroll

1

Berlin, Winter 1996

I am hungover and steer myself like a car through the crowds at Alexanderplatz station. Several times I miscalculate my width, scraping into a bin, and an advertising bollard. Tomorrow bruises will develop on my skin, like a picture from a negative.

A man turns from the wall, smiling and zipping up his fly. He is missing shoelaces and some teeth; his face and his shoes are as loose as each other. Another man in overalls, with a broom the size of a tennis-court sweeper, pushes disinfectant pellets along the platform. He makes arcs of green powder and cigarette butts and urine. A morning drunk walks on the ground like it might not hold him.

I'm catching the underground to Ostbahnhof to board the regional line down to Leipzig, a couple of hours from here. I sit on a green bench. I look at green tiles, breathe green air. Suddenly I don't feel too good. I need to get to the surface quickly and make my way back up the stairs. At ground level Alexanderplatz is a monstrous expanse of grey concrete designed to make people feel small. It works.

It's snowing outside. I move through the slush to where I know there are toilets. Like the train lines, these too are cut into the ground, but no-one thought to connect them to the station they serve. As I go down the steps, the sick smell of antiseptic is overpowering.

A large woman in a purple apron and loud makeup stands at the bottom. She is leaning on a glass-paned counter guarding her stash of condoms and tissues and tampons. This is clearly a woman unafraid of the detritus of life. She has shiny smooth skin and many soft chins. She must be sixty-five.

'Good morning,' I say. I feel awkward. I've heard stories of German babies having their input in food and their output in faeces weighed, in some attempt to get the measure of life. I have always found this kind of motherly audience inappropriate. I use the toilet and come out and put a coin in her dish. It occurs to me that the purpose of disinfectant globules is to mask the smells of human bodies with something worse.

'What's it like up there?' the toilet madam asks, nodding to the top of the steps.

'Pretty cold.' I adjust my little pack. 'But not too bad, not too much black ice.'

'This is nothing yet,' she sniffs.

I don't know if it's a threat or a boast. This is what they call *Berliner Schnauze*—snout. It's attitude: it's in your face. I don't want to stay here, but I don't want to go up into the cold either. The disinfectant smell is so strong I can't tell whether I am feeling sicker or better.

'I've been here twenty-one years, since the winter of '75. I've seen much worse than this.'

'That's a long time.'

'Sure is. I have my regulars, I can tell you. They know me, I know them. I had a prince once, a von Hohenzollern.'

I think she must use the prince on everyone. But it works—I'm curious. 'U-huh. Before or after the Wall came down?'

'Before. He was over on a day trip from the west. I used to get quite a few westerners you know. He invited me'—she pats her large bosom with a flat hand—'to his palace. But of course I couldn't go.'

Of course she couldn't go: the Berlin Wall ran a couple of kilometres from here and there was no getting over it. Along with the Great Wall of China, it was one of the longest structures ever built to keep people separate from one another. She is losing credibility fast, but her story is becoming correspondingly better. And, suddenly, I can't smell a thing any more. 'Have you travelled yourself since the Wall came down?' I ask. She throws her head back. I see she is wearing purple eyeliner which, at that angle, phosphoresces.

'Not yet. But I'd like to. Bali, something like that. Or China. Yes, China.' She raps her painted nails on the glass cabinet and dreams into the middle distance over my left shoulder. 'You know what I'd really like to do? I'd really like to have me a look at that Wall of theirs.'

From Ostbahnhof the train pulls out and finds its cruising speed. The rhythm soothes like a cradle, hushes my tapping fingers. The conductor's voice comes through speakers reciting our stops: Wannsee, Bitterfeld, Lutherstadt Wittenberg. In northern Germany I inhabit the grey end of the spectrum: grey buildings, grey earth, grey birds, grey trees. Outside, the city and then the country spool past in black and white.

Last night is a smoky blur—another session at the pub with Klaus and his friends. But this is not one of those hangovers where you write the day off to darkness. It is the more interesting kind, where destroyed synapses are reconstructing themselves, sometimes missing their old paths and making odd, new connections. I remember things I haven't remembered before—things that do not come out of the ordered store of memories I call my past. I remember my mother's moustache in the sun, I remember the acute hunger-and-loss feeling of adolescence, I remember the burnt-chalk smell of tram brakes in summer. You think you have your past filed away under subject headings but, somewhere, it waits to reconnect itself.

I remember learning German—so beautiful, so strange—at school in Australia on the other side of the earth. My family was nonplussed about me learning such an odd, ugly language and, though of course too sophisticated to say it, the language of the enemy. But I liked the sticklebrick nature of it, building long supple words by putting short ones together. Things could be brought into being that had no name in English— *Weltanschauung*, *Schadenfreude*, *sippenhaft*, *Sonderweg*, *Scheissfreundlichkeit*, *Vergangenheitsbewältigung*. I liked the sweeping range of words from 'heartfelt' to 'heartsick'. And I liked the order, the directness that I imagined in the people. Then, in the 1980s, I came to live in West Berlin for a while and I wondered long and hard what went on behind that Wall.

A barrel-stomached woman opposite me unwraps black bread sandwiches. So far she has managed to pretend I am not here, although if we weren't careful our knees could touch. She has painted on her eyebrows in arches of surprise, or menace.

I think about the feeling I've developed for the former German Democratic Republic. It is a country which no longer exists, but here I am on a train hurtling through it—its tumbledown houses and bewildered people. This feeling needs a sticklebrick word: I can only describe it as horror-romance. It's a dumb feeling, but I don't want to shake it. The romance comes from the dream of a better world the German Communists wanted to build out of the ashes of their Nazi past: from each according to his abilities, to each according to his needs. The horror comes from what they did in its name. East Germany has disappeared, but its remains are still at the site.

My travelling companion takes out a packet of West cigarettes, which seem to be the most popular brand here since the fall of the Wall. She lights up and directs her breath of smoke over my head. When she's finished she butts out in the flip-top bin, clasps her hands around her middle and falls asleep. Her expression, fixed with pencil, doesn't change.

I first visited in Leipzig in 1994, nearly five years after the Wall fell in November 1989. East Germany still felt like a secret walled-in garden, a place lost in time. It wouldn't have surprised me if things had tasted different here—apples like pears, say, or wine like blood. Leipzig was the hub of what everyone now calls *die Wende*—the Turning Point. The *Wende* was the peaceful revolution against the Communist dictatorship in East Germany, the only successful revolution in German history. Leipzig was the start and the heart of it. Now, two years later, I'm on my way back.

In 1994 I found a town built by accretion. The streets wound crookedly, there were crumbly passages through buildings that led unexpectedly into the next block, and low arches funnelled people into underground bars. My map bore no resemblance to how life was lived in Leipzig. People in the know could take hidden short cuts through buildings, or walk along unmarked lanes between each block, moving above and below ground. I got thoroughly lost. I was looking for the Stasi museum in the Runden Ecke, or 'round corner' building which had formerly been the Stasi offices. I needed to see for myself part of the vast apparatus that had been the East German Ministry for State Security.

The Stasi was the internal army by which the government kept control. Its job was to know everything about everyone, using any means it chose. It knew who your visitors were, it knew whom you telephoned, and it knew if your wife slept around. It was a bureaucracy metastasised through East German society: overt or covert, there was someone reporting to the Stasi on their fellows and friends in every school, every factory, every apartment block, every pub. Obsessed with detail, the Stasi entirely failed to predict the end of Communism, and with it the end of the country. Between 1989 and 1990 it was turned inside out: Stalinist spy unit one day, museum the next. In its forty years, 'the Firm' generated the equivalent of all records in German history since the middle ages. Laid out upright and end to end, the files the Stasi kept on their countrymen and women would form a line 180 kilometres long.

Eventually, I found the Runden Ecke, and it was huge. A set of steps led up to vast metal-clad double doors with studs on them. I shrank like Alice. To the right there was a pale rectangle in the cement facade, a bit of the building that hadn't been tanned by smog. A plaque saying 'Ministry of State Security—Leipzig Division' or something like it had hung there. It had been removed in a kind of fearful joy during the revolution and has not been seen since.

I walked around inside. All the desks were just as they were left the night the demonstrators took the building—frighteningly neat. Dial phones sat in breeding pairs. Shredding machines had been thrown out the back after collapsing in the Stasi's final desperate attempt to destroy the most damning files. Above one desk was a 1989 calendar with a picture of a woman naked from the waist up, but mostly there were just Communist insignia on the walls. The cells were open, set up as if prepared for more prisoners. Despite the best efforts of Miss December, the building felt damp and bureaucratic.

The citizens' committee administering the museum had mounted displays on cheap particleboard screens. There was a print of the famous photograph from the autumn 1989 demonstrations. It showed a sea of people holding candles, their necks craned up to the building, staring their controllers in the face. They knew it was from here that their lives were observed, manipulated and sometimes ruined. There were copies of the increasingly frantic telexes from the Berlin headquarters of the Stasi to here, where the officers had barricaded themselves in with tin on the windows. 'Secure all Ministry Premises', they read, and 'Protect all Covert Objects'.

My favourites were the pictures of protesters occupying the building on 4 December 1989, squatting in the corridors with the surprise still on their faces, as if half-expecting to be asked to leave. As they entered the building, the Stasi guards had asked to see the demonstrators' identity cards, in a strange parody of the control they were, at that very moment, losing. The demonstrators, in shock, obediently pulled their cards from their wallets. Then they seized the building.

Large and small mysteries were accounted for when the files were opened. Not least, perhaps, the tics of the ordinary man in the street. This document was on display:

SIGNALS FOR OBSERVATION

1. Watch Out! Subject is coming
   —touch nose with hand or handkerchief

2. Subject is moving on, going further, or overtaking
   —stroke hair with hand, or raise hat briefly

3. Subject standing still
   —lay one hand against back, or on the stomach

4. Observing Agent wishes to be terminate observation because cover threatened
   —bend and retie shoelaces

5. Subject returning
   —both hands against back or on stomach

6. Observing Agent wishes to speak with Team Leader or other Observing Agents
   —take out briefcase or equivalent and examine contents.

I pictured the street ballet of the deaf and dumb: agents signalling to each other from corner to corner: stroking noses, tummies, backs and hair, tying and untying shoelaces, lifting their hats to strangers and riffling through papers—a choreography for very nasty scouts.

Towards the back of the building, three rooms housed Stasi artefacts in glass cases. There was a box of fake wigs and moustaches alongside small tubes of glue to affix them. There were women's vinyl handbags with built-in microphones disguised as flower petals in a studded decoration. There were bugs that had been implanted in apartment walls and a pile of mail that never reached the west. One of the envelopes had a child's handwriting on it in coloured pencil—a different colour for each letter of the address.

One glass case contained nothing but empty jars. I was staring at it when a woman approached me. She looked like a female version of Luther, except she was beautiful. She was fiftyish, with high cheekbones, and a direct gaze. She looked friendly, but she also looked as if she knew I had been making mental ridicule of a regime which required its members to sign pledges of allegiance that looked like marriage certificates, confiscated children's birthday cards to their grandparents and typed up inane protocols at desks beneath calendars of large-breasted women. This was Frau Hollitzer, who runs the museum.

Frau Hollitzer explained to me that the jars in front of us were 'smell samples'. The Stasi had developed a quasi-scientific method, 'smell sampling', as a way to find criminals. The theory was that we all have our own identifying odour, which we leave on everything we touch. These smells can be captured and, with the help of trained sniffer dogs, compared to find a match. The Stasi would take its dogs and jars to a location where they suspected an illegal meeting had occurred, and see if the dogs could pick up the scents of the people whose essences were captured in the jars.

Mostly, smell samples were collected surreptitiously. The Stasi might break into someone's apartment and take a piece of clothing worn close to the skin, often underwear. Alternatively, a 'suspect' would be brought in under some pretext for questioning, and the vinyl seat he or she had sat on would be wiped afterward with a cloth. The pieces of stolen clothing, or the cloth, would then be placed in a sealed jar. The containers looked like jam bottling jars. A label read: 'Name: Herr [Name]. Time: 1 Hour. Object: Worker's Underpants.'

When the citizens of Leipzig entered this building, they found a large collection of smell samples. Then the jars disappeared. It was not until June 1990 that they turned up—in the 'smell pantry' of the Leipzig police. But they were empty. Apparently, the Leipzig police had taken them for their own use, even in the period after the fall of the Wall when democracy was beginning here. The jars still bore all their meticulous labels. From these it was clear that the Leipzig Stasi had collected smell samples of the entire political opposition in this part of Saxony. No-one knows who has these scraps of material and old socks now, nor what they might be keeping them for.

Later, Frau Hollitzer told me about Miriam, a young woman whose husband had died in a Stasi remand cell nearby. It was rumoured the Stasi orchestrated the funeral, to the point of substituting an empty coffin for a full one, and cremating the body to destroy any evidence of the cause of death. I imagined paid-off pallbearers pretending to struggle under the weight of an empty coffin, or perhaps genuinely struggling beneath a coffin filled with eighty kilos of old newspapers and stones. I imagined not knowing whether your husband hanged himself, or whether someone you now pass in the street killed him. I thought I would like to speak with Miriam, before my imaginings set like false memories.

I went home to Australia, but now I am back in Berlin. I could not get Miriam's story, the strange second-hand tale of a woman I had never met, out of my mind. I found a part-time job in television, and set about looking for some of the stories from this land gone wrong.

2

Miriam

I work at the overseas television service in what was West Berlin. The service was set up by the government after the war to beam benign Germanness around the globe. My job is to answer letters from viewers who've been beamed at and have some queries.

At Viewer Post I am a cross between an agony aunt, a free research assistant and a receptacle for messages in bottles. 'Dear Viewer Post, I am looking for the address of the clinic of Dr Manfred von Ardenne to try his new ultra-high temperature cancer treatment for advanced stages as featured in your program…'; 'Dear Viewer Post, Many thanks for your interesting program on asylum seekers in your country. I am sixteen years old and living in Akra. Could you please send me informations on asylum…' The occasional neo-Nazi from Missouri or Liverpool writes wanting information on 'mother groups' in East Germany. A man from Birmingham, Alabama sent me a photograph of himself in uniform at the liberation of Bergen Belsen concentration camp in 1945 standing behind corpses. He wrote, 'Thank you for your program on the fiftieth anniversary of the peace. I would like you to know that I recall with great fondness the welcome we Americans received from the ordinary German people. In the villages they had nothing, but when we came they shared it with us like family…' I write contained and appropriate responses. Sometimes, I wonder what it would be like to be German.

Alexander Scheller is my boss. He's a tall man just on forty who has a picture of a tight-faced blonde wife, a glass ashtray and a permanent cup of coffee on his vast and otherwise empty desk. He taps incessantly, fidgety with caffeine and nicotine. To his credit, he does me the honour of behaving as if my work answering viewer correspondence is as important as that of the journalists and professional people here. A month ago I sat on the other side of that desk because he had made time for a meeting I called myself.

Scheller's off-sider Uwe Schmidt was there too. Uwe's main job as adjutant is to make Scheller seem important enough to have an adjutant. The other part of his job is to appear busy and time-short, which is more difficult because he has hardly anything to do. Scheller and Uwe are both westerners.

Uwe has a similar amount of TV-journo energy to Scheller, only Uwe's is sexual not chemical. Uwe's girlfriends are always leaving him and he is, therefore, at most times of day and in almost any company, deeply distracted by desire.

I like Uwe and feel sorry for him because I know that in looking for the reason why his girlfriends leave him he has started to wear himself out from the inside. I recently saw him singing 'You're once, twice, three times a layayadeee' in English in his car at the lights with tears on his face. Now, over the other side of the desk, he caught himself looking at me like food, and I knew he hadn't heard what I was saying.

'Pardon?' he said.

I decided to start from the beginning. 'We've had a letter from a German living in Argentina in response to the item on the puzzle women.'

'Puzzle women? Puzzle women?' Uwe said, trying to remember the story.

'They sit in Nuremberg puzzling together the shredded files the Stasi couldn't burn or pulp.'

'Right. I'm with you,' Scheller said. He was tapping the eraser end of a pencil on the desk.

'This man says he left Dresden after the war. He asks whether we might do an item on what things are actually like now for the East German people instead, as he says, of "always broadcasting what is being done for the poor cousins".'

'Puzzle women,' Uwe muttered.

I took a deep breath. 'And I agree with him—we're always talking about the things that Germany is doing *for* people in the former GDR. It would be great to do an item from the eastern point of view. For instance, to find out what it's like to wait for part of your file to be pieced together.'

'You know we don't broadcast domestically,' Scheller said, 'so there's no point us doing items on the Ossis for their gratification.'

I looked to Uwe, off to one side with his feet up on Scheller's acreage of desk. He was rolling a fountain pen over his knuckles, lost in a reverie. Puzzling over women.

'I know, I know,' I said to Scheller. 'But East Germany—I just think we should show some of the stories from there. From here, I mean.'

'What sort of stories?' Scheller asked. Behind him the computer gave off a glockenspiel beep signalling new email.

'I don't know,' I said, because I really didn't know. 'There must be people who stood up to the regime somehow, or who were wrongfully imprisoned.' I felt myself warming up, a little dangerous. 'I mean, after World War II people searched high and low for the smallest signs of resistance to Hitler—as if a tiny piece of national pride could be salvaged and tied onto a couple of student pacifists and a bunch of old Prussian aristocrats. What about here? There must have been some resistance to the dictatorship?'

'They aren't a nation.' Scheller was tetchy now.

'I know, but it was a nation.'

'Look,' he said, 'they are just Germans who had Communism for forty years and went backwards, and all they want now is the money to have big TV sets and holidays in Majorca like everyone else. It was an experiment and it failed.'

'Well, what do you suggest I write to this guy?' I could hear my voice getting higher. 'Should I tell him that no-one here is interested in East Germans and their stories, because they don't form part of our overseas image?'

'For God's sake!' Scheller said. 'You won't find the great story of human courage you are looking for—it would have come out years ago, straight after 1989. They are just a bunch of downtrodden whingers, with a couple of mild-mannered civil rights activists among them, and only a couple at that. They just had the rotten luck to end up behind the Iron Curtain.' He tilted his head. 'What has gotten into you?'

Uwe put his feet down. 'Are you all right?'

Uwe walked back to my desk with me, solicitous as a doctor with a patient who's had bad news. That he did this made me realise I had gone over the top. He said, 'He's simply not interested.'

'No-one is interested in these people.'

'Look.' Uwe touched my forearm gently, turning me towards him like a dance partner. His eyes were green and slanted up, his teeth short and neat, little pearls. 'You're probably right. No-one here is interested— they were backward and they were broke, and the whole Stasi thing…' He trailed off. His breath was minty. 'It's sort of…embarrassing.'

I replied to the Argentinian thanking him for his suggestion but telling him that 'regrettably the station's remit is only for current affairs and news, and we are therefore unable to investigate more personal, "point-of-view" stories.'

A week ago he wrote back. He was angry, telling me that history is made of personal stories. He said that issues were being swept under the carpet in East Germany, and people along with them. It took twenty years after the war, he said, for the Nazi regime even to begin to be discussed in Germany, and that that process is repeating itself now. 'Will it be 2010 or 2020 before what happened there is remembered?' he wrote. And, 'Why are some things easier to remember the *more* time has passed since they occurred?'

The woman opposite me wakes up as the train pulls into Leipzig. Because there is something intimate about watching another person sleep, she now acknowledges my existence. '*Wiedersehen*,' she says as she leaves the compartment.

Miriam Weber stands at the end of the platform, a small still woman in the stream of alighting passengers. She holds a single rose in front of her body so I will know who she is. We shake hands, not looking too closely at first, talking about trains, trips, rain. It feels like a blind date, because we have described ourselves to each other. I know she has not told her story to a stranger before.

We drive through Leipzig. The city has been transformed into a building site, a work in progress with some new goal. Cranes are picking over holes open as wounds. People ignore them, weaving head-down along footpaths and alleyways. On one of the concrete towers a large Mercedes emblem rotates, waltzing to the new tune here.

Miriam's apartment is in the roof of her building. There are five flights of stairs, broad sweeping stairs with a graceful dark balustrade. I try not to puff too loudly. I try not to think about my damaged head. I try to remember when elevators were invented. When we reach it, the apartment is one big light space under the eaves, full of plants and lamps, with views over all of Leipzig. From here you could see anyone coming.

We sit in large cane chairs. Miriam, when I look at her straight, is a woman in her mid-forties with a cute short haircut, the bits on the crown sticking out like a cartoon boy, and small round glasses. She wears a long black sweater and pants, and curls her legs under her. She has a surprisingly big nicotine-stained voice. She is so slight that the voice comes from nowhere and everywhere at once: it is not immediately evident that it is hers; it fills the room, and it wraps us up.

'I became, officially, an Enemy of the State at sixteen. At six-*teen*.' Miriam looks at me through her glasses, and her eyes are wide and blue. In her voice is a combination of pride in how she became such a fiend, and disbelief that this country created enemies of its own children. 'You know, at sixteen you have this sort of itch.'

In 1968 the old University Church in Leipzig was demolished suddenly, without any public consultation. Two hundred and fifty kilometres away the Prague Spring was in full swing, and the Russians had not yet brought the tanks into the streets to crush the demonstrators for democracy. The demolition of the church in Leipzig provided a focus for the expression of a widespread malaise the Leipzigers had caught from their Czech cousins. Twenty-three years after the end of World War II, the next generation was asking questions about the way their parents had implemented Communist ideals.

The Leipzig demonstrations were interpreted by the East German regime as a sign of the times, a cinder likely to ignite. The police doused people with fire hoses and made many arrests. Miriam and her friend Ursula thought this was not right. 'At sixteen you have an idea of justice, and we just thought it was wrong. We weren't seriously against the state— we hadn't given it that much thought. We just thought it wasn't fair to rough people up and bring in horses and so on.'

The two of them decided to do something about it. At a stationer's they bought a child's stamp set with ink, small rubber letters and a rail to put them in.

'You could buy that sort of thing?' I ask. I know that roneo printers, typewriters and later photocopiers were strictly (if not particularly effectively) controlled by licence in the GDR.

'Not after what we did,' she smiles. 'The Stasi had them taken off the shelves.'

Miriam and Ursula made leaflets ('Consultation, not water cannon!' and 'People of the People's Republic speak up!') They stuck them up around town one night. The girls wore gloves so as not to leave fingerprints. 'We had read as many novels as the next person,' she says, laughing. Miriam had the posters tucked in her jacket; Ursula had a tub of paste and a brush hidden in a milk crate. They were clever—they slapped the leaflets up in telephone booths over the instructions and at tramstops over the timetables. 'We wanted to make sure people read them.' They made a circle around the town, and then they went straight through it.

The girls passed the Communist Party Regional Headquarters. Things were going well. 'We just looked at each other and we couldn't resist.' They marched in and told the guard on duty they were there to see Herr Schmidt, on the off-chance that someone by that name was in the building. They didn't stop to think what they would have done had a Herr Schmidt come out.

The guard made a call. He put the phone down. 'Uh no, Comrade Schmidt's not here at the moment.' The girls said they would come back the next day.

'On the way out there were these beautiful smooth columns…'

Miriam is convinced, however, that had they left it at that they would have gotten away with it, but on the home stretch they went one step too far. Passing a building where some of their classmates lived, they put leaflets in the letterboxes of two boys they knew. The next day, one of the parents rang the police.

'Why would you call the police about some junk mail?' I ask.

'Because they were silly, or maybe they were in the Party, who knows?'

'It seems so harmless,' I say.

Miriam comes back quiet but strong. 'At that time it was not harmless. It was the crime of sedition.'

In East Germany, information ran in a closed circuit between the government and its press outlets. As the government controlled the newspapers, magazines and television, training as a journalist was effectively training as a government spokesperson. Access to books was restricted. Censorship was a constant pressure on writers, and a given for readers, who learnt to read between the lines. The only mass medium the government couldn't control was the signal from western television stations, but it tried: until the early 1970s the Stasi used to monitor the angle of people's antennae hanging out of their apartments, punishing them if they were turned to the west. Later, they gave up: the benefits of soporific commercial programming apparently outweighed the dangers of news bulletins from the free world.

Sedition was handled by the secret police, not the ordinary *Volkspolizei*. The Stasi were methodical. They questioned all the classmates of the boys who had received the pamphlets. They talked to the principal, teachers, parents. Several days went by. Miriam and Ursula agreed on an arrest and incarceration plan: neither would admit anything. The Stasi arrived at a shortlist of suspects. Men with gloves and dogs combed Miriam's house.

'And we thought we had been so careful, thrown everything out and destroyed all the evidence.'

The Stasi found some of the little rubber letters in the carpet. Miriam's parents told the officers they did not know how such a thing could have happened in their house.

Both girls were placed in solitary confinement for a month. They had no visits from their parents or from lawyers, no books, no newspapers, not a phone call.

In the beginning they stuck to their plan. 'No sir, I don't know either how the leaflets got there, no, it couldn't possibly have been her.' 'But eventually,' Miriam says, 'they break you. Just like fiction. They used the old trick and told each of us that the other had admitted, so we might as well too. After no visits, no books, nothing, you think: well, she probably did say it.'

The girls were let out to await their trials. When she got home Miriam thought, there's no way they're going to put me back in that place. The next morning she got on a train for Berlin. It was New Year's Eve 1968, and Miriam Weber was going over the Wall.

Bornholmer Bridge

It takes less than two hours to get from Leipzig to Berlin but Miriam had never been there in her life. Alone in the big city, she bought herself a map at the station. 'I wanted to have a look at the border in a few places. I thought: this cannot be for real, somewhere or other you just must be able to get over that thing.'

At the Brandenburg Gate she was amazed that she could walk right up to the Wall. She couldn't believe the guards let her get that close. But it was too flat and too high to climb. Later she found out that the whole border paraphernalia only started behind the Wall at that spot. 'Even if I had been able to get up there, I could only have put my head over and waved "Hello" to the eastern guards.' She waves with both hands, and shrugs her shoulders.

By nightfall the chances were looking slim. 'I hadn't found any holes in it,' Miriam says. She was cold and unhappy. She sat in the suburban train on her way to Alexanderplatz station to catch the regional line home.

It was dark and she was going back to prison. The train sluiced between buildings, high up on its stilts. Buildings on both sides, flat concrete render facades with rectangular windows, five storeys high. Some lit, some dark, some with plants, some without. Then the vista changed. It took Miriam a moment to notice it in the dark, but suddenly she was going past high wire-mesh fencing.

'I thought: if I am travelling along here, and there's this big wire fence right next to me, then West Berlin would have to be just over there on the other side.' She got off the train, crossed the platform and caught another train back. It was as she had thought: a tall wire fence. She got off again and went back, this time getting out at Bornholmer Bridge station.

Later, I looked up the Bornholmer Bridge on a street map. I had heard of it, and thought it might have been one of the places East and West Germany used to exchange each other's spies. Now, I see nothing but this bridge each time I open a street map. It is like once you notice someone has a cast in his eye, that's all you can see in his face.

A western train line and an eastern train line met rarely in divided Germany. At Bornholmer Bridge the western train line still swoops down from the northwest to the southwest, and the eastern one up from the southeast to the northeast. The shapes they make on the map are like figures in profile doing a Maori nose-kiss.

At Bornholmer Bridge the border ran, in theory, along the space between the tracks. In other places in Berlin the border, and with it the Wall, cut a strange wound through the city. The Wall went through houses, along streets, along waterways, and sliced underground train lines to pieces. Here, instead of cutting the train line, the East Germans built most of the Wall's fortifications in front of the train line on the eastern side, letting the eastern trains run through to the furthest wall at the end of the death strip.

'I had a look at the lie of the land and decided: not too bad.' Miriam could see the border installation, the cacophony of wire and cement, asphalt and sand. In front of where it began was a hectare or so of fenced-in garden plots, each with its own little shed. These handkerchief gardens are a traditional German solution to apartment dwellers' yearning for a tool shed and a vegetable garden. They make a patchwork of green in odd corners of urban land, along train lines or canals or, as here, in the lee of the Wall.

Miriam climbed through and over the fences separating the gardens, trying to get closer to the Wall. 'It was dark and I was lucky—later I learned that they usually patrolled the gardens as well.' She got as far as she could go but not to the Wall, because there was this 'great fat hedge' growing in front of it. She rummaged around in someone's tool shed for a ladder, and found one. She put it against the hedge and climbed up. She took a good long look around.

The whole strip was lit by a row of huge street lamps on poles, their heads bent in submission at exactly the same angle. Overhead, fireworks had started to fizz and pop for the New Year. The Bornholmer Bridge was about a hundred and fifty metres away. Between her and the west there was a wire mesh fence, a patrol strip, a barbed-wire fence, a twenty-metre-wide asphalt street for the personnel carriers and a footpath. Then the eastern sentry huts stretched out about one hundred metres apart, and behind them more barbed wire. Miriam takes a piece of paper and draws me a mess of lines so I can see it too.

'Beyond all of that, I could see the wall I had seen from inside the train, the wall that runs along the train line. I assumed that there, behind it, was the west, and I was right. I could have been wrong, but I was right.' If she had any future it was over there, and she needed to get to it.

I sit in the chair exploring the meaning of dumbstruck, rolling the word around in my mind. I laugh with Miriam as she laughs at herself, and at the boldness of being sixteen. At sixteen you are invulnerable. I laugh with her about rummaging around for a ladder in other people's sheds, and I laugh harder when she finds one. We laugh at the improbability of it, of someone barely more than a child poking about in Beatrix Potter's garden by the Wall, watching out for Mr McGregor and his blunderbuss, and looking for a step-ladder to scale one of the most fortified borders on earth. We both like the girl she was, and I like the woman she has become.

She says suddenly, 'I still have the scars on my hands from climbing the barbed wire, but you can't see them so well now.' She holds out her hands. The soft parts of her palms are crazed with definite white scars, each about a centimetre long.

The first fence was wire mesh with a roll of barbed wire along the top. 'The strange thing is, you know how the barbed wire used to be looped in a sort of tube along the top of the fence? My pants were all ripped up and I got caught—stuck on the roll! I just hung there! I cannot believe no-one saw me.' A Pierrot doll hanging on display.

Miriam must have come unstuck, because next she got down on all fours and started her way across the path, across the wide street, and across the next strip. The whole area was lit as bright as day. 'I just got down on my knees and went for it. But I was careful. I was very slow.' After the footpath she crossed the wide asphalt road. She could not feel her body, she was invisible. She was nothing but nerve endings and fear.

Why didn't they come for her? What were they doing?

She reached the end of the asphalt and they still hadn't come. There was a cable suspended about a metre off the ground. She stopped. 'I had seen it from my ladder. I thought it might be some sort of alarm or something, so I went down flat on my belly underneath.' She crawled across the last stretch to a kink in the wall and crouched and looked and did not breathe. 'I stayed there. I was waiting to see what would happen. I just stared.' She thought her eyes would come loose from her skull. Where were they?

Something shifted, right near her. It was a dog. The huge german shepherd pointed himself in her direction. That cable was no alarm: it had dogs chained to it. She could not move. The dog did not move. She thought the guards' eyes would follow the pointing dog to her. She waited for him to bark. If she moved away, along the wall, he would go for her.

'I don't know why it didn't attack me. I don't know how dogs see, but maybe it had been trained to attack moving targets, people running across, and I'd gone on all fours. Maybe it thought I was another dog.' They held each other's gaze for what seemed a long time. Then a train went by, and, unusually, it was a steam train. The two of them were covered in a fine mist.

'Perhaps then he lost my scent?' Eventually, the dog walked away. Miriam waited another long time. 'I thought he would come back for me, but he didn't.' She climbed the last barbed-wire fence to reach the top of the wall bordering the train line. She could see the west—shiny cars and lit streets and the Springer Press building. She could even see the western guards sitting at their sentry posts. The wall was broad. She had about four metres to cross on top of it, and then a little railing to get under. That was all there was. She couldn't believe it. She wanted to run the last few steps, before they caught her.

'The railing was really only so high,' she says, putting an arm out to thigh height, 'all I had to do was get under it. I had been so very careful and so very slow. Now I thought: you have only four more steps, just RUN before they get you. But here'—she marks an X, over and over, on the map she has drawn me—'here, was a trip-wire.' The voice is very soft. She marks and re-marks the X till I think the paper will tear. 'I did not see the wire.'

Sirens went off, wailing. The western sentry huts shone searchlights to find her, and to prevent the easterners from shooting her. The eastern guards took her away quickly.

'You piece of shit,' a young one said. They took her to the Berlin Stasi HQ. They bandaged her hands and legs, and that was the first time she noticed her blood or felt any pain. The blood was on her face and in her hair.

'But they really hadn't seen me. No-one had even seen me.' She came so close.

In the west the neon shone and overhead fireworks destroyed themselves in the air.

Miriam was returned to Leipzig in the back of a paddy wagon. The Stasi officer questioning her told her they had contacted her parents, who no longer wanted anything to do with her.

'Did you believe him?'

'Hmm. Well, no. Not really, no.' It was very hard to be sure of anything, of anyone. Miriam pauses. It was an uncomfortable question. 'I think they probably demoted that dog, poor thing,' she says. 'Either that or shot him.'

Miriam was held in a cell in Dimitroffstrasse, which has been re-created in the nearby Stasi Museum. The cell is two metres by three, and at one end there is a tiny window of dull frosted glass recessed very high up. It has a bench with a mattress, a toilet and a sink. The door is thick, with metal bolts across it, and a spyhole for the guard to watch you. It is hung in a wall so deep I felt I was going into an airlock.

Again, Miriam was allowed no telephone calls, no lawyer, no contact with the outside world. She was sixteen and back in solitary. 'When they came to take me to interrogation,' she says, smiling, 'at least it was something to do. But that,' she pauses, 'that is when the whole miserable story really took off.' Back in Leipzig, the Stasi let her have it.

During the Korean War in the 1950s myths circulated of obscene torture methods practised on American POWs. After they were captured, the men would be taken to a camp, reappearing as little as a week later on a platform, mindlessly mouthing their conversion to Communism for the cameras. After the war it was revealed that, contrary to rumour, the Korean military's secret was neither traditional nor high-tech—it was sleep deprivation. A hungry man can still spit bile, but a zombie is remarkably pliable.

The interrogation of Miriam Weber, aged sixteen, took place every night for ten nights for the six hours between 10 pm and 4 am. Lights went out in the cell at 8 pm, and she slept for two hours before being taken to the interrogation room. She was returned to her cell two hours before the lights went on again at 6 am. She was not permitted to sleep during the day. A guard watched through the peephole, and banged on the door if she nodded off.

'Once in a while I'd look at the eye in the peephole as he was hitting the door and I'd think, "Why don't you just piss off for a change?" and keep dozing. Then he'd come in, shake me, and take the mattress off the bench so there'd be nothing left to sit on. They really made sure that I didn't sleep. I cannot explain how kaput it makes you.'

Afterwards, I looked it up. Sleep deprivation can mimic the symptoms of starvation, particularly in children—victims become disoriented and cold. They lose their sense of time, becoming locked in an interminable present. Sleep deprivation also causes a number of neurological dysfunctions, which become more extreme the longer it continues. In the end, your waking hours take on the logic of a dream, where odd things are connected, and you are just angry, angry, angry with the world that will not let you rest.

For the Stasi it was beyond comprehension that a sixteen-year-old with no tools, no training, and no help, could crawl across their 'Anti-Fascist Protective Measure' on her hands and knees. Involuntarily revealing his admiration, the guard who first took her to the interrogation room wanted to know what sports clubs she was in. She wasn't in any.

But the main point of the questioning, night after night, was to extract the name of the underground escape organisation that had helped her. They wanted the names of members, physical descriptions. Whose scheme was it to go on New Year's Eve, when the night was full of noise? How did she know to go to the Bornholmer garden plots if she had never been to Berlin before? Who had taught her to climb barbed wire? And, most insistently, who told her how to get past the dogs?

'They just could not fathom how I'd got past that dog,' she says. 'Poor dog.'

They were not above spite. Miriam was told that even if she had made it over she would have been sent back because she was underage. She protested. 'There's no way the westerners would have sent me back here,' she told the interrogating officers. 'Because I am a refugee from political persecution by you people which all started when I put up leaflets.' Miriam puts her chin out, imitating a cheeky kid who still thinks there is a safety net to catch her.

There was one main interrogator, Major Fleischer, but sometimes there were two of them. They both had moustaches and bristly short haircuts, grey uniforms done up tight. The younger one was so stiff he could have had a baking tray stuffed down his coat. Major Fleischer had hair in his ears. Sometimes he pretended to be her friend, 'like a good uncle'. Other times he was threatening. 'There *are* other ways we could do this, you know.' Her answers remained the same. 'I got a train from Leipzig, I bought a map at the station, I climbed over with a ladder, I went under on my belly, and then I made a run for it.'

Ten times twenty-four hours in which you hardly sleep. Ten times twenty-four hours in which you are hardly awake. Ten days is time enough to die, to be born, to fall in love and to go mad. Ten days is a very long time.

Q: What does the human spirit do after ten days without sleep, and ten days of isolation tempered only by nocturnal threat sessions?

A: It dreams up a solution.

On the eleventh night, Miriam gave them what they wanted. 'I thought, "You people want an underground escape organisation? Well, I'll give you one then."'

Fleischer had won.

'There then,' he said, 'that wasn't so bad now, was it? Why didn't you tell us earlier and save yourself all this trouble?' They let her sleep for a fortnight, and gave her one book each week. She read it in a day, then started memorising the pages, walking up and down in the cell with the book to her chest.

'In retrospect it's funny,' Miriam says, 'but at the time it was pure, unalloyed frustration. I cooked them up a story I would not have believed myself, even then. It was utterly absurd. But they were so wild about getting an escape organisation that they swallowed it. All I wanted to do was sleep.'

Auerbach's Cellar is a famous Leipzig institution. It is an underground bar and restaurant with oak bench tables in long alcoves under a curved roof, just like a cellar. The walls and ceilings are covered with dark painted scenes from Goethe's *Faust*: Faust meeting Mephistopheles, Faust betraying Margarethe, Faust in despair. Goethe used to drink here. It is a good place to meet the devil.

This is the story Miriam told the Stasi.

It all began when she was going to meet a friend in Auerbach's Cellar to eat goose-fat rolls. Her friend did not appear, so she sat down at one of the long tables by herself, and started in on the food. The place was full; it was nearly Christmas. Four men came and asked if they could share the table. They sat down to eat. Miriam listened to them talk. One of them had a Berlin accent in which '*gut*' is 'yut' and '*ich*' is 'icke'.

Miriam is enjoying herself at this point. She looks at me and her face is bright. She is imagining herself at sixteen and it makes her happy.

'So I said to the man—the one who looked like the leader, "Are you from Berlin?"

'And he said, "Yes."

'"How is it going in Berlin then?" I said.' Miriam's eyes widen and she looks like the cartoon boy again.

'"Fine thanks."

'"Where do you live in Berlin then?"

'"Pankow."

'"Is, uh, is that near the Wall?"

'"Actually, it is...You're not thinking of making a run for it are you?"

'"Yes, I am."

'"Well! You can't just front up to the Wall and expect to find a spot to climb over! Come with me and I'll give you a tip."'

Miriam said, 'OK.' So the five of them left and jumped in a cab. They travelled in a southerly direction, but she wasn't sure where because it was already dark. They went to an apartment on the second, or was it the third storey of a building? Hard to remember exactly. There was no name-plate on the door so unfortunately she couldn't say whose place it was. The man and his accomplices produced a map of Berlin, and showed her the spot to get over. Then they called another taxi, dropped her back at Auerbach's Cellar and she caught the tram home.

Miriam is laughing. She looks at me as if to say, 'Have you ever in your life heard such a ridiculous story? Can you believe they swallowed that?' I look back, confused. I try to rearrange my face. What is so improbable about someone offering handy hints on wall-jumping? I feel I am about to have something basic explained to me. My head is cocked like a dog watching TV: it can't make out what's happening, but it sure is interesting.

Miriam explains, gently, that in the GDR it was inconceivable that a person would ask a stranger, a total stranger whether they lived near the border. It was also inconceivable that the stranger would ask you whether you were thinking of escaping. And it was more inconceivable still that they would then proffer handy escape tips on the spot. Relations between people were conditioned by the fact that one or other of you could be one of *them*. Everyone suspected everyone else, and the mistrust this bred was the foundation of social existence. Miriam could have been denounced by the man for having asked a question about the border and admitting she was thinking of going over, and she could have denounced him in turn for offering to show her how. Underground escape organisations existed in the GDR, but you needed an intermediary to communicate with them. It would never happen so blithely over goose-fat rolls and beer.

Fleischer wanted a name. 'That I couldn't tell you,' she told him. 'I didn't hear them call each other by any name.'

'What did he look like, the leader?'

'Well,' she said, 'he was about so tall.' She puts her hand in the air above her head. 'And strong looking, well-built, you know.' She is smiling, enjoying her fantasy of a man. 'I told him that he was totally bald. Oh, and he had remarkably small feet.'

I am laughing hard now, enjoying the child's-eye detail.

'Yep, there you have it. It was pretty much the chrome dome with the remarkably small feet! What's more, I told Fleischer I had the impression he was a regular at Auerbach's Cellar.' She laughs too, pulling on a cigarette as she adjusts herself in her chair.

Miriam had thought it all through—no matter how many small-footed bald men they found for a line-up, she would fail to recognise any of them.

Two weeks passed before her next interrogation. She was summoned to Fleischer, not at 10 pm but in the afternoon. He had both hands on the table as if restraining himself from throwing it.

'My people,' he bellowed, 'have gone and got themselves a case of frostbite on your account. How dare you tell such tales! What could have possessed you to make up such a story?'

'I wanted to sleep.'

Fleischer said her conduct amounted to Deception of the Ministry, which was a criminal offence. She would now be up for an even longer sentence. And it was going to be bad enough for her, considering she could have started a war.

Miriam thought he must be crazy. Had she jumped over the last railing, he continued, the East German soldiers would have shot at her from behind, and the West Germans would have shot back. She could have been responsible for the outbreak of civil war. Then he softened. 'But for your sake I will take this little episode out of your file. Never let it be said we didn't give you a fair go.'

Later, it was clear to Miriam that he had been protecting himself. Had she been asked in court why she invented such a story, she would simply have said, 'Because they wouldn't let me sleep.' Apparently, even in the GDR, sleep deprivation amounted to torture, and torture, at least of minors, was not official policy.

As it was, the judge gave her one and a half years in Stauberg, the women's prison at Hoheneck. And at the end of the three-day trial he said to her, 'Juvenile Accused Number 725, you realise that your activities could have started World War III.'

They were all crazy and they were locking her up.

4

Charlie

'When I got out of prison, I was basically no longer human,' Miriam says.

On the first day at Hoheneck Miriam was required to undress, leave the clothes she came in and take in her hands the blue and yellow striped uniform. She was led naked down a corridor, into a room with a deep tiled tub in it. Two female guards were waiting. This was the Baptism of Welcome.

It was the only time she ever thought she would die. The bath was filled with cold water. One guard held her feet and the other her hair. They pushed her head under for a long time, then dragged her up by the hair, screaming at her. They held her down again. She could do nothing, and she could not breathe. And up: 'You piece of filth. You little upstart. You stupid traitor, you little bitch.' And under. When she came up the insults were what she breathed. She thought they would kill her.

Miriam is upset. Her voice is stretched and I can't look at her. Perhaps they beat something out of her she didn't get back.

Miriam says the prisoners were brutal to each other too. She says the criminal prisoners received privileges for abusing the politicals. She says that for eighteen months she was addressed by number and never by name. She says there was a hoard-and-barter system, in fact a whole economy, in sanitary napkins. I can't stay focused on the awfulness of it all, and my mind wanders, disobediently, to sitcoms. I think of the old TV series 'Prisoner', set in a women's prison: clanging metal gates before each ad break and a kindly lesbian in the laundry, steaming away.

But Miriam has found her stride again. She tells me at Hoheneck the prisoners worked in a sweatshop making sheets. An ordinary day started at 4.30 am with an alarm. When the warden's key rattled in the door all the prisoners stood to attention against the wall. This was roll call by number. They were counted as well. They went to breakfast, and then to the workroom, where they were counted again. 'To make sure no-one had run off between the cell and the canteen.' If Miriam wanted to go to the toilet, she stood to attention and called, 'Juvenile Prisoner Number 725 requests toilet permission.' When she got back she stood to attention again. 'Juvenile Prisoner Number 725 requests permission to resume.' Before going to lunch they were counted. After lunch they were marched around a yard for exercise and then counted again. The prisoners were counted and re-counted from the moment they woke to the moment they went to sleep, and, as Miriam says, chuckling, 'You know what?—the numbers were always right. Everyone was always there.'

'Prison left me with some strange little tics.' She has taken all the doors off their hinges in all the apartments she has lived in since. It's not that she has anxiety attacks about small spaces, she says, it's just that she starts to sweat and go cold. 'This apartment is perfect for me,' she says, looking around the open space.

'How about elevators?' I ask, recalling the schlepp up the stairs.

'Exactly,' she replies, 'I don't like them much either.'

One day, years later, her husband Charlie was fooling around at home, playing the guitar. Miriam said something provocative and he stood up suddenly, lifting his arm up to take off the guitar strap. He was probably just going to say 'That's outrageous', or tickle her or tackle her. But she was gone. She was already down in the courtyard of the building. She does not remember getting down the stairs—it was an automatic flight reaction. Charlie came out to coax her back up. He was distraught. She surprised them both with her tics in the first years they were together.

All of a sudden I am very tired, as though my bones have gone soft. I look up and it is dark outside. I want someone to give her a rub. I want someone to give me a rub. I want the benevolent prison governess of TV land to have existed, I want the lesbian with the heart of gold to have protected the little girl, and I think of what is still to come.

When Miriam was released, in 1970, she was seventeen and a half. Her sister took her to a lake to bathe. The lifesaver asked her out but she was unable to respond. His name was Karl-Heinz Weber, but everyone called him Charlie. When Miriam didn't answer, he pursued her through her sister. He thought she was so odd, and so quiet. He wanted to get to the bottom of it.

'What were you like?' I ask her.

'Well, you'd really need to ask him that,' she says. 'He was the one who brought me round again.' Miriam crosses the room to a worn suitcase, which spills her photographs onto the floor. She finds one of Charlie. It is of a man in his twenties, with light brown hair and a neat face, looking straight at the camera. He is positioned oddly close to the left-hand edge of the photo.

'Oh, that's because I cut myself out of it,' Miriam says. Then she says, 'That was our wedding photo.' I want to ask but I sit tight.

Miriam and Charlie moved in together. Charlie had trained as a sports teacher, studying physical education and biology. In the GDR, sport was closely linked with politics. The government screened youngsters for their potential and fed them into training institutes for the glory of the nation.

'Did he know about the doping?' Children at sports schools were given hormones under the guise of vitamins. In a scandal that has come to light since the Wall fell, the pills accelerated growth and strength, but turned the little girls halfway into boys.

'Yes, he knew from two different people about that. I remember he once told friends of ours to keep their daughter out of one of those institutes. But that wasn't why he left teaching.'

In his early twenties, Charlie and a friend holidayed up on the Baltic Sea. When a Swedish boat came near the coast, they decided to swim out to it just to see how far they could get.

'I don't think they wanted to board it or anything,' she says. 'It was a bit provocative, but it was just a game.'

The authorities brought them in on suspicion of wanting to leave the country. That was the beginning of Charlie Weber's pursuit by the Stasi.

Charlie didn't feel that he could represent to his students the state that was doing this to him. He left teaching and started to write. He wrote articles for the underground satirical publication *Eulenspiegel*, and treatments for television programs. He had jobs as a line producer on films, and some work in the theatre. He wrote 'a small book', Miriam says, called *Gestern Wie Heute* (*Yesterday, Like Today*), 'about the way that one dictatorship here is the same as another'. He sent it to West Germany where it was published.

'After we started living together—me, an ex-criminal, and he under surveillance—they would come over and search the house from time to time,' she says. 'When our neighbour, an old woman, saw this happening she offered to keep a trunk of our books and Charlie's manuscripts at her place, because they'd never suspect her. We made some mistakes though. I remember one time they were here, young blokes going through all our drawers, everything on the desks, the record collection. One of them was up a ladder searching the bookshelves when he found Orwell's *Animal*

Farm, which, of course, was blacklisted. We held our breath as he pulled it off the shelf. I remember the cover clearly: it was the pigs, holding a red flag aloft. We watched as this young man looked at it, the pigs and the flag. Then he put it back. Afterwards we laughed! We could only think that he saw the pigs—that was bad—but that they were holding a red flag, and they seemed to be on a collective farm—he must have thought that meant it was all right!

'I was prohibited from studying. And I couldn't get any kind of job at all,' Miriam says. 'Everything I applied for, the Stasi made sure I was turned down. Employers had to check my personal file and the instruction was always "not her". I used to take a lot of photographs. Eventually, all I could do was to send them to magazines with friends' names on them, and my friends would pass on the money they got for my work.' She ruffles her hair. 'In a way though, how we lived was quite good—we didn't have to submit ourselves to the sorts of structures and authority that we couldn't trust here. We managed.'

In 1979 Miriam's sister and her husband tried to escape to West Germany concealed in the boot of a car. Charlie drove them to meet the courier who was to smuggle them over the border. The Stasi followed every move; the couple received prison terms, and Charlie was placed on a type of probation.

In September 1980 the West German chancellor Helmut Schmidt was scheduled to visit the GDR. At that time the Solidarity movement in Poland was a source of tension for Eastern Bloc governments, because it was a focus of hope for many under their rule. Then Schmidt's visit was cancelled because of East German government concern that it would lead to demonstrations for democracy in front of the western television cameras.

Nevertheless, the East German authorities had prepared for the visit. They had rounded up and locked away anyone who might protest, or might in some way embarrass the government.

By this time Charlie stood under formal suspicion of the crime of

'Attempting to Flee the Republic'. He and Miriam had put in applications to leave the GDR. Such applications were sometimes granted because the GDR, unlike any other eastern European country, could rid itself of malcontents by ditching them into West Germany, where they were automatically granted citizenship. The Stasi put all applicants under extreme scrutiny. People who applied to leave were, unsurprisingly, suspected of wanting to leave which was, other than by this long-winded and arbitrary process, a crime. An 'application to leave' was legal, but the authorities might, if the fancy took them, choose to see it as a statement of why you didn't like the GDR. In that case it became a *Hetzschrift* (a smear) or a *Schmäschrift* (a libel) and therefore a criminal offence. On 26 August 1980 Charlie Weber was arrested and held in a remand cell.

At first Miriam's only contact with him was by letter. She was permitted no visits, and he could not call. Eventually, a half-hour visit was scheduled for Tuesday 14 October. The day before, Miriam's most recent letter to Charlie came back to her, marked in handwriting: 'Postal Permission Terminated.' With it there was a Stasi card in the letterbox: 'Visit Authorisation for 14.10.1980 Withdrawn.'

On Wednesday 15 October, an ordinary policeman in his green uniform knocked on their apartment door. 'Is this the house of Herr Weber?'

'Yes.'

'And you are Frau Weber?'

'Yes.'

'Well, you need to report to the district attorney's office and collect your husband's things, because he is dead.'

He was gone before Miriam could find any words.

The German Democratic Republic paid lip service to the institutions of democracy. There were district attorneys, whose job it was to administer justice, and lawyers, whose job it was to represent clients, and judges, whose job it was to pass judgment. There were, at least on paper, political parties other than the ruling Socialist Unity Party. But really there was just the Party, and its instrument, the Stasi. Judges often got their instructions from the Stasi which, in turn, passed them on from the Party—right down to the outcome of judgment and the length of the sentence. The connection of the Party, the Stasi and the law went from the ground up: the Stasi, in consultation with school principals, recruited obedient students with an appropriately loyal attitude for the study of law. I once saw a list of dissertation topics from the Stasi Law School at Potsdam, which included such memorable contributions to the sum of human knowledge as 'On the Probable Causes of the Psychological Pathology of the Desire to Commit Border Infractions'. There was no room for a person to defend themselves against the State because all the defence lawyers and all the judges were part of it.

Miriam went to Major Trost, the district attorney who was responsible for investigating Charlie's death. Trost told her Charlie had hanged himself. Trost said he was very sorry, in fact they were all deeply, deeply shocked. He said he had been called to the cell immediately.

Miriam asked what Charlie had hanged himself with. What had he hanged himself from? 'I know those cells,' she tells me, 'there are no exposed pipes. Everything is smooth inside. There are not even bars over the windows—they are too small.'

Trost said he didn't know.

'But you were called to the cell. How can you not know? You must have seen what a man is hanging from.'

'No.'

Miriam shakes her head imitating his dismissiveness. 'Well, what with, then?' She would not give up. That day Trost told her Charlie had hanged himself with the elastic from the waistband of his trousers. Miriam didn't believe it. She kept going back to his office, and kept asking. They were being surprisingly gentle with her. Trost's deputy told her Charlie had hanged himself with his underwear. Another time Trost said it was a torn-up piece of bedsheet.

She confronted him. 'Underwear or bedsheet? Underwear or bedsheet? The least you people could do is get your story straight.'

Major Trost lost his cool. He said if she didn't leave the room he would have her arrested.

Miriam found out Charlie's body was being held in forensics at the morgue. She went there, but no-one would let her in. She felt she was being followed.

She went to see Charlie's lawyer Herr X, who was the Leipzig representative for Dr Wolfgang Vogel in Berlin. Vogel was the government lawyer responsible for trade in people between East and West Germany. He ran a list of names, and negotiated with the West German government the prices at which they would be, as it was called, 'bought free' (*freigekauft*). There was a scale of prices which varied, apparently according to the education of the person being bought. A tradesperson or clerical worker came more cheaply than someone with a doctorate. The exception was for clergy—a pastor cost nothing because they were often independent anti-regime thinkers, and it was worth it to the regime to be rid of them. For East Germany, trading in humans was a source of hard currency and at the same time a means of getting rid of those who would not conform.

One way of getting on to Vogel's list, and thereby having a chance of getting out of the GDR, was to become a client of one of his regional representatives. That is why Charlie Weber had engaged X. By the time Miriam went to see him, X had had the Weber matter (now the investigation of a death in custody) for eight weeks. Miriam sat down in his office and asked him to tell her what he had found out.

When he opened his file on the desk, it contained only a single sheet of paper: the delegated authority from Vogel to take on the case. Instead of telling her anything, he asked, 'Mrs Weber, why don't you tell me what *you* know?'

Miriam was wild. For days, she says, she had experienced the kind of anger that makes you not care any more, say things you would usually put a brake on. She replied that it was his job to investigate, so he should really be finding out and telling her. If he had done nothing for Charlie while he was in prison, she said, he could at least find out how he died.

'Do I look insane to you?' the lawyer said, very cold. 'Do I? You don't truly think I am going to trot down there and ask what happened, do you? For that you had better find yourself another fool, young lady.'

Miriam is upset again. Here, across the desk, was the face of the system itself: a mockery of a lawyer, making a mockery of her.

On Tuesday 21 October 1980, a Stasi man came to the door to tell Miriam that the corpse had been released from forensics, and that the ministry would like to be of service to her with the funeral arrangements. Miriam said she could manage on her own.

'Of course, Mrs Weber,' the man said, 'but do you have a particular funeral parlour in mind?'

She told him to go to hell, and found a smallish funeral establishment. The woman behind the desk was old and kind. She said, 'You know, Mrs Weber, you would really be better off going to the Southern Cemetery, because they will organise the whole thing from start to finish, and fill in all the forms on your behalf and so on. It would mean much less running around for you.' Miriam didn't think anything of it. She left, and went to the Southern Cemetery offices. She knocked on the door, and was told to come in.

'You're late—we were expecting you earlier,' the man behind the desk said.

'What? Who told you I was coming? I didn't know myself I was coming here until half an hour ago.'

'Uhh, I don't know, don't remember.'

First of all, he suggested cremation instead of burial.

Miriam said no.

Well, actually, they said, it was going to have to be cremation, because they had no coffins left.

Miriam bluffed: 'I will bring you a coffin.'

The man left the room for a moment, then reappeared. 'Today, Mrs Weber,' he said, 'is your lucky day. We have one last coffin left.' Unfortunately, however, he added, it was not going to be possible to lay out the body for mourners to pay their last respects. He gave no reason.

'If that's the way it is,' Miriam said, 'I'm going to another funeral establishment and another cemetery.'

'No, no, no, Mrs Weber, no need for that, we'll see what we can do about a laying-out then.'

The day before the funeral Miriam and a friend took some of the wreaths she had received to the gravesite—there were too many to carry them all the next day. She noticed a fellow standing around, smoking, doing nothing much, watching.

A woman in the uniform of a cemetery official came up to her. 'Are you with the Weber funeral?'

'Yes.'

'Well, I just wanted to say, don't you get too upset tomorrow if there's no laying-out, because it may just be that there isn't.'

Miriam got her in full view, the smoker within earshot. 'Let me tell you now, if there is no laying-out, there will be no funeral. I will call the whole thing off with everyone standing around here—I will make the kind of ruckus you have never seen. DO YOU UNDERSTAND ME?'

The next day there was a laying-out. Miriam says the coffin was far away, behind a thick pane of glass, and the whole thing was lit from below with purple neon light. 'Even in that terrible light, I could still see his head injuries. And I could see his neck—they'd forgotten to cover it up. There were no strangulation marks, nothing.' She looks across at me. 'You'd think they would make sure to cover his neck if they wanted to stick with their story that he hanged himself, wouldn't you?' From there the coffin was sunk to another level and reappeared on a trolley wheeled by cemetery employees to the gravesite. All these details are slowed down in time, stuck in the amber of memory. In the minutes between the coffin sinking from view and re-emerging, she says, there would have been time for a body to be taken out.

'A great many people were at the funeral,' Miriam tells me, 'but I think there were even more Stasi there.' There was a van with long-range antennae for sound-recording equipment parked at the gates. There were men in the bushes with telephoto lenses. Everywhere you looked there were men with walkie-talkies. At the cemetery offices building work was going on: Stasi agents sat in pairs in the scaffolding.

'Everyone, every single one of us was photographed. And you could see in advance the path the procession was to take from the chapel to the grave: it was marked at regular intervals all along by the Stasi men, just standing around.' When they reached the grave, there were two of them sitting there on a trestle, ready to watch the whole thing. 'As soon as the last person threw on their flowers,' Miriam says, 'the cemetery people started piling on the earth and it was too quick. It was just too quick.'

Miriam walks barefoot across the room to a desk and picks up some papers in a plastic sheath. 'I made a copy of this for you,' she says, coming back to the table. It is part of the Stasi file on Charlie Weber: a handwritten report signed by a Major Maler. In it all the divisional plans are set out for the organisation and surveillance of the Weber funeral: Miriam's telephone is to be tapped; she is to be called in for a 'Clarification of Circumstances' the day before; sound recording technology is to be used at the site; a 'photographic documentation' of the event is to be made; citizens of the Federal Republic of Germany attending the funeral are to be supervised to ensure they leave the GDR before curfew at the end of the day. 'The name of the pastor who will conduct the service regrettably could not be ascertained by this operative. Should negative-enemy behaviour occur during the funeral all men are given orders to use force to quell it on the grounds that such actions would contravene the dignity of the cemetery premises.' Major Maler noted that the head of the Southern Cemetery, a Herr Mohre, had guaranteed the Stasi complete freedom of movement for the Weber 'action', and that should any of the Stasi officers be questioned by workers at the cemetery, they should be referred to Colleague Mohre. Mohre knows that Maler is an officer of the Stasi, and also knows him by his true name, not his undercover identity.

All of this Miriam could have guessed, from what she saw on the day. She points to the next line and reads it aloud: 'No definitive information is available as to the date for the cremation. This date can be ascertained from Colleague Mohre on or after 31.10.80.'

Miriam hands the file to me. 'On 30 October we buried a coffin. We buried a *coffin* and they are setting the date for *cremation* the next day. Either there is no-one inside that thing, or there is someone else in it.'

Miriam went to the Interior Ministry, and added the claim of 'Transportation of Coffin' to her application to leave the GDR. She wanted to get out, and she wanted to rebury Charlie in West Germany.

Every month or so she would be called in to the Stasi for a chat. It went on for years. 'What's all this about transportation of the coffin?' they asked her. 'What do you want with the coffin?'

'What do you think I want with the coffin? To take it for a Sunday stroll? I want to do with the coffin what one does with a coffin: I want to bury it.'

In 1985 they said to her, 'You probably want to have the contents examined, do you?'

'What if I do? What am I likely to find other than that he hanged himself, as you say?'

'You know there will be nothing left in the coffin. You won't be able to prove anything.'

'Well, why are you so preoccupied with it, then?' she said, and took it as an admission of guilt. After a time Miriam stopped obeying the cards that appeared in her letterbox summoning her to their offices to clarify some circumstances. The only thing that ever got clearer was that they had the power, in the circumstances.

'It was silly. I stopped thinking I'd ever get out. They were playing with me like a mouse.'

At 8 am one morning in May 1989, Miriam's phone rang. It was the Stasi. They couldn't say why, but she was required to report to them without delay, this day, and bring her identity papers.

Miriam thought if it wasn't cards in her letterbox summoning her to clarify circumstances they were giving her wake-up calls. She had had a late night. She slept some more, then got up and had a shower, made the first cup of tea.

At midday the doorbell sounded. A Stasi man, Division of the Interior. 'Why are you still here?' he said.

'This is my home.'

'You are required to report immediately to the ministry, and bring your identity papers with you.'

'There's plenty of time. The day is still long, my friend.'

He stationed himself outside her door.

She went down to the offices. An official took her ID papers, and said she was to go to a photographer, and that after that she had an appointment with a public notary. Then, she was to come back to collect her travel authority. 'You are on a train tonight,' he said.

'That was when I understood,' Miriam says. 'I was in shock. I said to them, "It's been eleven years since we lodged the application to leave, and now I can't even say goodbye to my friends?"'

'Mrs Weber, the travel authority you have been issued is valid until midnight tonight. If you are found to be on GDR territory after that time, you will be here illegally, and you will be arrested. I would remind you,' he said holding them up to her in his hand, 'that you no longer have any identity papers for this country.'

The train that night was crammed full of people being expelled from the GDR. It was as though anyone who might catch the glasnost virus had to be put over the Wall. Miriam had a small carrybag with two changes of clothes in it, and she was leaving her life behind. Her friends were going to pack up her apartment for her. For all she knew, she would never be back. No-one had any idea that the Wall would fall that November.

'Essentially, the deportation came eleven years too late,' she says, 'and six months too early.'

Night has fallen, and the city lights are spread out beneath us. In the dark, this could be any city, in any normal place.

Some people are comfortable talking about their lives, as if they can make sense of the progression of random events that made them what they are. This involves a kind of forward-looking faith in life; a conviction that cause and effect are linked, and that they are themselves more than the sum of their past. For Miriam, the past stopped when Charlie died. Her memories of picnics or cooking meals or holidays, her real life, are memories where 'she' is a 'we' and those are the things she and Charlie did together. It is as if the time after his death doesn't count; it has been a non-time, laying down non-history. She is brave and strong and broken all at once. As she speaks it is as if her existence is no longer real to her in itself, more like a living epitaph to a life that was.

'Why did you come back to Leipzig?' I ask.

'Well, in this matter I've got going at the moment, it is better that I am here. It only takes me an hour to get to the offices of the investigators in Dresden,' she smiles. 'And I am hoping,' she says, and I see that under the smile she is fighting back tears, 'I am really hoping that the puzzle women in Nuremberg find out something about Charlie in all those pieces of files.'

Miriam wants Charlie's body exhumed, so she can know for sure what happened to him.

I look out at the lights. She continues, 'I don't believe he would have killed himself. I don't think he did. Of the two of us, he was always more worried it'd be me who would crack under all that pressure.'

Not knowing what happened to Charlie is so hard, because if it was suicide, she was abandoned. I wonder what will happen to her when they dig up the coffin. If he was cremated, there will be nothing there, or someone else's remains. If it's Charlie what could that tell her? Will she be released into a new life? Or will the current one lose its purpose?

Miriam can't afford to have the exhumation performed privately, so she hopes it will be done in the course of the criminal investigation into his death that is now, apparently, being undertaken by the authorities of united Germany. But twice they have tried to suspend the investigation, and twice she has travelled to Dresden to 'bang on their desks'. 'You know, they just want to stop thinking about the past. They want to pretend it all didn't happen.'

Most recently, the DA wrote to Miriam saying that the investigation was to be suspended because a former employee of the Southern Cemetery had 'credibly assured' him that there had been nothing untoward about the Weber funeral. She sent him in the file, highlighting the parts that referred to the body coming from 'Anatomie' (code for the Stasi mortuary, as if somehow the corpses coming from custody were coming from the medical school); the surveillance detail for the funeral; the part about Herr Mohre knowing the true identity of the Stasi man who was making arrangements with him; and the part about the cremation, scheduled to take place the next day. 'That stopped them,' she says. 'I wrote, "Do you still think there was 'nothing untoward' about the Weber funeral?"' The DA replied that he hadn't yet read that section of the file. When Miriam inquired at the Stasi File Authority she found that he hadn't even lodged a request to see it.

'Do you ever run into any Stasi men you recognise in the street?' I ask. I think that is what would terrify me, in the nonsensical way in which it is horrible to run into someone who has wronged you.

'No, thank goodness. But I did try to find the people involved in Charlie's case.'

Shortly after the revolution in 1989 Miriam went to the cemetery to find Herr Mohre, but he had vanished as soon as the Wall came down. 'The Stasi cremated a lot of people at the Southern Cemetery,' she says.

Miriam did find Major Maler. She rang him and said she would like to meet to discuss the Weber case. They met in a cafe. Miriam took a friend along so she would have a witness. The friend sat at the next table, unknown to Maler.

Maler said he didn't know anything. 'No, the name Weber doesn't say anything to me.'

'Well why did you come here then?' Miriam asked.

'Uhh, I just wanted to see what you wanted.'

'But I told you on the phone that what I wanted was to talk about the Weber matter.'

'Oh, I thought you were going to tell *me* something.'

Did he want to know how much she knew, whether he was going to be uncovered, or whether he was to be blackmailed?

'It is amazing,' Miriam says, 'what a revolution can do to people's memories.' A cloud of smoke covers her head and the high back of the chair. 'There are some compensations though, for being here. This apartment, for one,' she says, and she's right. A siren wails past and subsides. She is a maiden safe in her tower.

'And I think about those Stasi men. They would never in their lives have imagined that they would cease to exist and that their offices would be a museum. A museum!' She shakes her head and butts out her cigarette. 'That's one thing I love to do. I love to drive up to the Runden Ecke and park right outside. I just sit there in the car and I feel…*triumph*!' Miriam makes a gesture which starts as a wave, and becomes a guillotine. 'You lot are gone.'

The Linoleum Palace

It's past midnight when I get back to Berlin. I've been on a tram, a regional train, the local line, and then walked through the park where things are only shapes, dark on dark. Miriam's story has winded me. My head, no longer consumed by listening, started to pulse again as soon as I left her apartment. I dislike being made aware that my heart is just a small pump, pushing all that blood around. I am beyond tired. As I reach my place I'm in slow motion, crossing a finishing line.

My building is covered in grey sprayed-on concrete, but still has grand arched doors at its entrance. At the end of the carriage hall a matching set of doors leads into the yard with its chestnut tree and weedy cobbles. I live on the first floor past the letterboxes up the stairs on the right. I don't check the mail but turn on the hall light and go straight up. The stairwell walls are covered in bright but inscrutable spraycan graffiti which could be expressions of joy or pain depending on how you look at them, but I don't. I hurry to get my key in the lock before the hall bulb goes off its automatic timer. Home free, home safe.

Inside, the lights are on.

A voice shrieks, 'Don't be frightened! Don't be frightened!'

I am terrified.

'Sorry, sorry,' says the voice.

The pump in my chest pumps, hard. I drop my pack.

A woman up a ladder holds a large screwdriver. It's Julia, from whom I rent. 'I'm really sorry,' she says, turning towards me and lowering the screwdriver.

'That's OK,' I say slowly, puffed.

'I know exactly how it is,' she says. 'Sometimes you just want to get home and be by yourself.' That would probably be, I think, because I live by myself. I don't say anything.

'I'm just unscrewing here,' she says. 'I'm taking these bookshelves, I hope you don't mind.'

'I don't mind.'

'I need them at my place, there are none there.'

I have been living in this apartment for six months, and I am still not used to this. I think it must stop at some point, and I hope it's while I still have a little furniture left. Julia worked at the rental agency I visited when I was looking for a place. She offered to sublet the apartment she'd been living in until her lease ran out. It had been a share house, but everyone was moving. The apartment was much too big for me, but it was in the old east where I wanted to be, and I could afford it.

And it was furnished if, as Julia warned me, 'only sparsely'. This is even truer now.

I know Julia is concerned about how long it is taking her to move out, about the steady denuding of the apartment. I have comforted her before, saying all I need is a bed, a desk, a chair and a coffee pot. I meant it at the time, but two days ago when I found a pile of screwed up papers and old tissues and cassette wrappers I'd thrown under the desk where the waste-paper basket used to be I thought I must say something to her. Only right now I'm too too tired.

'Where've you been?' she asks.

'Leipzig.'

'Ah,' she says, 'where it all started.'

'Julia, I'm sorry, but I'm knackered. I need to go to bed. How about a cup of coffee some time? Why don't you come over?' During the day, I think.

She says she will, but we don't make a time because Julia regards fixed appointments as intolerable constraints on her freedom. Which may account for how she lit upon this hour of the night for some home renovation.

I fall into bed and she continues her nocturnal disassembly so quietly I don't hear a sound when she leaves with the boards and L-hooks and screws balanced in the basket of the bicycle she must have carried down the stairs.

In the morning the first thing I notice is that I can see my breath. One day without heating and the air here congeals with cold. My head is clear, but yesterday feels like a different country. The second thing I notice is that opposite the bed, where there were two blue milk crates that served as a bedside table-cum-dressing stool, is a freshly exposed piece of brown linoleum.

When I moved in I was pleased by the spareness of the place. I had two bedrooms, a huge living room with windows at tree height looking into the park, and a kitchen on the other side looking over the yard. This apartment was converted under the Communists into a place of concrete render on the outside and, on the inside, practical lino brownness, washed and waxed and charmless. But it was summer then and to me it was a place of air and light, with green on both sides.

I soon realised everything here was either broken or about to be. Each item had started life as a utilitarian piece of furniture in an eastern home well over a decade ago. After the Wall fell the students had moved in, and nothing that remains was good enough even for them to take when they left. The couch in the living room has developed lumps and is covered in a dark cloth I fear to disturb; the cord for the kitchen blind is permanently tethered to a plastic chair in order to stop it crashing down; my mattress springs are inching their way through the ticking; and the bathroom, windowless and painted Extreme Dark Green, has plumbing that needed to be learnt.

In the hallway Julia has left a tin bucket full of coal. She must have gone down last night to the pitch-dark cellar to fill it. I feed firelighters and coal into the brown tiled heater. Although it will take hours to heat up, her kindness warms me already.

I don't really hold it against Julia that she comes to take this flotsam from here. I know she has nothing better where she is now—a one-roomer at the back of a block not far away. I know that in summer the smells from the garbage bins in her yard rise up to her, almost visible. I know that year-round her neighbours are unfriendly, both to each other and within their households, and that she hears their squabbling as it reverberates around the yard. I know that she needs to be alone but suffers from it too and that her room is choked with cheap and broken things she feels she may want at some point in life but may not be able to afford if she abandons. And I know that her small cat is incontinent, which makes her place smell, somehow, of anxiety.

So I cannot resent it if she still has keys, and comes back to her old life, every now and again. I accustom myself to each unexpected absence— the rubber bathmat, the coffee machine, and now the milk crates. I acclimatise to the thinning of the atmosphere. I wear dust-free tracks on the linoleum from kitchen to desk, from bathroom to bed.

All I feel today in fact, as I pass where the bookshelf used to be in the hall, is the sudden predominance of linoleum in my life. Altogether I can count five kinds of linoleum in this once grand apartment, and they are all, each one of them, brown. Degrees of brown: dark in the hallway, fleck in my bedroom, a brown in the other bedroom that may have once been another colour before succumbing to house rule, brown-beige in the kitchen and, my favourite, imitation parquetry-in-lino in the living room.

In the kitchen I make coffee in the thermos. What surprises me about living here is that, no matter how much is taken out, this linoleum palace continues to contain all the necessities for life, at the same time as it refuses to admit a single thing, either accidentally or arranged, of beauty or joy. In this, I think, it is much like East Germany itself.

I take my cup to the living-room window. In the park there is snow on the ground and the trees, light on light. My breath mixes with coffee steam on the glass. I wipe it away. In the distance lies the city, the television tower at Alexanderplatz like an oversized Christmas bauble, blinking blue.

I can't see it but I know that just near there, on the site of the old Palace of the Prussian Emperors pulled down by the Communists, is the parliament building of the GDR, the Palast der Republik. It is brown and plastic-looking, full of asbestos, and all shut up. It is not clear whether the fence around it is to protect it from people who would like to express what they thought of the regime, or to protect the people from the Palast, for health reasons. The structure is one long rectangular metal frame, made up of smaller rectangles of brown-tinted mirror glass. When you look at it you can't see in. Instead the outside world and everything in it is reflected in a bent and brown way. In there, dreams were turned into words, decisions made, announcements applauded, backs slapped. In there could be a whole other world, time could warp and you could disappear.

Like so many things here, no-one can decide whether to make the Palast der Republik into a memorial warning from the past, or to get rid of it altogether and go into the future unburdened of everything, except the risk of doing it all again. Nearby, Hitler's bunker has been uncovered in building works. No-one could decide about that either—a memorial could become a shrine for neo-Nazis, but to erase it altogether might signal forgetting or denial. In the end, the bunker was reburied just as it was. The mayor said, perhaps in another fifty years people would be able to decide what to do. To remember or forget—which is healthier? To demolish it or to fence it off? To dig it up, or leave it lie in the ground?

Between the Palast der Republik and my apartment lies the neighbourhood of Mitte, the old centre of Berlin, with its grey buildings and white sky and naked trees. Streets near here are being renamed: from Marx-Engels-Platz to Schlossplatz, from Leninallee to Landsberger Allee, from Wilhelm-Pieck-Strasse to Torstrasse, in a massive act of ideological redecoration. Most of the buildings though, are not yet renovated. They have largely lost their plaster and are scraped back to patches of brick; they look like tattered faces after plastic surgery. They are as they were before the Wall fell, except for the sprouting of domestic-size satellite dishes from the window-frames; a sudden white fungus, tuned to outer space. The trams are western now—they were among the first things to cross over here after the Wall came down. They are a flash of sighing yellow suspended from strings, shifting through this greyscape.

A tram stops right outside my apartment. It obeys a set of lights here under the window, though on the other side of the street there are none to match. I see the driver has the tabloid—screaming red-and-black headlines—on the control dash. Behind him sit tired-looking people for whom this day has come too soon.

I cannot fathom why these lights make the tram halt under my window. The stop itself is half a block away at the corner. Right here, the doors never open for passengers; they just sit, arrested and accepting. It is odd, the sight of a tram with a row of cars behind it stopped here for no pedestrians, no passengers, no reason, while on the other side vehicles continue unimpeded up the hill into Prenzlauer Berg. The lights change and the driver, still looking at the paper, moves a lever and slides the tram into action.

I go out for the paper and bread, and walk through the park. In summer this park is festooned with motley groups of drunks and punks.

In winter the punks claim the underground stations for warmth, while the drunks install themselves in tram shelters. Today the corner stop is occupied by an old man with a mane of matted locks, a huge felt beard and flowing black robes. His belongings, in plastic bags around him, double as pillows. He is timeless and grand like someone walked in from another century—a Winter King. As passengers alight from trams he acknowledges them as if they were supplicants paying their respects to his throne, nodding to each and waving them on their way.

I cross to the bakery past a billboard that reads 'Advertising Makes Better Known'. My baker holds, to some extent, with tradition. He makes wholegrain and rye and country loaves, stacked as oblong bricks on the back wall. But now, freed of state-run constraints on his ingenuity, he appears to be conducting his own personal experiment in bestsellerdom. On the left-hand side under the glass counter are the baked goods: iced donuts and cheesecake and blueberry crumble. On the other side, also under the glass and laid out just as neatly, is a bewildering assortment of fat paperbacks with embossed titles.

I am served by a woman with a bad perm. She's wearing a T-shirt which has a lion's face on it—the lion has winking sequins for eyes placed exactly where her nipples must be. I buy half a loaf of rye and ask no questions about the books. When I reach my building I see that the Winter King has crossed here to the place where the tram stops for no reason. He waits, but no passengers emerge for him to receive. Instead, as I approach, he turns to me and bows, long and dangerously low.

Over the next week I think about Miriam and I think about Stasi men. I am curious about what it must have been like to be on the inside of the Firm, and then to have that world and your place in it disappear. I draft an advertisement and fax it to the personal columns of the Potsdam paper.

Seeking: former Stasi officers and unofficial collaborators for interview. Publication in English, anonymity and discretion guaranteed.

6.

Stasi HQ

The next day the phone calls start very early in the morning. I hadn't thought it through—I hadn't imagined what it would be like to have a series of military types, who had lost their power and lost their country, call you up at home.

I'm asleep. I pick up the phone and say my name.

'*Ja*. In response to your notice in the *Märkische Allgemeine*.'

'*Ja*…' I fumble for my watch. It is 7.35 am.

'How much are you paying?'

'*Bitte?*'

'You must understand—,' the voice says. I sit up and pull the covers around me.

'To whom am I speaking?'

'That doesn't matter for the moment.' The voice is assured. 'You must understand that it is very hard for some of us now to get jobs in this new Germany. We are discriminated against and ripped off blind from one minute to another, in this—this *Kapitalismus*. But we learn fast: so I ask you, how much you are prepared to pay for my story?'

'I don't know, if I don't know what sort of story it is.'

'I was IM,' he says.

I am tempted. The 'IMs' were *'inofizielle Mitarbeiter'* or unofficial collaborators. I know I probably won't find many who will speak to me. They are the most hated people in the new Germany because, unlike the uniformed Stasi officers and administrative staff who went off to their bureaucratic jobs each day, these informers reported on family and friends without them knowing. *'Moment, bitte,'* I say, and I put the phone in my lap. I remember Miriam telling me that informers routinely argue that their information didn't harm anyone. 'But how can they know what it was used for?' she asked. 'It is as if they have all been issued with the same excuses manual.'

I pick up the receiver and say no. How can I reward informers a second time around? And besides, I don't have the money.

The phone keeps ringing. I make a series of assignations with Stasi men: in Berlin, in Potsdam, outside a church, in a parking lot, in a pub and at their homes.

My kitchen overlooks the yard. I often see movement behind the windows of the other apartments. Today in one of them a man stands, staring out absent-mindedly. He is naked. I'm on the telephone and I look away, hoping he has not felt observed. When I turn to put the receiver down he's still there—for a moment I think he may not have seen me. But then I notice he has pulled the curtain across his penis, where he holds it in a gesture of static modesty, a polyester toga.

I need to get out of the house, and away from the phone.

Outside the cold is bitter and soggy. There's no wind; it is as if we have all been refrigerated. In the stillness people trail comets of breath. I catch the underground to the national Stasi Headquarters at Normannenstrasse in the suburb of Lichtenberg. The brochure I picked up at the Runden Ecke shows a vast acreage of multi-storey buildings covering the space of several city blocks. The picture is taken from the air, and because the buildings fold in at right angles to one another the complex looks like a gigantic computer chip. From here the whole seamless, sorry apparatus was run: Stasi HQ. And, deep inside this citadel was the office of Erich Mielke, the Minister for State Security.

On 7 November 1990, only months after the citizens of Berlin barricaded this complex, Mielke's rooms, including his private quarters, were opened to the public as a museum. The 'Federal Commissioner for the Files of the State Security Service of the former GDR' (the Stasi File Authority) has taken control of the files. People come here to read their unauthorised biographies.

I see through a window into a room where several men and a woman sit each at their own small table. They look at pink and dun-coloured manila folders and take notes. What mysteries are being solved? Why they didn't get into university, or why they couldn't find a job, or which friend told Them about the forbidden Solzhenitsyn in their bookcase? The names of third parties mentioned in the files are crossed out with fat black markers so other people's secrets are not revealed (that Uncle Frank was unfaithful to his wife, that a neighbour was a lush). But you are entitled to know the real names of the Stasi officers and the informers who spied on you. For the moments that I stand there at least, no-one is crying or punching the wall.

I make my way to the main building like a rat in a maze. I want to get a sense of the man who ran the place, before meeting some of his underlings face to face.

The name Mielke has now come to mean 'Stasi'. Victims are dubiously honoured to find his signature in their files; on plans for someone to be observed 'with all available methods', on commands for arrest, for kidnapping, instructions to judges for the length of a prison term, orders for 'liquidation'. The honour is dubious because the currency is low: he signed so many. Mielke's apparatus, directed largely against his own countrymen, was one and a half times as big as the GDR regular army.

After the Wall fell the German media called East Germany 'the most perfected surveillance state of all time'. At the end, the Stasi had 97,000 employees—more than enough to oversee a country of seventeen million people. But it also had over 173,000 informers among the population. In Hitler's Third Reich it is estimated that there was one Gestapo agent for every 2000 citizens, and in Stalin's USSR there was one KGB agent for every 5830 people. In the GDR, there was one Stasi officer or informant for every sixty-three people. If part-time informers are included, some estimates have the ratio as high as one informer for every 6.5 citizens. Everywhere Mielke found opposition he found enemies, and the more enemies he found the more staff and informers he hired to quell them.

Here, at Normannenstrasse, 15,000 Stasi bureaucrats worked every day, administering the activities of the Stasi overseas, and overseeing domestic surveillance through each of the fourteen regional offices in the GDR.

Photos show Mielke to be a small man with no neck. His eyes are set close together, his cheeks puffy. He has the face and the lisp of a pugilist. He loved to hunt; footage shows him inspecting a line of deer carcasses as he would a military parade. He loved his medals, and wore them pinned over his chest in shiny, noisy rows. He also loved to sing, mainly rousing marches and, of course, 'The Internationale'. It is said that psychopaths, people utterly untroubled by conscience, make supremely effective generals and politicians, and perhaps he was one. He was certainly the most feared man in the GDR; feared by colleagues, feared by Party members, feared by workers and the general population. 'We are not immune from villains among us,' he told a gathering of high-ranking Stasi officers in 1982. 'If I knew of any already, they wouldn't live past tomorrow. Short shrift. It's because I'm a humanist, that I am of this view.' And, 'All this blithering about to execute or not to execute, for the death penalty or against—all rot, comrades. Execute! And, when necessary, without a court judgment.'

Mielke was born in 1907, the son of a Berlin cartwright. At fourteen he joined the Communist youth organisation, and at eighteen the Party.

Through the 1920s and early 1930s, the political situation in Germany was volatile—there were street fights between the Communists and the Nazis, and the Communists and the police. The 1931 death of a Communist in a skirmish in Berlin prompted the Party to order revenge. On 8 August, at a demonstration at Bülowplatz, Mielke and another man killed the local police chief and his off-sider by shooting them in the back at point-blank range.

Mielke fled to Moscow. There, he attended the International Lenin School, the elite training ground for Communist leaders, and worked with Stalin's secret police, the NKVD. In January 1933 the Nazi Party came to power in Germany. Some of the Communists responsible for the Bülowplatz murders were sentenced to death, others to long jail terms. A warrant was issued for his arrest.

Mielke stayed out of Germany. In the late 1930s he was active in the Spanish Civil War; by his own account, he was interned in France during World War II. But afterwards Stalin decorated him with medals for service: it seems clear that from the mid-1930s, wherever he was, Mielke was a hatchet man in Stalin's secret service.

When the war was over he returned to the Soviet sector of Berlin, where he was safe from prosecution. He worked in the internal affairs division of the Soviet-run police force. In 1957 Mielke engineered a coup against its leader, and then he took over as Minister for State Security. He proceeded to consolidate his power within the Party and over the country. In 1971 he helped organise the coup which brought Erich Honecker to power as Secretary-General. Honecker rewarded Mielke with candidacy for the Politbüro, and a house in the luxurious Party compound at Wandlitz. From that time on the two Erichs ran the country.

Mielke was an invisible man, but Honecker's picture was everywhere. It was in schools, in Free German Youth halls, in theatres and over swimming pools. It was at the universities, in police stations, at holiday camps and in the border guards' watchtowers. He always wore a suit and tie, large dark-rimmed glasses and his hair, first dark then grey, combed back off a high forehead. Other than being small, Honecker was unremarkable-looking, except for his strange, full-lipped mouth which seemed to widen, only partially, for a smile.

Honecker's background was not dissimilar from Mielke's. His father was a miner, and he joined the 'Jung-Spartakus-Bund' at eleven, and the Communist Youth at fourteen. He was apprenticed as a roof-tiler, before spending 1930–31 at the Lenin School in Moscow, then working underground for the Communists against the Hitler regime. In 1937 he was arrested by the Gestapo and sentenced to ten years imprisonment for 'preparation of high treason'. He escaped shortly before the end of the war, when he began, steadily, to make his career in the Party running East Germany.

The Stasi's brief was to be 'the shield and sword' of the Communist Party, called the 'Socialist Unity Party of Germany' (*Sozialistische Einheitspartei Deutschlands*) or SED. But its broader remit was to protect the Party from the people. It arrested, imprisoned and interrogated anyone it chose. It inspected all mail in secret rooms above post offices (copying letters and stealing any valuables), and intercepted, daily, tens of thousands of phone calls. It bugged hotel rooms and spied on diplomats. It ran its own universities, hospitals, elite sports centres and terrorist training programs for Libyans and the West Germans of the Red Army Faction. It pockmarked the countryside with secret bunkers for its members in the event of World War III. Unlike secret services in democratic countries, the Stasi was the mainstay of State power. Without it, and without the threat of Soviet tanks to back it up, the SED regime could not have survived.

The foyer of Stasi HQ is a large atrium. Soupy light comes through the windows behind a staircase that zigzags up to the offices. A small woman who reminds me of a hospital orderly—neat hair, sensible white shoes—is showing a tour group around. The visitors are chatty, elderly people, who have just got off a bus with Bonn numberplates. They wear bright colours and expensive fabrics, and have come to have a look at what would have happened to them had they been born, or stayed, further east.

The group is standing around a model of the complex, as the guide tells them what the demonstrators found here on the evening of 15 January 1990 when they finally got inside. She says there was an internal supermarket with delicacies unavailable anywhere else in the country. There was a hairdresser with rows of orange helmet-like dryers, 'for all those bristle-cuts'. There was a shoemaker and, of course, a locksmith. The guide crinkles her nose in order to push her glasses up its bridge; a reflex which doubles as a gesture of distaste. She explains that the neighbouring building—the archive—was invisible from outside the complex, and a copper-lined room had been planned for it, to keep information safe from satellite surveillance. There was a munitions depot here, and a bunker underneath for Mielke and a select few in the event of a nuclear catastrophe. She says Berliners used to refer to this place as the 'House of One Thousand Eyes'.

I start to look about the atrium. An arrow points towards a library, another up the stairs to an exhibition room. It smells of dust and old air.

Then I hear the guide say something about a 'biological solution'. The westerners are silent. She says instead of waiting for a revolution she and her friends had pinned their hopes on the old '*Marxisten-Senilisten*' in power dying off. After all, she says wrinkling her nose, the GDR had the oldest leadership in the world, 'We have got to have broken some kind of a record there.' But unlike in China, where the leaders were wheeled out virtually dead for display, the old men here showed remarkably little sign of physical decay. 'They were up to it all,' she explains, 'injecting sheep cells, ultra-high doses of oxygen, you name it. Those blokes wanted to live forever.' She starts to talk about the beginning of the end.

Mielke and Honecker grew up fighting the real evil of Nazism. And they kept on fighting the west, which they saw as Nazism's successor, for forty-five years after the war ended. They had to, as a Soviet satellite state, and the Eastern Bloc's bulwark against the west. But in East Germany they did so more thoroughly and with more pedantic enthusiasm than the Poles, the Hungarians, the Czechs, or the Russians themselves. They never wanted to stop.

When Mikhail Gorbachev came to power in the Soviet Union in 1985 he implemented the policies of *perestroika* (economic reform) and *glasnost* ('openness' of speech). In June 1988 he declared a principle of freedom of choice for governments within the Eastern Bloc and renounced the use of Soviet military force to prop them up. Without Soviet backup to quash popular dissent, as there had been at the workers' uprising in Berlin in 1953, in Hungary in 1956, and in Prague in 1968, the GDR regime could not survive. The options were change, or civil war.

By comparison with other Eastern Bloc countries, East Germany never had much of a culture of opposition. Perhaps this was in part due to the better standard of living, perhaps to the thoroughness of the Stasi— or, as some put it, to the willingness of Germans to subject themselves to authority. But mostly it was because, alone of all Eastern Bloc countries, East Germany had somewhere to dump people who spoke out: West Germany. It imprisoned them and then sold them to the west for hard currency. The numbers of dissidents could not reach a critical mass until 1989 when the changes in the Soviet Union gave ordinary people courage and they took to the streets.

But the men running the GDR were ossified. They were not interested in reform. As late as 1988, they disallowed Soviet films and magazines in an attempt to stop the people being infected with new ideas. And they cracked down, exiling waves of 'negative-enemy' elements to West Germany. Miriam's summary expulsion in May 1989 was one of the last of these purges.

They couldn't, however, all be thrown out. That would be impractical, and, worse, might amount to giving the people the freedom they craved. 'So,' the guide says, 'the old men had another scheme: they would contain the dissenters at home.'

Documents found after the Wall fell reveal meticulous plans, current throughout the 1980s, for the surveillance, arrest and incarceration of 85,939 East Germans, listed by name. On 'Day X' (the day a crisis, any crisis, was declared), Stasi officers in the 211 local branches were to open sealed envelopes containing the lists of the people in their area to be arrested.

The arrests were to be carried out quickly—840 people every two hours. The plans contained exact provisions for the use of all available prisons and camps, and when those were full for the conversion of other buildings: former Nazi detention centres, schools, hospitals and factory holiday hostels. Every detail was foreseen, from where the doorbell was located on the house of each person to be arrested to the adequate supply of barbed wire and the rules of dress and etiquette in the camps: armbands, 'green, 2cm wide' for the oldest in the room, 'green, three stripes 2cm wide' for the oldest in the camp, yellow with the letters 'SL' in black for the Shift Leader to be worn on the left upper arm. And there were written instructions for packing to be given upon arrest to each prisoner:

```
2 p. socks
2 towels
2 handkerchiefs
2 x underwear
1 x woollens
1 x toothbrush & paste
1 x shoe cleaning gear
Women:
In addition, sanitary supplies
```

They would be locked up indefinitely and for no reason at all, but they would have clean shoes, teeth and underwear.

By mid-1989 the demonstrations after Monday prayer meetings at

Leipzig's Nikolaikirche were spreading all over the country to Erfurt, Halle, Dresden, Rostock. People were protesting against travel restrictions, shortages of basic goods and the falsification of election results. Their protests took them to the offices of most obvious representatives of the regime: not the Party, but the Stasi. They cried, 'Democracy, Now or Never!', 'Stasi Out!' and 'SED. You're hurting me!'

In August, the Hungarians cut the barbed wire at their border with Austria, creating the first hole in the Eastern Bloc. Thousands of East Germans flocked there and ran, crying with relief and anger, across the border. Thousands more travelled to the West German embassies in Prague and Warsaw and set up camp, creating a diplomatic nightmare in German–German relations. Finally, the regime agreed to let them out, on condition that the trains taking them to West Germany travel through the GDR. Honecker hoped to humiliate the 'expellees' by confiscating their identity papers. And he wanted them to fear (as they did) that he would stop the trains and arrest the passengers.

Honecker's plans backfired. The people on the trains ripped up their identity papers with tears of joy. Thousands flocked to the stations to see if they could climb aboard, and to cheer on their compatriots.

In early October, Leipzig was at a flashpoint. Petrol-station attendants were refusing to refill police vehicles; the children of servicemen were being barred from creches. Those who worked in the centre of town near the Nikolaikirche were sent home early. Hospitals called for more blood. People made their wills and said things they wanted their children to remember, before going out to demonstrations. There were rumours of tanks and helicopters and water cannon coming, but then so were the postcards from friends who had already reached the west. The people went on to the streets.

Honecker ordered that the 'counter-revolutionaries' in Leipzig were to be 'nipped in the bud'. 'Nothing,' he said, 'can hinder the progress of socialism.' On 8 October Mielke began to activate the plans for 'Day X', sending out orders to the local Stasi branches to open their envelopes. But things were already too far gone. Instead of incarcerating the people, the Stasi, hiding in their buildings, locked themselves up. In the regional offices they had 60,000 pistols, more than 30,000 machine guns, hand grenades, sharpshooter's rifles, anti-tank guns, and tear gas. Fears of lynching ran high. Leipzig police were shown photographs of a Chinese policeman immolated by the mob at Tiananmen Square and told, 'It's you or it's them.' But they were also ordered not to shoot or use violence unless it was used against them.

On 7 October 1989 the GDR celebrated its forty years of existence with lavish parades in Berlin. There was a sea of red flags, a torchlight procession, and tanks. The old men on the podium wore light-grey suits studded with medals. Mikhail Gorbachev stood next to Honecker, but he looked uncomfortable among the much older Germans. He had come to tell them it was over, to convince the leadership to adopt his reformist policies. He had spoken openly about the dangers of not 'responding to reality'. He pointedly told the Politbüro that 'life punishes those who come too late'. Honecker and Mielke ignored him, just as they ignored the crowds when they chanted, 'Gorby, help us! Gorby, help us!'

In Leipzig the extraordinary courage of the people didn't waver, and it didn't break out into anything else. On 9 October 70,000 protesters went out in the dark, in big coats and carrying candles. They stood outside the Runden Ecke with their demands. 'Reveal the Stasi informers!' 'We are not Rowdies—We are the People!' and the constant, constant call of 'No Violence!' From that night on the demonstrations grew, footage of them was smuggled to the west and Leipzig came to be known as 'the City of Heroes'.

There were now protests outside Stasi offices all over the country. But even in the smallest towns, the Stasi men in them continued their meticulous work, faithfully sending back to Berlin reports of the demands of the crowds outside: 'Stasi to the factories!' (heard at Zeulenroda), 'We earn your money!' (from Schmalkalden) and the prescient 'Your days are numbered!' (Bad Salzungen). In Leipzig the demonstrators had started to shout, 'Occupy the Stasi Building Now!' and 'We're staying here!'

The Party belatedly tried to change its image. On 17 October Honecker was ousted by his deputy Egon Krenz, who, although younger, was just as disliked. Proceedings were started against Honecker on 8 November for abuse of office and corruption.

On 9 November, thinking to deal with the crisis, the Politbüro met and decided to relax travel restrictions. People would be allowed to travel freely and be prohibited from leaving the country only in 'special exceptional circumstances'. The session went into the night. At this stage the regime had taken to holding a regular press conference with the international media. That evening, Politbüro member Günter Schabowski needed to get to it. He hadn't been at the session, but was hastily given a note of its decision to read out at the press conference.

When he finished, there was no visible reaction among the journalists in the room; all pens were poised, the boom mikes floated in the air. Then a question came from the floor: 'When will this new provision come into force?' Schabowski has baggy eyes and a face like a bloodhound. Embarrassed, he looked at the paper. He turned it over but found no answer. 'It will come into force...to my knowledge, immediately,' he said.

The decision was to have become operable the next day, after the border guards had been instructed on its implementation. But as soon as Schabowski had spoken it was too late. Within hours of his blunder 10,000 people were at the Bornholmer Bridge checkpoint on foot and in their Trabant cars, thronging the Wall. The light from the death strip showed up breath, exhaust. There was a symphony of horns. The guards stood at trigger point, but no orders came. Eventually, the supervisor decided to let the people through, on one condition. The guards were to place the exit stamp to the left of the passport photographs of 'the most importunate' (those at the front of the queue), so that they could later be identified, and refused re-entry.

The people didn't know and they didn't care. They streamed through into West Berlin. When the first few came back with cans of western beer to show where they'd been, the guards tried to stop them coming home but it was too late, it was all over, and people from east and west were climbing, crying, and dancing on the Wall.

The Smell of Old Men

Here, at the Normannenstrasse headquarters, there was panic. Stasi officers were instructed to destroy files, starting with the most incriminating—those naming westerners who spied for them, and those that concerned deaths. They shredded the files until the shredders collapsed. Among other shortages in the east, there was a shredder shortage, so they had to send agents out under cover to West Berlin to buy more. In Building 8 alone, members of the citizens' movement found over one hundred burnt-out shredders. When the Stasi couldn't get any more machines, they started destroying the files by hand, ripping up documents and putting them into sacks. But this was done in such an orderly fashion—whole drawers of documents put into the same bag—that now, in Nuremberg, it is possible for the puzzle women to piece them back together.

On 13 November, Mielke, aged eighty-one, became desperate about the waning of his world. He made his first and only address to the parliament. It was broadcast live. 'Dear Comrades,' he opened, and the booing began. Cries of 'We are not your comrades!' came from the newly independent minor parties. Then, as if he simply could not understand why he might be disliked, Mielke stammered into the microphone. 'I love,' he said, '—but I love all people. I put myself out for you...' When they think of Mielke, East Germans like to think of this. Perhaps there is something healing about ridicule. It is a relief, anyway, from terror and anger.

On 3 December, along with Mielke, Krenz was expelled from the Party. Hans Modrow, a politician from Dresden, became leader. Modrow decided to change the name of the 'Ministry for State Security' to the 'Office of National Security' (*Amt für Nationale Sicherheit*) a cosmetic reform resulting in the deeply unfortunate acronym, 'Nasi'. Nobody was fooled.

The group of West Germans touring the building has become tighter. The quiet jokes among the men have stopped, the looks between the wives. The guide asks whether they would like to see upstairs, but they shuffle and shake their heads, and say they probably don't have time, today.

'Well then,' she says, 'we come now to the end of our story.' With her bossy manner and her twitching nose, she is not going to let these westerners go until she has told them how the people took this building.

She says that in January 1990 when the Berliners saw the smoke coming out of the chimneys they came here to protest. They brought bricks and rocks and built a symbolic wall around the building, to get the Stasi to stop burning the files. She says it is extraordinary that, with all those stones, not one was thrown and that, conversely, not one shot was fired from this building. 'There were a lot of Stasi agents mingled in among the demonstrators,' she sniffs, 'and maybe that's why they didn't fire—fear of hitting a colleague.' Eventually, after the Stasi had done all they could to remove or destroy the files, they opened the doors to the demonstrators.

The denunciations against Mielke began as soon as he lost power—and how could they not, his people being trained to the highest level in denunciation. The Berlin prosecutor's office received a note accusing Mielke of using public funds to build his hunting estate. In January 1990 more counts were added to the indictment: suspicion of high treason; collaboration to subvert the constitution in that he, along with Erich Honecker had instituted a 'nationwide system of post and telecommunications surveillance'; and having 'contrary to the law' denied people their freedom by locking them up in 'protective custody' on the occasion of the GDR's fortieth birthday.

Mielke was taken into remand. Through 1990 and 1991 he was in and out of custody in various Berlin prisons including Hohenschönhausen, where he had sent most of his political detainees. Further counts were added, including the charge of murdering the police officers in 1931. Mielke's trial began in 1992 but by the time it ended the only accusations remaining concerned the Bülowplatz murders. For his part in those, he was sentenced to six years in prison. The guide says to her flock, 'It was ridiculous to get him for those old murders.' Many people felt though, at least it was something. He was released on health grounds in August 1995, and lives now not far from this building.

Honecker fared worse. In early 1990 he was arrested on suspicion of corruption and high treason, but released from remand. In November of that year he was accused of responsibility for killings at the Wall but fled to Moscow, from where he told the press he had no regrets, and protested the arrest of former colleagues. In July 1992 he was extradited to Berlin to face trial, which was suspended the following January due to his terminal liver cancer. Honecker and his wife left for Chile, where he died in May 1994.

As the Party was losing its grip on the country, it started negotiating with the *Runden Tisch*, the consortium of East German citizens' rights activists and church groups. But even these were riddled with Stasi informers. Nevertheless, when the *Runden Tisch* passed a resolution at its first meeting on 7 December 1989 demanding that free elections be held, and that the Stasi be dissolved under civilian control, most of the informers voted in favour. It seems they felt compelled, in order to maintain their cover, to vote for measures to destroy the regime that employed them.

From 1989 to October 1990 debate raged hot in Germany as to what to do with the Stasi files. Should they be opened or burnt? Should they be locked away for fifty years and then opened, when the people in them would be dead or, possibly, forgiven? What were the dangers of knowing? Or the dangers of ignoring the past and doing it all again, with different coloured flags or neckerchiefs or helmets?

In the end, some files were destroyed, some locked away, and some opened. The *Runden Tisch* decided the *Hauptverwaltung Aufklärung* (the overseas arm of the Stasi) could disband itself. Too many files concerning too many foreign countries, not least the West German administration which had been infiltrated by Stasi spies, were in this trove, and they were too dangerous.

That left the files the Stasi kept on the people inside the GDR. Many East Germans, particularly those who had been in power, or were informers, argued against making them available. The West German government argued this too. Did it fear embarassment from what the files might reveal—its own dealings which supported the regime? Or would there be indiscriminate bloodletting, as people took revenge on informers?

In August 1990 the first and only elected parliament of the GDR passed a law granting the right for people to see their own files. But the West German government, in its draft Unification Treaty for the two countries, prescribed that the files would all be delivered to the Federal Archives in Koblenz, West Germany, where, most likely, they would be locked away.

Ordinary people in the GDR were horrified. They feared that all this information about them might continue to be used, or that they would never know how their lives had been manipulated by the Firm. Protests began. On 4 September 1990 campaigners occupied the lobby here, and a week later they began a hunger strike. The protesters were successful, and provisions were included in the Unification Treaty regulating access to the files.

On 3 October 1990, the day of German reunification and the day that the GDR ceased to exist, the East German pastor Joachim Gauck took office as head of the newly formed Stasi File Authority. It was a close call, but Germany was the only Eastern Bloc country in the end that so bravely, so conscientiously, opened its files on its people to its people.

The group leaves, not even muttering among themselves any more. I imagine they are in a hurry to get back to the international-style West Berlin hotel that reminds them of nothing, and I don't blame them. The guide comes over and asks me about my interest in this place. I explain that after the Runden Ecke in Leipzig, I wanted to see the Stasi head-quarters. I say though, that I'm looking to speak with people who confronted the regime, as much as those who represented it. 'In that case then,' she says, 'you need to meet Frau Paul.' I follow her into her office, a small space lined with binders of files, and she gives me a phone number.

I make my way up the stairs in the foyer. On the landing, glass cases display objects that hid tape recorders and cameras in order to document the 'enemy'. There is more variety than I saw in Leipzig: a flower pot, a watering can, a petrol canister, and a car door, all with cameras of varying sizes hidden in them. There's a thermos with a microphone in its lid, a hiking jacket with a camera sewn into the lapel pocket and an apparatus like a television antenna that could pick up conversations fifty metres away in other buildings, or while you were in your car, stopped at lights.

On the next landing I pass a black bust of Marx on a pedestal, god-like with flowing hair. One of the offices has been converted into a trophy room for Stasi trinkets. There are banners for each regiment, ribbons and medals for service and buttonhole pins as signs of senior-ity. There are miniature pointy-bearded Lenins in a range of sizes, and a long row of clenched plaster fists sticking up for international social-ism. There are trophies and vases and beer mugs with the GDR's hammer-and-compass insignia on them. A miniature boxed book set contains the life and deeds of Comrade Erich Honecker and there's a locket-sized portrait of Mielke himself in, of all things, enamel. A carpet hangs on the wall bearing the woolly triumvirate of Marx, Engels and Lenin in profile next to a lurid hand-worked mat with the Stasi insignia in red, yellow and black acrylic. The rugs fascinate me. They demonstrate, I think, the value of labour over everything else here, mostly aesthetics and utility.

A smaller room leads off from this one. At first I think it's going to be more revolutionary kitsch, but here there are just books and medals under glass. In fact, mostly there seem to be papers. But when I read them, I see why they deserve a room of their own. They are the 1985 plans of the Stasi, together with the army, for the invasion of West Berlin.

The plans are methodical. They include the division of the 'new territory' into Stasi branch offices, and figures for exactly how many Stasi men should be assigned to each. And there's a medal, cast in bronze, silver and gold by order of Honecker, to be awarded, after successful invasion, for 'Courage in the Face of the Western Enemy'. No-one in the west had imagined the extent of the Stasi's ambitions.

Mielke's quarters are on the second storey. There's no-one around. My shoes make a plasticky noise on the lino, till I reach his office where the floor is parquetry. It's a spacious room, with the feel of well-kept impoverishment. It is the same sense you might get visiting someone who bought their furniture as a bride in the 1950s but never had the means to update it. In fact, everything seems to be in that particular fifties yellowy-green colour, nuclear mustard.

The main feature of the room is a middling-sized veneer desk. As I approach I pass a portrait of Lenin. His eyes follow me across the room. The only things on the desk are two telephones and a white plaster death mask of Lenin. Life-size, his head seems small compared with all the exaggerated versions of it in wool and paint and marble in the treasure chamber downstairs. It also looks very dead—a *memento mori* in this belief system, like a crucifix in another. Aside from his presence though, this place could be the mayor's office in the down-at-heel council chambers of a small but proud rural town whose people recall fondly the days when wool prices were high.

The light is so bad now that outlines are blurring. I walk further, through Mielke's private quarters (a daybed and chair) and personal bathroom (a plain tiled affair) to a larger anteroom which now has cafeteria tables for tourists. It, too, is empty. There are a couple of old lounge chairs in one corner; a video plays on a television set. I move towards it, a source of light, and sit down to watch.

The film shows amateur footage of demonstrators storming this building on the cold night of 15 January 1990. They walked through the offices, the supermarket, the hairdressers, opening locked rooms and staring at the sacks and sacks of paper. They didn't seem jubilant; they didn't even show much bravado. Their faces wore instead a quiet mixture of disgust and sadness. I have heard this particular feeling described as not knowing whether you want to laugh or throw up.

It's cold in here, and the air tastes recycled. I pull my coat collar up to my ears. I think that there is no parallel in history where, almost overnight, the offices of a secret service have gone from being so feared they are barely mentionable, to being a museum where you can sit in an easy chair next to the boss's private pissoir and watch a video on how his office was stormed. There's a footfall behind me and I start. A small blonde woman in jeans and rubber gloves stands holding a canister of cleaning spray.

'Are you closing up now?' I ask. 'Should I go?'

She smiles and pats the air with a pink plastic hand. 'You're all right,' she says. 'We're the last people left, so we might as well leave together when I'm done.'

She starts spraying the tables with perfumed ammonia. I turn back to the film. It shows footage of the Stasi mortuary in Leipzig—bodies on slabs, including that of a young man with no apparent injuries. It switches to an interview with a worker at the Southern General Cemetery who explains that, 'about twenty or thirty times' he'd had a call to leave a certain oven open 'so that the Stasi could do their business'. The man looks uncomfortable, but he also shrugs as if to say, 'it was just my job'. The voice-over comments that some thirty urns were found at the Leipzig Stasi offices, unlabelled and unclaimed. I wonder whether Miriam knows this. I think I should call her.

The next item is an interview with a man with neat hair and a red moustache who was a Stasi psychologist. He is accounting for the willingness of people to inform on their countrymen, which he calls 'an impulse to make sure your neighbour was doing the right thing'. He doesn't bat an eyelid. 'It comes down to something in the German mentality,' he says, 'a certain drive for order and thoroughness and stuff like that.'

Stuff like that. There's a cough behind me.

'Of course *I* lived normally,' the cleaning woman says. I turn around. She has a smoker's lined face and hollow-chested thinness. 'I conformed, just like everybody else. But it's not true to say the GDR was a nation of seventeen million informers. They were only two in a hundred.'

'Yes,' I say, and then I'm stumped. Even with one informer for every fifty people, the Stasi had the whole population covered.

She gives up on me. 'Can't get these tables clean,' she says, and turns back to her work.

When she finishes we start moving out through Mielke's private quarters, his bathroom and his office. She locks the doors behind us as we go. 'You know, there's no real unity in this country,' she says, 'even after seven years. I don't feel like I belong here at all. Did you know that in the suburb of Kreuzberg in West Berlin they wanted the Wall back! To protect them from us!' She lights a cigarette. 'Can you understand this German thinking?'

I hope it's a rhetorical question. All I understand is that it only took forty years to create two very different kinds of Germans, and that it will be a while before those differences are gone.

We pass a toilet with 'H' for *Herren* on it. 'They only needed a men's bathroom,' she says. 'Women couldn't get past colonel rank and there were just three of them anyway. This was a *Männerklub*.'

She puts her head into a small room for a sentry. 'Have a look at this,' she says. Over the desk a calendar is still on January 1990. 'No, over there.' She points to the other wall, behind the desk. There's a smudge on the paintwork. 'That's where the fella would have leant back on his chair and rested his fat greasy head on the wall.' She's disgusted. 'Won't come off.'

We move on, down the zigzag stairs past Marx and his billowing hair. The only sound is of our footfalls, and the only light now is from over the entrance downstairs. 'Do you get spooked here, by yourself at night?' I ask.

'Sometimes,' she says, 'but it was much worse back when we had just opened. At that time the whole building smelled—we cleaned and cleaned and we just couldn't get rid of the smell.'

She stops walking and turns her face up to me. Even in the half-light her eyes are cornflower blue and pretty. She winces. 'Do you know it?' She does not wait for an answer. 'It was the smell,' she says, 'of old men.'

Telephone Calls

The phone rings. I steel myself for another Stasi man. But it's a woman's voice.

'Anna, Anna is that you?' Something turns itself over in my chest. It's Miriam.

'Yes, Miriam, hello, I've been meaning—'

'I'm just calling,' she says, 'to say thank you for the other day. I wanted to thank you very much.'

What is she thanking *me* for? Suddenly I know I should have called her earlier. 'No, please, I thank you,' I say. Something is odd here. A retreat from intimacy is taking place.

'It was very nice to meet you,' she says. 'And I wish you good luck with your work.'

This sounds final. I want to ask whether she has heard about the unclaimed urns at the Runden Ecke, but it feels wrong. 'Perhaps we could meet again,' I say, 'at some point.'

'I'd love to,' she says quickly. 'I'd love you to come down, sometime. We could visit my friends who have a sculpture garden. It's very beautiful, and I'd like you to meet them, and…' She trails off. 'Just call me and we'll go there.'

'I will,' I say, 'and thanks. For everything.'

I replace the handset. If I were Miriam and had told the most painful and formative parts of my life to someone, I'm not sure I'd want to see that person again either. Especially if my life had already been written down by other people, stolen and steered. The phone is made of black plastic. It's not a walk-around model but as a compromise some nifty student attached an extremely long extension cord to it. I walk back through the bare and broken apartment, retracing the lead to its source.

I've dragged my mattress into the living room, to be closer to the heater. Every evening I watch television until I fall asleep. It is a canny box which receives only three channels but they are of its own choosing, and one of them, although I have no dish, is a satellite channel. They are all black and white, and the terrestrial ones have constant snow.

Late at night there's a program called 'PEEP!' Guests are interviewed and quizzed about their sex lives in seamy catch-22 hypotheticals ('If your girlfriend brought her sister home to play with would you…?' 'Is there anything you have had to give up since the reassignment?'). Footage is shown to tempt the censorship provisions—about sex expos, sex experiments, sex revues and sexual art.

Tonight there's a feature about a Leipzig stripper named Heidi, aka Yasmina. Yasmina is stocky and firm-bodied with blue eyes and fake blonde hair. This evening she and her brood are doing a 'horror-erotic' show inspired by *Walpurgisnacht*, the night when witches meet to revel with the Devil. On the stage young witches, wearing latex masks, leopard-skin and lace, are undressed by skeletons till they are nothing but rubber faces and sequinned G-strings in the dry ice gloom. The camera zooms dizzyingly in and out from breasts and crotches. Then there's an interview with Yasmina, who has pushed her witch's face onto the top of her head so that the nose droops a little over her forehead, nodding when she speaks. The interviewer wants to know what it was like to have had the only strip school 'back in the GDR', and, 'is it true'—he puts the microphone closer to her face—'that you stripped for the Politbüro?'

Yasmina smiles and flutters a taloned hand. 'I always want to offer my public something a little different,' she says, 'then as now.' She winks, the nose nods, and the program cuts abruptly to the next segment: plaster casts of body parts. The first is a female torso, the second a pair of long-nailed fingers either side of a clitoris. An unctuous man's voice says, 'PEEP!-Special! For 250 marks you too can have your most intimate parts preserved forever in plaster of Paris.'

I'm no longer capable of making sense of this. The whiteness of the plaster reminds me only of the dead Lenin's head on Mielke's desk. I switch channels and find my favourite program. It is manna for insomniacs, people like me who do not want to stay still. A camera is attached to the top of a vehicle. As it drives the pictures glide over the roads and lanes and highways of eastern Germany in glorious summer. The footage is mesmerising: flying bodiless through villages, down the main streets, and then out into the countryside again. The shops are open or closed, aproned women sweep footpaths where people sit drinking coffee, mothers run from under the umbrellas after straying children, road workers lean around in overalls. This is the world unfrozen. It's black and white and snowing on my screen, but I know that it is really the bright yellow of rape, the green haziness of wheat, and the heavier green of summer oaks lining the road. Occasionally we stop at traffic lights, level with the hooded eye. Then on and on, moving magically through village after thawed village, places I have never been and may never go.

In my sleep I continue soundlessly through the countryside, exhilarated by the wind on my skin. Suddenly I am joined by another woman flying at the same height. There is a blur where her face should be, but that doesn't bother me at all. She is naked, apart from pink rubber gloves. Her nipples are puckered a deeper pink and her pubic hair is luscious gold. I'm startled that I'm not alone in the air, that she's naked. 'The gloves, of course, are for driving,' she says. I nod, and I look at my hands. I have no gloves. Then I look at my body and see that I am naked too. My feeling of wellbeing evaporates. I glance down over the main street of a village— there are people beneath us. The church bell starts to ring, it rings and rings and will not stop and soon I know I'll drop—I have no driving gloves!—and they'll all see me, fallen and naked and pointless.

I wake up to get the phone. The clock says 2.30 am—heart attack hour, the hour of bad news from home. Or another Stasi man? Telephone harassment is common, but I can't be high on their list. It must be the fifteenth ring by the time I find the black phone, the duvet wrapped around me.

'Hello?'

'Hello my friend.' A lubricated voice from my local pub, coming down the line through a mouth with a pipe in it, a thick Saxon accent and a beard. It's Klaus. By the sound of it he's holding his chin up with the receiver.

'How'd you pull up after last time?' he asks, 'Feel like another drinking session?'

'Klaus, it's 2.30 in the morning.'

'Come on,' he says, 'this time the other night you were just getting into it.'

I have no wish to be reminded of other nights. In my view one of the conventions among decent drinking partners is that where there isn't actual amnesia it should be simulated. The other night we filled the air with words and smoke that are all gone now. My only memory is of the hangover I took with me to Leipzig.

'I had a big day.'

'It's nice here,' he says. 'They're playing our song.'

This is not a come-on. He means they're playing *his* song.

Klaus Renft is the legendary 'Mik Jegger' of the Eastern Bloc. He lives around the corner from me in a one-room apartment lined with videos and posters of his band, the Klaus Renft Combo. There are always sports bags full of beer and every kind of smoking equipment known to man. We are both regulars at the local pub, which we use, effectively, as a living room. The pub sound system is pumping out the plaintive and beautiful song '*Hilflos*', re-recorded on their recent comeback album.

'You still there?' he says.

'Yep. And I'm staying here.'

'Sweet dreams then, kiddo,' he slurs. When he hangs up the receiver misses its cradle and dangles upside-down in the air. I take the phone back to bed. I lie listening to '*Hilflos*', and then I hang up.

I wake to the phone ringing. It's morning.

'*Guten Tag*. You put an advertisement in the *Märkische Allgemeine*.'

'Yes. Thank you for calling. I am looking to speak with people who worked for the ministry, in order to be able to represent what it was like. I'm writing about life in the GDR.'

There is a pause. 'The notice said you were Australian.'

'Yes.'

'You are Australian?'

'Yes.'

'You are from Australia?'

'That's right.'

In the GDR a great swathe of geography remained theoretical because people couldn't travel outside the Eastern Bloc. If easterners thought about Australia at all, it was as an imaginary place to go in the event of a nuclear catastrophe.

'You are writing in English or in German?'

'In English.'

'I will meet with you,' he says. 'In order to set the record straight. It is possible that in Australia your media has not tainted people against us, and that there at least, we can put our side. With objective information and analysis. Are you available tomorrow?'

'Yes.'

'In Potsdam, in the afternoon?'

'Yes.'

'Then I will meet with you as follows: I will be outside the church on market square at fifteen hundred hours. I will have tomorrow's *Märkische Allgemeine* rolled up under my left arm. Understood?'

'Yes,' I say obediently, although I am incredulous that this man wants to play spy games seven years after the fall of the Wall. And then I ask, 'What is your name?'

Another pause. 'Winz.'

'Till tomorrow then, Herr Winz.'

I'm early to the church and stand alone in its forecourt. The sky is blanket-grey and close. I am wearing all-purpose black boots and a black coat with fake fur trim and I stand out a mile. I have so obviously nothing to do but wait for an assignation. At the market next to the church, women in bright scarves and woollen gloves push their strollers around caravan stalls, nosing under the red-and-white striped awnings. They buy potatoes and pickles from vats, and chunks of pink liverwurst. At the deli a man with ham-hock forearms serves a council worker a sausage and a piece of bread on a paper plate. The bells chime three times. I hop from one cold leg to the other.

After ten minutes a man approaches with a newspaper rolled under his left arm. He's about sixty, paunchy and jowly as a hound-dog. He's wearing a foreign-looking tweed suit coat. When he takes the newspaper from under his arm to greet me, I see it even has leather elbow patches: he is disguised as a westerner.

'The parking here is terrible,' Herr Winz says by way of apology for being late, but also as if it were my fault. He speaks in authoritative barks. 'I suggest we go to a neutral place,' he says. 'I usually use the Hotel Merkur.'

Neutral? Usually? 'Fine by me, Herr Winz,' I say, and we set off on foot to the hotel, a good fifteen minutes from here. It occurs to me that he has hidden his car somewhere so that, should I succumb to the urge, I can't tail him. I'm glad to get moving anyway.

The hotel has a low-ceilinged lobby with brown booth seats and a lot of plastic plants. There is no-one else here. We order coffee from a waiter with a strawberry mark over one side of his nose and I start to explain to Herr Winz my interest in speaking with former Stasi employees. He waves me silent. He waits until the waiter is well out of earshot. Then he leans forward. 'One cannot be too careful these days,' he says, tapping his nose and glancing towards the waiter's back. Then he eyeballs me. 'First, please show me your ID,' he says.

'*Bitte?*'

'I would like to see your identity card,' he says.

'I don't have one.'

'What do you mean?' he asks.

'In Australia we don't have ID cards.'

He is speechless. He looks at me as though all his suspicions are confirmed: I come from a place so remote, so primitive that the people there have not yet been labelled and numbered.

I give in. 'But I have a passport,' I say and pull it out of my bag. There are a great many things one cannot do anonymously here—from buying a mobile phone card to travelling on a train. I have had to prove my identity so frequently that I now carry my passport around with me like a fugitive.

He reads my date of birth and checks me against my younger self. Then he flicks through its pages to see where I have been in the last few years. 'Ah, Czechoslovakia,' he mutters at one point. Then he sees that back in 1987 I was in the GDR. 'So you visited my country,' he says approvingly.

'Yes, I came here to Potsdam and I went to Dresden,' I say, 'and I went to a party once with some friends in East Berlin.'

I remember a cold grey day in Potsdam like this one, the streets deserted. Our busload of undergraduates visited only the paved and gilded parts of this show-town, selected streets made into a neat sheep-run for tourists. In Dresden we were shunted up a hill in a cable car and fed a meal, which, including the steak substitute, came entirely from tins. At my East Berlin party, the host, a Jewish journalist of impeccable Communist pedigree, was revealed after the Wall fell to have been an informer. I may gain credibility in this man's eyes from having a couple of hammer-and-compass stamps in my passport, but it could not be said that I knew his country. I visited it only long enough to wonder what was being kept from me.

I ask to see Herr Winz's ID too, but he fobs me off with a laugh and a dismissive gesture. Behind him the waiter starts, as if this could be a summons, but I catch his eye and shake my head slightly. He slides his notepad back into his apron pocket.

Herr Winz opens his briefcase and takes out papers and pamphlets and a thesis bound in a springboard cover. Then he places a small hardback book on top of the pile. It is Karl Marx and Friedrich Engels' *The Communist Manifesto*.

He tells me he worked from 1961 to 1990 at the ministry in Potsdam, exclusively in counter-espionage. He picks up the thesis and reads its title:

> The Work of the Ministry for State Security on the Defence Against Intelligence Infiltration by the Secret Services of the NATO States against the GDR. Presented from the Viewpoint of a Member of the Division for Counter-Espionage, Regional Administration, Potsdam.

'This is a discussion paper I wrote based on my work at the ministry. If you read this, you will learn a lot of what you want to know.'

I flick to the front page, and see that the paper was written in 1994 for the 'Potsdam Working Group of the *Insiderkomitee* for the Re-examination of the History of the Ministry for State Security, Inc.'

'This was written for the *Insiderkomitee*?' I ask.

'Yes.'

'You are a member?'

'Yes, but we have changed our name to the "Society for the Protection of Civil Rights and the Dignity of Man".'

The *Insiderkomitee*. Civil Rights and the Dignity of Man? I have heard of this group. It is a more or less secret society of former Stasi men who write papers putting their side of history, lobby for entitlements for former Stasi officers, and support one another if facing trial. They have close links to the successor party to the SED, the Party of Democratic Socialism, and it is alleged that together they may have access to the tens of millions of marks which belonged to the SED and remain unaccounted for.

It is widely suspected, however, that these men also harass people who they fear may uncover them. A former border guard who appeared on a television talk show was threatened with an acid attack and had to be placed under police protection. Home-delivered harassment is popular: one man had a ticking package delivered to his doorstep; wives have had to sign for porn not ordered by their husbands. The strangest incident I heard of was when a man was delivered a truckload of puppies, yelping outside his door and the driver demanding a signature. Car brake-leads have been cut, accidents and deaths reverse-engineered. The child of an outspoken writer was picked up from school by a person or persons unknown and taken to drink hot chocolate, just for an hour or so. Detaining people clearly has its own pleasures; a habit hard to break.

I look at Herr Winz and suddenly the landscape here seems crowded with victims: of the Nazis, of Stalin, of the SED and the Stasi; and now this lot, wannabe victims of democracy and the rule of law.

'What does the *Insiderkomitee* do?' I ask.

'We try to present an objective view of history,' he says. 'To combat the lies and misrepresentation in the western media.'

'It is said that the *Insiderkomitee* is also a front to co-ordinate action against those working to uncover what the Stasi did to people.'

'I wouldn't know about that.'

'Why not?'

'I am a small fish,' he says. 'I am here to tell you about the excellent work—the masterful work—of the Stasi in counter-espionage. That is where I spent my life.'

Either Herr Winz doesn't know much, or he's not telling. He won't respond to my questions about the *Insiderkomitee* or talk about himself either. Each time I ask him about the reality of life in the GDR he returns to the beauties of socialist theory. I think he hopes, through me, to sow the seeds of socialism in an untainted corner of the world.

'We had people everywhere!' he says. His main interest seems to have been placing young committed East Germans into lives in West Germany, where they would eventually come into the sights of the West German security service and be recruited. 'We had them very high up! We had Günter Guillaume as Chancellor Brandt's secretary and Klaus Kuron in West German counter-intelligence and the woman who prepared Chancellor Kohl's daily intelligence briefings!' This is true, but it is widely known. I find it hard to believe that Herr Winz was personally involved at a high level. He's too underconfident and unconvincing with all his spy play-acting to have ever done it for real. I try to imagine what he probably did do, because he won't tell me. The best I can come up with is that he wrote procedural manuals.

But Herr Winz is warming to his tale. 'The CIA—now they were bandits! A very nasty crew. Did you know they made twenty attempts on Fidel Castro's life?'

'They couldn't have been very good then,' I smile. He looks startled. He is not amused.

'Bandits!' he shouts, 'I said they were bandits!'

I cast a look behind him in the direction of the waiter, shuffling busily at his station. If he had any curiosity about this man's origins, it is now well and truly sated.

'How are you treated today, as a former Stasi man?' I ask. I would like to find out why he is disguised as a westerner.

'The foe has made a propaganda war against us, a slander and smear campaign. And therefore I don't often reveal myself to people. But in Potsdam people come up and say'—he puts on a small sorry voice—'"You were right. Capitalism is even worse than you told us it would be. In the GDR you could go out alone at night as a woman! You could leave your apartment door open!"'

You didn't need to, I think, they could see inside anyway.

'This capitalism is, above all, exploitation! It is unfair. It's brutal. The rich get richer and the masses get steadily poorer. And capitalism makes war! German imperialism in particular! Each industrialist is a criminal at war with the other, each business at war with the next!' He takes a sip of coffee and holds his hand up to stop me asking any more questions.

'Capitalism plunders the planet too—this hole in the ozone layer, the exploitation of the forests, pollution—we must get rid of this social system! Otherwise the human race will not last the next fifty years!'

There is an art, a deeply political art, of taking circumstances as they arise and attributing them to your side or the opposition, in a constant tallying of reality towards ends of which it is innocent. And it becomes clear as he speaks that socialism, as an article of faith, can continue to exist in minds and hearts regardless of the miseries of history. This man is disguised as a westerner, the better to fit unnoticed into the world he finds himself in, but the more he talks the clearer it becomes that he is undercover, waiting for the Second Coming of socialism.

He pulls himself together and lowers his voice, leaning towards me in a conspiratorial way. His breath is hot and bitter from coffee and small flecks of brownish spittle spray over the cardboard thesis cover. 'Have this.' He passes me *The Communist Manifesto* from the top of his pile. It looks well-loved. 'You should read it,' he hisses. 'Then you will understand a great deal more. There is, even today, no better analysis of capitalism. It's a present from me.' He takes out a pen and inscribes it to me 'as a memento of our Potsdam discussion'.

'Thank you very much.'

Herr Winz collects his material and stands up to go. Then he puts one set of knuckles down on the table and pushes his face close to mine. 'You can take it from me,' he says. 'I have lived through a revolution already—in 1989—and I know the signs.' His voice is getting louder. I can see the veins in his forehead. 'This system is on its last legs! Its days are numbered! Capitalism will not last! The revolution'—he raises his fist off the table—'is coming.'

Then he marches through the lobby out the front door, and the waiter brings me the bill.

A cheery voice: 'No-one can come to the phone right now, but if you leave a message, someone will call back as soon as possible. If it's good news, even sooner. Bye.'

'Miriam, it's Anna,' I start. Then I hear the electronic beep. I start again. 'Miriam, it's Anna calling. Just to say hello really. No news. I'll call back another time, or you can reach me on the Berlin number. Hope all's well.' I can't think of any other small thing to say. 'Bye.'

For a few days afterwards each time the phone rings I think it might be her, but it's mostly Stasi men. After a week or so, despite the Stasi men, I somehow remain hopeful when the phone rings. Another week passes and this feeling coagulates into something grimmer: have I offended her? I fill her silence with possible scenarios: 'she's lost my number', 'she's on holiday' and even the full-blown, 'now that she has re-lived her story it's all too much and she's swinging from a rope in her tower'. Despite the vividness of this last, I decide to give it another fortnight or so before I call again. At some level, at least, I am aware that I am following a person who has been hounded enough.

Does telling your story mean you are free of it? Or that you go, fettered, into your future?

9

Julia Has No Story

After work I catch the underground to Rosenthaler Platz and then walk home through the park. Away from the corner the grass slopes into a hill, rare for this swamp city. At the top there is a community centre with a terrace café that serves coffee and beer. Saturday afternoons the centre fills with dancing pensioners moving in tender, timeless coupledom.

The pensioners are just visiting—the park belongs to the drunks and the punks. The drunks dress either in tracksuits or old business suits. Each morning they emerge from the corners of the park and shuffle together in an amphitheatre arrangement around the statue of Heine. All day long they hold what look like philosophical discussions, gesticulating slowly with their free hands and clasping tins of beer with the other. They seem to share knowledge of a world where each of them once had a place.

Closer to the station are the young people. Here, there are women as well as men. They have as much beer and as many cigarettes as the drunks, but a lot more rancour. Their heads are partially shaved or covered with dreadlocks in blue and deep black, their faces pierced, limbs tattooed. Their appearance says both 'Look at me' and 'Fuck off'. There are fights and tears; terrible pain, public in the park. Sometimes they ask for money. Unlike the drunks who claim the benches and tram shelters, the young people sit or sleep on the ground, with only their dogs for warmth. The dogs often look better groomed than the humans. But this afternoon, passing one young man, I realise I probably underestimate the effort required to maintain a cockscomb of eight 12-inch cones of hair erect and green, every day.

My door is unlocked. Pushing it open, I can see through to the living room. It looks like a giant cat has pissed, twice, on the lino. Then I hear a sound I know instinctively from my childhood: possums in the roof. Only the roof of this building is four storeys higher. I turn around and there's a ladder set up against the wall in the hallway to the height of the mezzanine, about a metre under the ceiling.

'Only me, only me,' a muffled voice says. A small behind in army pants is backing out. 'I came over to water the plants,' Julia turns to me. 'I thought I'd just get some of this old stuff while I was here.' She passes me a bike pump like a relay baton and climbs down with a shoebox under one arm.

'Old love letters,' she says apologetically, and to my surprise she turns red. The blush begins at the neck and moves rapidly up to her yellow hair. This used to happen to me until some merciful god put an end to it so I don't look, but walk straight through to the kitchen.

Julia has started to use the plants as a reason to drop by, both as if she is saving me the trouble of watering them, and by way of gentle rebuke. 'The plants' are two skinny crooked bald-trunked palm things in pots in the living room and not only is it true that I forget to water them—I forget their existence altogether. Subconsciously I have come to think of this apartment as some kind of closed and self-sustaining universe, with its own laws of nature. It tolerates my presence but demands as little interference from me as possible. I just keep to my tracks: bed to bath, window to desk.

Julia comes through to the kitchen. Along with the army pants, she is wearing her usual assortment of black: black boots, black baggy jumpers and a black scarf twisted like a dishrag around her neck. Right now she is black, red and yellow, uncharacteristically patriotic in the colours of the German flag.

'Coffee?' I ask.

'Love some. I ran out two days ago.'

I look at her and I know that under all those layers of black is a wiry body and a sharp-sharp mind, but there is something about Julia that breaks my heart. She has an honesty I have started to think of as East German, a transparent fairness with all things that leaves her so open. But it's not that. She is a hermit crab, all soft-fleshed with friends but ready to whisk back into its shell at the slightest sign of contact. It's not that either. I don't know what it is.

'I've been thinking lately about all the drunks and the homeless in the park,' I say.

'There were no drunks before the Wall came down,' Julia says. 'I mean,' she corrects herself, 'in the park. No-one was homeless as they are now.'

They might not have been in the park, but there certainly were drunks. Per capita the East Germans drank more than twice as much as their West German counterparts. Sometimes they had to live in untenable arrangements because of the lack of housing: divorced couples still together, or newlyweds with the in-laws. Whatever the other shortages were, you could always, always buy beer and schnapps. People were drunk on the job, drunk after work, and drunk at home putting up with one another in a place from which there was no escape.

Julia adds, 'You should be careful of those bums, you know.'

'Oh, the drunks at least seem harmless enough.'

'Well they're not,' she says. 'One of them once climbed up that tree outside the living-room window and got in here.'

'Really? What for?' I realise I think of the road outside as some kind of moat between me and the park.

'He took a cassette recorder.'

'How do you know who it was?'

'The neighbour said she saw him leaving the building,' she says. 'You shouldn't leave those front windows open.'

I find it hard to picture one of the rubber-legged drunks making his way across the road and shimmying up the ash tree into here.

'It's getting worse, I find,' she says. 'I mean not only that sort of thing, but just being on the street you get harassed nearly every day.' She flips a lank piece of hair off her face, and it flips back.

Whatever and whoever they are, those drunks are not aggressive. Fuelled by beer, they have reached another world where their potency, albeit limitless, is entirely imaginary. They have never done anything more than nod a greeting as I walk by. Perhaps Julia needs to be able to pin down aggressors, to know exactly who and where they could be. But I am willing to admit that I notice staring men on the street. 'I think that sort of thing happens to me more here than at home,' I tell her. 'Although it might be just that I notice things more here than at home.'

'That would be because men can tell you're foreign,' she says.

'What do you mean?' I have always assumed I inherited enough from my Danish forebears to pass here incognito.

'Well,' Julia says, 'You don't look German.'

'Oh?'

'You're too pale.' I feel the colour draining from me. 'Your skin is too pale. Your eyes are too pale. When a German has blue eyes for instance, they are really blue. Not your kind of pale colour.'

I am fading, blending in with the kitchen walls, which were once white but seem to me now an odd, remarkably flesh-like colour. I look at Julia and she reminds me of myself—straggly fair hair she doesn't care much about, grey-green eyes and slightly crooked teeth that have seen a bit much nicotine. I wonder whether she started off a true German, much brighter. I don't know what to say, but she's lost in thought anyway.

'I think it's because my first boyfriend was such a macho,' she's saying, 'that might be one reason I react so strongly to harassment.'

I'm still gazing at her, wondering just how it is that we can have such wrong ideas of what we look like, our colour and shape and the space we take up in the world.

'Actually,' Julia is chuckling, 'he was *macho autentico*—he was Italian.'

'How on earth did you find an Italian boyfriend?' This conversation is getting weirder. Julia could never have travelled in the 'non-socialist abroad', as the rest of the world was known, and there was no Italian immigration into the GDR. Involuntarily, an Italian boyfriend of my own flashes to mind: an ice-cream vendor with a beautiful voice and a truck with bells, sweet Mr Whippy.

'Long story,' she mutters. 'You know,' she says, looking into her mug, 'having lived in both east and west without moving house, I think I can tell you that there's a difference between sexual stalking, and stalking, neat.'

She sits framed by the window onto the yard. The late afternoon light comes through her wisps of hair, illuminating them like live things around her head. In the yard sparrows wheel and duck through the empty chestnut tree. The sky hangs, pale and veined, over the rooftops.

'Oh?' I ask.

'Yes. For instance, when we were teenagers the local lads would come by in summer time—my sisters and I would be on the balcony sunbaking. They'd hoon up and down on their motorbikes. Sometimes they'd take their shirts off for us. There was nothing scary about it. But there was also a car—for the GDR an expensive car, a Russian Lada—that would sometimes come and crawl slowly along the street in front of our house. We lived in a detached house a bit outside the town, and there were no other houses around. The Lada had two men in it. That was creepy.'

'Yes,' I say. I have decided not to ask questions. I am hoping Julia will not slip back inside her shell. 'Must have been different though if there were four of you—some safety in numbers.'

'That car,' she says deliberately, 'was there for me.'

'What?'

'Long story…' She takes a sip of coffee and is silent for a moment. 'It had to do with the Italian boyfriend, actually.'

The laws of love I assume, like the laws of gravity, apply everywhere. We are back to boyfriends. 'Things can end so badly,' she says.

'Not wrong there,' I say, though I have been generally of the belief that the young heart is rubbery and unlikely to scar.

'It was funny, really, I guess. I ended it with my Italian boyfriend when we were on holiday in Hungary.'

'That would have been one great holiday.' She ignores me.

'…But that wasn't the end of it at all.'

'Never is really, is it?'

'No, no,' she says, 'I mean something else. I ended up at the police.'

'What?'

'At least I thought I was at the police.'

'How——?'

'Long story,' she says again. I am realising this is code for 'no story'. Instead, she asks me about my trip to Leipzig. I tell her I met a woman whose life was shadowed and controlled by the Stasi, and about the row of Stasi men now lined up in my life. I say I'm looking out for other people too, who lived through Communism, the twentieth century's experiment on humans.

Julia glances away. 'I don't have any story of the Stasi, or anything like that,' she says.

The clock in this apartment works, and she looks up at it. 'Thanks for the coffee. I've got to go. Got a class.'

I am suddenly far away, thinking of old boyfriends, more experiments on humans. I remember the freedom of youth to mount exploratory expeditions into deeply inappropriate territory: the misjudged, the flaky, the devastatingly dim, the latent homosexual, the baby rock star who sang flat. Afterwards, there's something one does to past lovers—a kind of post-mortem of memory manoeuvre that aspirates all the gooey parts leaving them dried and stable, unable to bite. The taxidermy of lost love. I don't want to be left here alone now with all those stuffed heads in my attic, shaking in high winds. Old boyfriends seem like safer ground than old Stasi men. I want her to stay.

Julia puts her shoebox of love letters on her lap and pushes her chair out.

I can't stop myself. 'Please stay,' I say.

She looks up and I can see that she's surprised by my neediness. 'OK then,' she says. She puts the shoebox back on the floor with a small cardboard thud.

'Right,' I say, and then the gods abandon me and I blush from collar-bone to brow, crimson.

I get up to heat more water in a saucepan on the stove. Standing, I can see the corner of the yard where the high stone walls meet, closing us in. A sandpit is tucked in there, and next to it a wooden table. Opposite, the crooked stables seem to be inching, almost audibly, towards the ground.

We drink more coffee and she stays. Later on we make a meal from what there is in the fridge—smoked halibut and bread and cheese, with fennel tea.

Julia and I were born the same year, 1966, which makes all kinds of maths in our parallel universes possible and immediate. She was twenty-three when the Wall fell, part of the fortunate younger generation which could catch up with its western contemporaries. She could get an education and a new life, instead, like many older people, of just losing her old one. But Julia is still studying some—by her own admission—obscure Eastern Bloc languages at Humboldt University, languages which can only be of use if she goes to hide out in the obscure places in which they are spoken. Students in Germany often stay at the university into their late twenties, but it seems to me she is never going to leave. I'm curious about her: a single woman in a single room at the top of her block, unable to go forward into her future.

'There are things I don't remember,' she says. I can't tell whether she means she makes it a practice not to think of them, or she cannot recall. To my relief she has started to talk anyway, and she has the kind of finely articulated voice you occasionally come across here, which can turn this barking language into a song of aching beauty and finesse.

Julia Behrend is the third of four girls. Her parents, born during the early years of the war, were both high-school teachers in a town in Thüringen, the small state tucked in the south-western corner of East Germany.

Like many families, the Behrends were ambivalent about their country. 'We weren't dissidents; we weren't in church groups or environmental groups or anything like that,' Julia says. 'We were an ordinary family. None of us had ever had a run-in with the state.' Nevertheless, they lived with a distinct sense 'from the minute we woke up', of what could be said outside the home (very little), and what could be discussed in it (most things).

Julia's parents had different ways of managing their relationship with the authorities. Her mother Irene is a practical woman. She didn't expect a great deal from the state, and she didn't rock the boat to change it. As a girl she had been a swimmer, a high jumper and a trapeze artist. She told her daughters they could be anything they wanted to be.

Julia's father Dieter is a sensitive man. He wanted to better what he saw as a flawed system, but one which, from its founding premise, was fairer than capitalism. Unlike his wife, he was a joiner: he joined the Free German Youth (the *Freie Deutsche Jugend*, or FDJ—the Communist successor to the Hitler Youth) and later, as many teachers were encouraged to do, he even joined the Party.

For his pains, his country made him a pariah and his life a misery. 'Every Wednesday before the Party meetings Dad would be in a foul mood,' Julia says, 'really grim.' Dieter spoke up against things he disagreed with, such as recruiting eighth-graders for the army, or teaching boring Russian socialist-realist writers. He would come home hollow. 'They dressed him down like a child there.'

In the GDR people were required to acknowledge an assortment of fictions as fact. Some of these fictions were fundamental, such as the idea that human nature is a work-in-progress which can be improved upon, and that Communism is the way to do it. Others were more specific: that East Germans were not the Germans responsible (even in part) for the Holocaust; that the GDR was a multi-party democracy; that socialism was peace-loving; that there were no former Nazis left in the country; and that, under socialism, prostitution did not exist.

Many people withdrew into what they called 'internal emigration'. They sheltered their secret inner lives in an attempt to keep something of themselves from the authorities. After 1989 Dieter retired from teaching as soon as he could. He was depressed, and required medication. 'I think one could count him too, as a victim of the regime,' Julia says. Living for so long in a relation of unspoken hostility but outward compliance to the state had broken him.

Lately, a study has suggested that depressed people have a more accurate view of reality, though this accuracy is not worth a bean because it is depressing, and depressed people live shorter lives. Optimists and believers are happier and healthier in their unreal worlds. Julia and her family, like many others in the GDR, trod this line between seeing things for what they were in the GDR, and ignoring those realities in order to stay sane.

Ever since she can remember, Julia was interested in languages. Before she could read she was fascinated by the Roman and Cyrillic letter systems she'd find around the house. At school they were taught English ('very badly') and Russian. Julia won first prize in the state Russian competition: a trip to Moscow. Curious about the world, she had penpals in Algeria, the Soviet Union and India. Her spare time was spent formulating letters in French, Russian and English, and sending them off to the outside world.

Julia wanted to be a translator and interpreter. 'I was growing up in the 1980s at the height of the Cold War. People really thought that the US and Russia might start a nuclear confrontation, and in the GDR we were on the front line. It was sort of naïve, but I thought that by facilitating, even in this small way, communication among peoples I could make a contribution.' She shakes her head at herself, as if embarrassed by the extravagance of her hopes. But I don't see why a talented linguist who believed in her country should be embarrassed by this goal. Then again, I don't see in front of me a talented linguist who believed in her country. I see a woman who leaves her past in a box but then comes to collect it; and whose part-time study and part-time rental agency work keep her only part-attached to the world.

Like her father, Julia believed in East Germany as an alternative to the west. 'I wanted to explain to people overseas about the GDR—that Communism was not such a bad system.' She didn't want to leave. 'We watched a lot of western television and I knew about unemployment, about homelessness, about hard drugs. And prostitution—prostitution! I mean how is it people think they can just *buy* a person? That was incredible to me.' She doesn't seem bitter about her belief in the GDR now. She seems, somehow, nostalgic.

She shivers. I go down to the cellar for more coal to feed the heater. When I come back into the kitchen Julia has not moved. I'm relieved: I half-expected to find one of the yellow sticky-notes she sometimes leaves for me in her fine handwriting: *Just remembered an appointment. Sorry. J.*

But she wants to keep talking. The edge of the linoleum table has come loose and without thinking she is stroking it flat. The memories do not come in the right order. As I listen, I think this is because she has not voiced them much before. But there may be another reason: something her mind keeps returning to which she veers away from telling.

10

The Italian Boyfriend

When she was sixteen Julia worked in the holidays as an usher at the Leipzig Fair, the famous international trade fair for which, twice a year, East Germany opened itself up to the outside world. Exhibitors of machinery and books, photocopiers and kitchen appliances all visited, along with members of the western press. They stayed in the Hotel Merkur, or were billeted to families who fought over them and the news from outside they might bring. Julia's job, along with that of other young people—selected as much for their loyalty as their language skills—was to direct visitors around the fair and the city.

It was here that she met the Italian boyfriend. He asked her out almost immediately ('they all thought we were for sale'), and she declined ('I wasn't'). Eventually, as you do, she said yes—because he persisted, because it might be fun, because what harm could come of it?

The Italian boyfriend was a man of thirty representing a northern Italian computer firm. He and Julia fell into the kind of unreal long-distance relationship in which longing, sustained by enough time apart, ripens of its own accord into love. He came to visit her twice a year—at Easter and Christmas, and they met for annual holidays in Hungary. Hungary was relatively free then, 'for us almost like the west,' she says. The rest of the time they telephoned once a week and wrote frequent letters. He became her most intimate penpal.

'How long were you with him?' I ask.

'Two years. Oh God no, more like two and a half.'

Whenever he stayed with her, the surveillance was intense and overt. The couple could hardly leave the house without being stopped by the police and asked to account for themselves. Or the police would be waiting at a checkpoint on the outskirts of town. 'It didn't matter when we left the house, or where we were going, there'd be someone there to stop us,' she says. Sometimes they went through the car. 'If we said we were going to the pictures, they would disappear for long enough with my ID and his passport to make us miss the start.'

The Italian boyfriend was terrified at each search. 'He'd start to sweat, then he'd go all pale and literally shake with terror.' Julia, on her home ground, teased him while they waited to get their papers back. 'Look, it can't be that bad,' she'd say. 'What on earth do you imagine they are going to do with you? They're not going to kill you!—this isn't Latin America after all.'

'I lived with this sort of scrutiny as a fact,' she says. 'I didn't like it but I thought: I live in a dictatorship, so that's just how it is. It was clear to me as a simple act of GDR-logic: I am with a western foreigner; now I will be under observation.'

The Behrends had no telephone, so Julia went to her grandmother's for the weekly call from the Italian boyfriend. His calls had to be booked through the authorities, and they both imagined it was possible they were being overheard. 'When I hung up I'd say goodnight to him, then I'd say, "Night all," to the others listening in,' she chuckles. 'I meant it as a joke. I didn't let myself really think about whether there was another person on the line.'

It was a condition of sanity both to accept 'GDR-logic' and to ignore it. 'If you took things as seriously as people in the west think we must have, we would have all killed ourselves!' Julia laughs, but I am feeling agitated. The fluorescent light in the kitchen has started to vibrate. 'I mean you'd go mad,' she says, 'if you thought about it all the time.'

Julia topped her year in middle school, and wanted to go to a senior high renowned for its language teaching. Instead, for reasons never made clear, the authorities sent her far away to a boarding school with no reputation at all. Her mother complained bitterly, but was told that nothing could be done. 'I don't know if it was because of the Italian boyfriend, or the penpals. Maybe they thought I had too much contact with the west and needed to be isolated.' She has started to tap a pen on the table and not to look at me when she speaks. For a moment the only sounds are the tapping pen, the vibrating light.

She puts the pen down and smiles. She has found something lighter to tell. 'The school was strict,' she says. 'There were things about it that were seriously traumatic, such as what we used to call "TV-torture".'

By the 1980s most people in East Germany watched western television, especially the news bulletins. No-one watched the GDR news, despite the fact that it screened daily on both state-run television stations, in a long and a short version. Julia smiles. 'At that school every night without fail we were sat down and made to watch "*Aktuelle Kamera*" in the long version. It was hell.'

The news program was so long because each time Erich Honecker was mentioned, he was announced with every single one of his titular functions. Julia sits up straight with her hands on the table and puts on a media voice. In the flickering light and with her fly-away hair she is a newsreader from outer space, coming through static: 'Comrade Erich Honecker, Secretary-General of the Socialist Unity Party of the German Democratic Republic, First Secretary of the Central Committee, Chairman of the State Council and of the National Defence Council, leader of the Fighting Groups bladibla—'

We laugh and she pushes back onto two legs of the chair. She is a relaxed and confident mimic. 'And then the actual news item that came after all that would be null!' She straightens up again. '—today visited the steelworks such and such and spoke with the workers about the 1984 Plan targets which they have over-over-over-achieved by so and so per cent' or, 'today opened the umpteenth apartment built in the new district of Marzahn' or, 'congratulated the collective farm of Hicksville this morning for their extraordinary harvest results, an increase of so-and-so-many-fold on previous years.'

We are laughing and laughing under the strobing light. 'And the thing about it was,' she slaps the table with her fine white hand, 'it never told us anything that happened in the world!' She shakes her head at the wordiness of no-news.

Worse though than the no-news, was the anti-news. The students also had to watch '*Der Schwarze Kanal*' (The Black Channel), with Karl-Eduard von Schnitzler. I have heard about this man, the human antidote to the pernicious influence of western television. 'At home,' Julia says, 'everyone called him "Karl-Eduard von Schni—" because that was how long it took before one of us could jump up and change the channel.'

Von Schnitzler's job was to show extracts from western television broadcast into the GDR—anything from news items to game shows to 'Dallas'—and rip it to shreds. 'That man radiated so much nastiness he simply wasn't credible. You'd come away feeling sullied, as if you'd spent half an hour atrociously badmouthing someone.' Julia crosses her arms. 'I mean you might have your doubts about the west—I sure did—but we also felt that our own country was feeding us lies and that our futures depended on seeming to agree with it all.'

One day in 1984 the headmaster made an appointment to see Julia's parents at home.

'We should have guessed something at that point. That was unheard of.' The three of them sat for two hours with coffee and cake, quite formal. He had come to convince Irene and Dieter to influence Julia to break it off with the Italian boyfriend. People assumed, if they didn't know Julia, that he was her ticket out. The state was using every avenue it could to stop that from happening.

Julia's mother told the headmaster, 'Look, the girl is seventeen, she's just about an adult, and if she's decided that this is the man for her life, so be it.' But Irene also said, 'To tell the truth, we're not all that happy about it either. He's a lot older than she is, and we don't want our daughter to leave. But we will not stand in her way.'

The headmaster didn't get very far. 'He left dissatisfied,' Julia says. 'He was actually a nice man. It could be that he had been warned about the consequences for me, and was trying his best to help.'

In 1985 Julia matriculated with straight As. She went to Leipzig to sit the entrance exam for the university's translating and interpreting course. She failed. 'The written language exam was ridiculously easy and short. But then there was the political exam—'

'What do you mean, "political exam"? You wanted to do language training!' The light tube on the ceiling is still spluttering and hissing and I am bilious and annoyed. In this light, Julia's face is marble and her lips blue-rimmed.

'Well, we were asked about our political knowledge. It was intended that we'd work at the highest levels of government, even internationally. So I think that's quite OK.' Of course it is. It's standard practice in the west too, I am just oversensitised.

I get up and find some tea-light candles in the cupboard so I can kill the fluorescent. I put the candles, thimbles of light around the kitchen— on the sink, on the table, and on the windowsill behind Julia.

'I don't know with any certainty that it was organised by them that I fail,' Julia says. 'There were an awful lot of applicants, and I have to admit that I did pretty crap in that exam.' She says she didn't know things, 'things that were not just *faux pas*, but really serious mistakes.' She starts to laugh again.

She couldn't name, for instance, the political parties in the GDR. There were political parties other than the ruling Socialist Unity Party but they were parties in name only and the names were remarkably similar to those of the political parties that existed for real in West Germany: the Christian Democrats, the Liberals and so on. Julia says, 'I was terrified of getting them wrong. If I put a name that was actually a western party, I might well have failed.' She gives the loose table lino a flick. Julia was being asked to repeat her knowledge of socialist catechism, her belief in things that were hard to remember, because they were not real.

After the results were announced a former student of Dieter's took him aside. The man's wife and father-in-law were on the university board of examiners. 'Between you and me,' he said to Dieter, 'there's no point Julia trying again next year. I would strongly suggest to you she do something else. Get a job.'

'Maybe,' Julia says, 'like the headmaster, he was trying to do me a favour. Save me the trouble of reapplying.' She has started to look away from me, focusing her attention towards the dark corner of the room. 'But the strange thing was,' she says slowly, 'that afterwards I simply couldn't get a job. Any kind of job at all…' She fiddles with the scarf wrung around her neck. 'That was when it got hard for me.'

Julia thought she might work as a receptionist in a large hotel. That way, she could practise her languages. She applied to Berlin, to Leipzig, to Dresden. She was a top student who spoke English, Russian, French and a smattering of Hungarian. She always got an interview. She would present in her neat clothes, and accept the compliments of management. The hoteliers were invariably excited and impressed. They would send her away for a routine medical, shake her hand warmly, and say they looked forward to seeing her soon.

Sometimes a letter would come in the mail a week later: 'We regret to inform you that the position has been filled. Thank you for your interest…' Other times she would call up herself to be told that she had just missed out. Sometimes she didn't hear at all. In the end, she stopped ringing to be told the same, uncomfortable excuses. She tried to find a position as a waitress, also without success. Julia assumes now that every hotel and every restaurant was required to check the names of all new employees with the Stasi.

Her options were running out. She decided to enrol in a night course for a certificate as a *Stadtbilderklärerin* ('a Town Plan Explainer').

'A what?' I have never heard this word. Julia says that it means a 'tour group leader', but that in the GDR the word 'leader' (*Führer*) was forbidden after Hitler, *der Führer*. Because 'führen' also means 'to drive', this meant there were no traindrivers (a *Lokkapitän* or 'Locomotive Captain' instead) and no drivers' licences (but a *Fahrerlaubnis* or 'Permission to drive'). Being a Town Plan Explainer was an occasional way to earn pocket-money. It was not a living.

Julia went to the Employment Office, took a number and stood in an interminable line. She was among people who might have had similar experiences, both explicable and not, to her own. She turned to the man behind her and asked, 'So how long have you been unemployed?'

Before he could answer an official, a square-built woman in uniform, stepped out from behind a column.

'Miss, you are not unemployed,' she barked.

'Of course I'm unemployed,' Julia said. 'Why else would I be here?'

'This is the Employment Office, not the Unemployment Office. You are not unemployed; you are seeking work.'

Julia wasn't daunted. 'I'm seeking work,' she said, 'because I am unemployed.'

The woman started to shout so loudly the people in the queue hunched their shoulders. 'I said, you are not unemployed! You are seeking work!' and then, almost hysterically, 'There *is no* unemployment in the German Democratic Republic!'

In my mind I tote up further GDR fictions: that *der Führer* was excised not only from their history but also from their language; that the news was real on television; and, contrary to Julia's lived experience, that there was no unemployment. By no fault of her own, Julia Behrend had fallen into the gap between the GDR's fiction and its reality. She no longer conformed to the fiction. Loyal and talented as she was, she was now being edged out of the reality.

Julia could either think she had failed at everything she had tried, or that they were out to get her. Or, she could try not to think at all. 'It is true to say that from then on I sort of withdrew from things.' She slept later and later each day. 'I think I was depressed.' She enrolled in another night-school course, this time in Spanish, but it seemed to her more and more like learning secret codes used outside your cave, spoken in places you would never see. After class she went, 'nearly every night' to the local night-club. 'My parents just sort of let me go. There wasn't much else they could do. I think they felt sorry for me.'

It was at this time her younger sister Katrin noticed it. The car was white. She watched it three days in a row outside the house before she said anything. Julia hadn't seen it. 'As I said'—she looks at me—'I knew that car was there for me.'

She knew, too, that getting on with her life would mean leaving it behind. She was going to have to marry the Italian boyfriend and get out. The idea frightened her. 'That was part of my attraction for him—that I would be utterly dependent on him, in his home and his country and his language. At his mercy.'

She went to meet him for a holiday in Hungary. At the airport she was taken aside and her luggage searched. They unscrewed the hairdryer and emptied her boxes of tampons over the examination bench. In Hungary she told him it was over. 'He was so controlling, so jealous.' Now Julia had withdrawn from him, withdrawn into her home, and withdrawn from hope. This was more than internal emigration. It was exile.

11

Major N.

Then a card came in the letterbox. 'It seemed normal enough—a standard printed card as if I had to report to the police to have my ID renewed. It had spaces in it for them to handwrite my name, and the date and time of the appointment.'

She's not looking at me. She's hardly talking to me. Her eyes move around the room although there's not much to see: behind me the hot-water cistern over the sink with its little blue flame, to my left the door to the hall. Candlelight catches her face, etches cheekbone and chin. She is remembering as I watch, summoning presences more real than mine.

'There are some things—' she stops. 'I don't think I'll be able to remember this. I haven't remembered this.'

I stick to small facts. 'Did you know what the card was about?'

'I thought I had overstayed my visa in Hungary. Usually they would just restamp your ID at the border and let you back in. I started preparing excuses in my mind. At the same time I said to myself: look, it can't be that bad! What can they do to me? I mean I wasn't afraid they'd collect me in the night and lock me up and torture me.'

Julia analysed the situation from every angle. In its later stages the regime stopped, for the most part, direct action (arrest, incarceration, torture) against its people. It opted instead for other ways of silencing them, methods that Amnesty would find harder to chronicle. 'The typical thing that could happen to you in my day in the GDR—that your career was broken before it was begun—that had already happened to me! And now that I didn't even have the Italian boyfriend any more—what else could they want?'

The police station had a vast waiting hall. People stood silently in two long queues curled around the room, each one joined to a counter. The lines hardly moved. 'I took a number but then I realised I didn't know which queue was the right one,' she says. 'So I went up to the policewoman who was overseeing things. She looked at my card and said straight away: "Ah Miss Behrend. You don't need to queue at all. You are to go directly to Room 118."'

Julia laughs at herself. 'I was pleased at first! I thought I had got out of standing in line.'

Then she noticed that all the people in the queues were going into one of two rooms behind the counters, but neither of those was Room 118. 'I had to go by myself up several flights of stairs and down a long corridor, left around a corner and then left again. There were no other people around. I saw no-one enter or leave any of the rooms I passed. Room 118 was way over on the other side of the building.'

She knocked.

'Come in.'

There was a man alone behind a desk. The first thing she noticed was that he wore a western suit and a good tie. He stood up straight away, a small nod, his feet clicking together.

'Miss Behrend, I am N., Major,' he smiled and extended his hand. And then, clear as a bell, 'Ministry of State Security.'

She felt fear, she says, 'like a worm in my belly'.

The man was not yet forty, with a wide face, and receding hair. He wore small round eyeglasses. He had a glowing suntan. He was friendly—in fact for GDR standards, exaggeratedly polite. 'Please,' he said, 'do sit down.' They sat. She thought it might still, perhaps, be about the overstayed visa.

But N. began, 'Such an attractive, intelligent young woman as yourself, Miss Behrend, perhaps you could explain to me why it is,' he smiled, 'that you are not working?'

This was it. Up until this moment it could all have been a product of her imagination: the boarding school, the headmaster's visit, the constant street searches, the failed exam, the 'friend's' warning, the cruising Lada, the extraordinary unemployment.

She was in shock. She spoke slowly.

'You must know why I have no job,' she said.

His voice was soft. He did not stop smiling. 'How would I know that, Miss Behrend?'

Her mind flew. She could see where this was going: she was going to be kicked out of the country. 'I thought it was my last chance to stay home,' she says. So she told him, straight out, 'Look, please, I don't want—I don't want to go to the west. But I think you people are forcing me out.' She realised she was imploring him. 'I must work somewhere. I am, after all, unemployed.'

'But Miss Behrend,' he said, 'how can that be?' He laced his fingers together on the desk. 'There is no unemployment in the German Democratic Republic.'

She could not answer.

He reached across his desk to a pile of papers and pulled them to him. 'First, I have some questions,' he said, 'about these letters.'

Julia looked at his hand and saw, under it, her own handwriting. She was confused. She looked closer.

They were copies of her letters to the Italian boyfriend.

Julia had imagined all along that her mail might be being read. Sometimes letters she received from overseas had been brutally torn and taped back together with a sticker: 'Damaged in Transit.' 'It was ridiculous really,' she says. But, like all the other things, she had never thought about it for long.

Major N. laid the first letter flat on the desk and smoothed it out with both hands. He cleared his throat. To Julia's horror, he started to read it aloud.

I think of the shame I would feel sitting opposite Major So-and-So in his office with these intimate things in his fingers. Shame at hearing your words turn into the universal banalities of love in his mouth.

Julia and her boyfriend wrote to one another in English. Major N. had underlined in each letter the words he had not been able to find in his German-English dictionary.

'He sat there and he—' Julia stops and takes a sip of tea. It must be cold by now. It goes down the wrong way. She coughs and coughs, but puts her hand out to stop me helping, '—and he asked me,' she says in a choked voice, 'what they meant.'

The hairs on my forearms stand up. I have stopped looking at Julia now because in this dimness she ceased addressing her words to me some time ago. I am humbled for reasons I cannot at this moment unravel. I am outraged for her, and vaguely guilty about my relative luck in life.

Major N. took his time perfecting his translation. The words that were not in the dictionary were, mostly, the words of their private lovers' language. He asked her, 'what is the meaning of this?' and again, 'would you mind, please, explaining this term?' One long forefinger on her handwriting, or her lovers'. 'What about this?' he asked, touching the word *cocoriza* in a letter from her boyfriend.

'*Cocoriza*,' Julia told him, 'is the Hungarian word for corn.'

'What does this mean then, Miss Behrend, when your friend writes, "I want my little *cocoriza*"?'

She had to explain. On their holidays her hair had lightened to the colour of corn. *Cocoriza* was his pet name for her.

'Thank you, Miss Behrend.' Then, in his western suit, with his foreign manners and his exaggerated courtesy, Major N. proceeded through her relationship, one letter at a time.

'It took quite a while,' Julia says in a faraway voice. Her eyes are fixed in the middle distance. Major N. was thorough. There was a pile of her letters to the Italian. There was a pile of his letters back to her. This man knew everything. He could see when she had had doubts, he could see by what sweet-talking she had let herself be placated. He could see the Italian boyfriend's longing laid bare, and his invention, for his own pleasure, of his faraway girl.

N. insinuated he knew—as Julia surely also realised—that the Italian had an image of her that didn't quite hit the mark. He flattered her. 'You are more complex, I think Miss Behrend, and much more intelligent than he gives you credit for.' When he was done reading, pointing, probing, he straightened the two piles of letters and put them back to the side of the desk. 'Let us discuss your friend for a moment now,' he said, 'shall we?'

He started to tell Julia about her boyfriend. 'They weren't particularly spectacular things,' she says. 'But they were things I could not have known because I couldn't go to Italy and see for myself.' Julia assumes that the Stasi had people in Italy. 'He was even sort of witty about it, drawing me in as if we could both have a chuckle about aspects of my boyfriend's life, as if we were both on the same side, and it was my friend not I who was the object of observation.'

'As we know,' N. said, 'our friend is in the computer business.'

Julia nodded. 'I'd never understood much about the sort of business he was in,' she says, 'and with my East German mindset not at all! He had told me it was trade in computer components.'

N. specified it for her. 'He is a sales manager for the regional branch of the firm.' Then he described the boyfriend's family house in Umbria. He told her the make of car he drove. When he saw that this meant nothing to Julia, he interpreted it for her: in N's estimation it was a 'middle class' sort of car, 'so there's no thinking he's rich or anything'.

Julia wondered where this was going.

He opened his desk drawer and brought out a thick manila folder which he put, closed, on the desk.

'Now Miss Behrend,' he said, 'we come to you.'

He evaluated her life-in-progress. 'He knew everything about me,' she says. 'He knew all the subjects I'd taken and how I did in them. He knew all about each of my sisters, my parents. He knew my youngest sister wanted to study piano at the conservatory.' Major N. felt sufficiently informed to make some psychological assessments. He told her that there were clearly issues her father did not understand, that Dieter was 'problematic'. Irene, by contrast, was much more loyal to the state.

'It is clear to us on the evidence, Miss Behrend, that you take after your mother,' he said. 'Which, if I may be so bold as to say so, is a good thing.'

'He was showing me that he had me in the palm of his hand,' she says. Julia draws her knees up to her chest and places her heels on the seat. She stretches her jumper over the knees, making herself into a small black ball. 'The only thing—' she says, '—it's ironic but the only thing that they seemed not to know, was that I'd broken up with my boyfriend!' Since their split in Hungary, the Italian boyfriend had written several imploring letters. Julia had replied to the first one but then stopped writing.

'Or at least the Major acted as if he didn't know that we'd broken up,' she says. 'I thought it was strange that he didn't know. Maybe he'd been on holidays and had missed the last couple of letters.'

Or, I think, he might have known, and thought his prospects with her then were better.

N. put the manila folder to one side next to the love letters. He joined the tips of his fingers together and leant forward. 'As I'm sure you will have picked up, we are interested in your friend.' And then it came. 'We would propose,' he said, 'if you would assist us, that we meet every now and again. For a chat.'

Julia says, 'I thought it was absurd. I thought: what on earth could interest them in him?' She could not imagine that the Italian boyfriend was in any way a bigwig. 'He did not have any high-up connections he ever mentioned, or any special expertise or training at all.' It did not occur to her until she got home that it could have been her they wanted.

There was no question for Julia. She would not inform on him, or at all. 'I am terribly sorry,' she told Major N., 'but I can't help you because we split up on this last trip to Hungary. I want nothing more to do with him. He wanted to own me. I knew if I stayed with him I would not be able to determine my own life.' She added, 'I never want to see him again, even as a friend.'

N. smiled. 'If,' he said, 'after giving the matter some further thought you reach a different decision, you should not hesitate to call at any time.' He gave her his card with his phone number on it. 'Oh and Miss Behrend,' he said, 'one more thing. You must not discuss our little talk with anyone— not your parents, not your sisters, not your closest friends. If you do, we will know about it. This afternoon has not occurred. You have never been to Room 118. If you see me on the street you are not to acknowledge me— you must walk on past. All this for obvious reasons, as I'm sure you will have understood long ago.'

She nodded.

And that was it. He had shown her that with one phone call to him she could be in, or she could be out. She could be with them, or she could be gone.

'And then he let me leave.' The street was another world, the daylight bright and unnatural. Julia watched a class of small children being herded along the pavement. She felt sundered, suddenly and irrevocably, from life. 'It was as though all at once I was on the other side,' she says, 'separate from everybody.'

Julia seems to have run out of words, so I pick up the plates and place them behind me in the sink. I look in the fridge for something else to eat, as if it might yield possibilities missed at first glance. There's only a saggy old condom of liverwurst and an apple. I throw out the liverwurst and cut up the apple. Whilst I have my back to her, she starts to speak again. To listen to her is to witness the process, almost mechanical, of pulling things up from the past.

Her voice is slow. 'I think I'd totally repressed that entire episode,' she says. 'Maybe what came later, the whole 1989 story, was so severe that other things just fell away. Otherwise, I can't explain it.'

I don't know what she means by 'the whole 1989 story'. I say I think it is extreme, what happened to her.

'Yes, it is,' she says, 'when you become conscious of it. But the strange thing is it's only now, in this room, that I feel the shudder run down my spine. At the time I criticised other things—not being allowed to study or have a career. But looking back on it, it's the total surveillance that damaged me the worst. I *know* how far people will transgress over your boundaries—until you have no private sphere left at all. And I think that is a terrible knowledge to have.' She flicks her hair as if to get rid of something. 'At this distance I understand for the first time how bad it was what he did in that room.'

She takes a piece of apple and seesaws its fleshy arc between two fingers on the table. The empty fridge shudders and stops; the kitchen is a deeper quiet. 'People talk about the unconscious,' she says, 'and it becomes clear to me as I am telling you this, the effect this knowledge has had on my life.' She takes a small bite of apple. 'I think I am definitely psychologically damaged!' She laughs, but she means it. 'That's probably why I react so extremely to approaches from men and so on. I experience them as another possible invasion of my intimate sphere.' She watches my face. 'I think it's worse if you repress it.' To dig it up, or to leave it lie in the ground?

When she left Room 118 Julia was all right until she got home. Then her legs wouldn't hold her weight. She made it to the bathroom and vomited. When she came out she noticed her voice trembled and she couldn't set it straight. She told her parents and her sisters everything. That evening the family sat down to decide what to do.

'My mother is a very pragmatic person,' Julia says. 'Irene said, "Right, you ended it with the Italian—I didn't want to influence you, but I'm glad you didn't marry him. Now, though, you have to think very coolly about what you do next."'

Julia couldn't quite believe that this was happening, that they were sitting in the living room at home talking about how she might live out the rest of her life. She was twenty years old. 'We'd always discussed me going to live with the Italian boyfriend, as if it were an option. But that was more like a teenage adventure fantasy: thinking, I'm free to do that and no-one can stop me. Suddenly it was reality: I have to leave here forever—I have to leave my family, I will not see my sisters again, and I have to go to the west. Which, as I said, I had never wanted to do.' Julia has started to speak into the jumper wrapped over her knee. 'And I think too, I was disappointed in the state. I realised for the first time that it wasn't really the good father state you have in the back of your mind. I saw it can be so dangerous, so very dangerous, without me having done anything at all.'

She would not become an informer. That left only one real option. 'You'll have to find someone else to marry so you can get out,' Irene said. 'That's the only way.' Then she voiced all of their doubts. 'But do you really want to marry any old person?' she said. Dieter sat hunched in rage and sadness at the end of the table. No-one spoke.

'That's when I thought of it,' Julia says, 'I thought, if there's no way around it, we just have to crash through somehow. There was, apparently, this method called a *Staatsratsbeschwerde* for people to write directly to Erich Honecker if they needed something they couldn't get, or to make a complaint'—she shakes her head—'as if the citizen really did have a voice and rights. People would write saying they wanted to buy tiles for their bathroom or machine parts for their tractor and none had been available since August or whatever. Ordinary people would sometimes say, "Well, why don't you stop complaining and just write to Erich!" So I thought to myself, why don't we? I mean, if we examined it, what had happened was just not right.' I see the mimic in her again. 'I don't even have this boyfriend any more, and I want to study and I want to stay in the GDR, and why not? We can just write to Erich and complain.' She looks up at the ceiling. 'There was a certain naivety in this that I see today—back then we thought that the Party and the state were one thing, and the Stasi another.' She shakes her head and unravels herself from her jumper, placing both feet on the ground. She opens her hands wide. 'I thought, well, what can they do to me?'

Major N.'s card lay on the table between them all. 'You have the phone number,' Irene said. 'Call him up tomorrow and tell him that you and your parents are going to write to Honecker and make a complaint.'

'I will never forget that night,' Julia says. 'I said to my parents: right then, that's what we'll do, and I went to bed. I had nightmares like I have never had before or since.' Julia dreamt she was being pursued in a place where everything was familiar to her—the kitchen countertop, the view from her bedroom, the faces in a shop, the back of her sister's head. But no-one recognised her and she was not at home. Her father started to die, wilting like a plant and calling for her but he couldn't hear her responses, couldn't see where she was. When she woke she didn't know if she'd dreamt of where she was or wherever it was she was going. 'The night was terrible, terrible. I don't remember if I cried. I don't think I did. I just sweated and sweated till the bed was wet. I woke up many times. It was truly terrifying what I lived through.' She runs a hand through her hair. 'It was the loss of everything until I had disappeared too.'

The next morning after everyone left Julia picked up the card and took it to her grandmother's to make the call. She was alone in the house. She could smell disinfectant, and boiled potatoes. She looked at the numbers in black on the card. They moved. She saw her hand was shaking, and put the card down on the bench. In that moment she could no longer string together the reasons why she was making this call, how it came to this. She was just here, now, with this card and this name and the numbers that would make him speak to her again. She put her fingers in the loops to dial.

N. picked up straight away. When he realised what she was saying—you told others what we said? You are going to write *what*?—he was furious and demanded that Julia meet with him alone. She was to come to a covert apartment in town.

'It was over, of all things, the travel agency,' she says. She puts her lips together in a grim smile. 'Of course I'd gazed in that window many times. I knew exactly where it was.' N. told her there would be serious repercussions for her, and possibly for her family, from this breach of her undertaking of silence. He reminded her that her younger sister Katrin, was it not correct, dreamed of studying piano at the conservatory. He said he would contact his superior, the regional head, and see what action was to be taken from here.

The family waited a week before a card came in the letterbox. They were to be visited at home.

Two of them came: N. and his boss. 'But it was not at all what we anticipated,' Julia says. 'N. looked completely different to me. He was sweating and uncomfortable. His boss didn't look much better. We didn't know what was going on.'

Dieter told them there was no reason—what reason could there be?—for all the things that had happened to their daughter. They had always been good citizens. Irene told them flatly that they were going to write to Honecker.

The men held their hands up: there was no need to overreact here. Surely, they said, things had not gone so far that they couldn't be fixed locally—there was no need to get Berlin involved. This was a situation, they looked at Dieter and Irene, where the imagination of a young person—a good quality of course—might have come into play. Dieter and Irene and the girls were silent. Then the men asked to be given some time.

'We couldn't figure it out at first,' Julia says. 'But when they left we knew we'd won. We had never really known where the battle was,' she smiles, 'but we knew we'd won.'

Julia doesn't know why the Stasi was afraid of them complaining to Honecker. Possibly because both her parents were teachers, and outwardly conformist, or because the Stasi had no 'legal' basis for what it had done to her. Who knows? It is one of the very rare occasions when the bluff was called and someone 'won' against the Firm.

'The amazing thing was,' Julia says, 'the next week I was rung up about a job.' She was taken on as a receptionist in a hotel. It looked like she would work there for her lifetime.

But then came 1989.

'That's a whole other story.' She picks up her box of love letters. 'It's late, I should go,' she says. 'I thought I'd come and get these'—she pats the box—'and have a look at them. I'm seeing a psychotherapist and we've got up to my relationships with men. I'm trying to remember them—they seem like another life.' She smiles and the light catches her teeth. 'These letters from the Italian boyfriend will be an *aide memoire* to all that,' she says. I look at the box in her arms and know that you cannot destroy your past, nor what it does to you. It's not ever, really, over.

I see her out. In the hall she clicks the bike pump onto the crossbar of her beat-up bicycle and I open the door. As she goes down the stairs I feel there is something missing here. She does not seem like a girl who called their bluff, worked in a hotel for two years and was then liberated into her future by the 1989 revolution. No-one can tote up life's events and calculate the damages; a table of maims for the soul. But this is not the full sum of things, I think, as Julia rides back to her barricaded tower, full of things she can't leave, but can't look at either.

12

The Lipsi

'…you pigdogs think we all here forgotten what you nazis done and come in my home on my TV with you music and you news you fuckups better write me n—'

There's a knock on my office door. It's Uwe. 'How about a lift home?' he says.

'That would be great.' From some stupid impulse, I move to hide the letter in front of me, as if to spare him insult. I hold his gaze and pull it towards me across the desk. The printing is as large and uneven as a ransom note, so it catches his eye.

'What's that one?' he asks.

'It's, uh, actually a piece of hate mail,' I say.

'Oh,' he says, 'yes.' He knows immediately what that means: that the hate is not directed at a particular presenter or the station itself, but at the whole nation.

'We usually respond to those in a moderate tone,' he says, 'and say that the National Socialist dictatorship was a terrible thing that happened to us. That it caused untold pain and suffering and so on, and that whatever attempts there have been to make reparations, amends can never truly be made, etc, etc.'

'Yes,' I say. But what does he mean, 'that happened to us'? The Germans were wild about Hitler. It is true that after he was elected he changed the structures of power into a dictatorship, but it is also true that when the war was over the people might well have voted him in again. Everyone, always, is claiming innocence here.

'Well then?' he says. His eyes are red-rimmed. He doesn't give himself much rest. 'Do you want a lift?'

'Yes. Thanks. Great.'

I am rarely in a car in Berlin. The train network under the streets is so dense I can go anywhere on it, popping out of the earth in one place or another. It is a skein of arteries, pumping people around the city. The surface is another world.

The streets are cobbled. Uwe drives fast. He wears leather gloves with press-studs on the wrists. His car is a new silver VW Golf, shiny and smelling of pineapple deodoriser.

'Do you like Elton John?' he says. Before I can answer he turns on the tape-deck full blast. He lights a cigarette from the dash lighter. He starts nodding his head and tapping the beat with a leather hand on the leather-covered steering wheel. He's screaming down the streets, the tyres noisy over the cobbles. I hold onto the door handle with one hand and my little pack on my lap with the other. I wonder whether the pack might have some airbag effect. He's humming and smoking and tapping and ashing out the window in a frenetic demonstration of how laid-back he is. He shouts something through the music and smoke and din. All I catch is that he's taking drum lessons 'to get'—I watch his mouth—'better rhythm'.

'That's where I'm off to now,' he yells. 'My teacher lives in Mitte like you. Speaking of which, did you follow up any of those Ossi stories you were talking about?' He doesn't ask this as if I need to redeem myself from my outburst with Scheller. He seems genuinely curious. And he turns the music down.

'Yes, I did,' I say. 'I've been having Adventures in Stasiland.' He laughs, so I go on. 'I've been in a place where what was said was not real, and what was real was not allowed, where people disappeared behind doors and were never heard from again, or were smuggled into other realms.'

'Really? How did you find these people?'

'They're all around us, Uwe. This was the east, after all. And I've gone looking. I advertised for Stasi men—'

'You did what?' He looks at me and I wish he'd look back at the road.

'I put an ad in the paper, Uwe, it was no big deal. And other people I've just stumbled across. My landlady, for instance,' I say, and I tell him briefly about Julia's expulsion from life until the Stasi offered to redeem her if she would inform for them. 'And this was as late as the 1980s,' I finish.

'No shit,' Uwe says, and I can see that Julia's story is as strange and awful for him as it is for me. He slows to a stop. We have reached my place, intact. He turns to me. 'Two things,' he says, in his serious journalist's voice. 'There's a man around who as a young Stasi officer drew the line along the street where the Wall would be built, and he's prepared to talk about the whole thing. His name is Hagen Koch—we had him on a program once about Checkpoint Charlie. And what you said about turning one world into another made me think of someone else. There is a fellow called Karl-Eduard von Schnitzler—he was the chief propagandist for the regime. He might be interesting for you too.'

'Julia mentioned von Schnitzler. He's still alive then?'

'Yep. And fierce, from what I hear.'

'How can I find them?'

'I'll see whether we've got any contact details at work.' Uwe leans across me to open my door, which is sort of gentlemanly, but also unnecessary. He takes the opportunity to look up and check out my building.

'Thanks for the lift,' I say. 'And thanks for the tips.' He smells of smoke and fake pineapple, like a seedy Hawaiian.

'No problem.' He's still leaning across me, so I follow his gaze. In the bare tree outside my living room two white things float in the branches. One is a plastic bag, and the other, as we both stare up at it, reveals itself to be a pair of men's underpants. I shrug. I can tell Uwe would never live in a place like this. He leans back into his seat. 'Good luck in Stasiland,' he says. 'Take care there.'

A few days later Uwe does find me a number for von Schnitzler, but it's wrong. 'Lady,' the man who answers tells me, 'people like that don't want to be found.' Herr von Schnitzler is unlisted. I decide to call Herr Winz, to see if he can help. Herr Winz is chuffed to think I need him, and says he'll see what he can do. In the meantime, I decide to watch some of von Schnitzler's programs, 'The Black Channel'.

'The Black Channel' was broadcast in the east from 1960. It was intended as a countermeasure to the western program *'Das Rote Optik'* (The Red View), a critique of socialism being broadcast into the east from West Germany. On Monday nights *Deutsche Fernsehfunk*, then the single East German television station, screened beloved old movies from the heyday of the pre-war studios, and the Party decided that these, as well as the western programs, required commentary. Karl-Eduard von Schnitzler was given the job.

For a long time, workers in the power stations were on alert every Monday night. First, everyone tuned in at once to the movie, so they went into overdrive. Then, when 'The Black Channel' came on, the workers had to struggle to stop the power supply from collapsing under a back-surge as everyone, simultaneously, switched off their sets.

Karl-Eduard von Schnitzler became a one-man institution and the most hated face of the regime. At the end of 1989 when the demonstrators called out, 'We are the people!' and 'Free elections!' they also shouted, 'Say Sorry, Schnitzler!' and 'Schnitzler to the Muppet Show!' That was exactly what he was: a grumpy old puppet throwing scorn on proceedings from on high.

The East German television station was at Adlershof, an eastern suburb of Berlin. The complex is now being touted as a hot new multi-media centre but remains a cluster of cold grey buildings set in an expanse of gravel, like an industrial park. One of them houses the archive of programs broadcast in the GDR.

This place isn't really open to the public, and Uwe has made some calls to get me in. I enter what seems to be a back door and then walk along a grimy glass-sided gangway linking this building to the next. There are no people around. I come to double doors with an old security intercom. I ring in and they open for me. Ahead, there's a counter. In either direction, right and left, a long linoleum corridor stretches out, strewn with ancient editing equipment and piles of film reels.

Behind the counter I find the first signs of life. Two men in what look like matching brown cardigans are drinking coffee. They take a look at me and turn back immediately to one another.

'Good morning,' I say.

'Have you come for a parcel?' Cardigan One asks, staring straight at Cardigan Two.

'No,' I say. 'I've come to look at some tapes.'

'We wouldn't know anything about that,' Cardigan One says. He still doesn't look at me. There's a silence.

'Is Frau Anderson about?' I ask.

'She'd have to see Frau Anderson about that, wouldn't she?' One says to his silent companion. Two takes a sip. One reads this as agreement.

'Yes,' One repeats, 'she'd have to see Frau Anderson about that.'

I glance up and down the empty corridor.

'It's getting on for time,' he adds. 'We leave here at 4.25, you know.'

'Right,' I say.

Cardigan Two speaks. 'We're on a break,' he says to One.

'Right,' I say again. There's another silence. What is this, Beckett? I remember what the German absurdist poet Kurt Tucholsky said about his countrymen and counters: they all grovel in front of them, and aspire to sit behind them. I am tossing up whether to grovel like a native or to make a scene, foreign-style, when I am saved by footsteps coming along the corridor: Frau Anderson.

'There you are then,' Cardigan One says to Cardigan Two, as if this whole little episode had been a private bet between them, 'Frau Anderson.'

Frau Anderson is a woman in her mid-fifties. It is hard to tell what she really looks like because she is wearing makeup to disguise. Perhaps she used to be on the stage, or in television. She has shiny skin the consistency of cheesecake and lips painted on in a shape that departs, boldly and theatrically, from nature.

'*Ach*, Herr von Schnitzler,' she says as she leads me down the corridor. 'He was a one. You've got to give it to him: at least he has stuck with what he said back then. Not a damn turncoat like the rest of them these days.' Her bitterness and nostalgia shock me. It is part of the nostalgia for the east (*ost*) which has given rise to a new sticklebrick word: *Ostalgie*. Clearly only those demonstrably loyal to the state worked here, and Frau Anderson is still one of them.

The corridor is fluorescent-lit, without a chink of natural light. The linoleum is beige, and either mottled or marbled. The walls are a peeling bilious yellow. There's a stale smell. It is like being inside some old beast. We walk the length of the corridor and I count, from habit or obsession or just not wanting to get lost, fifteen steel doors on each side before we get to the last one. Frau Anderson opens it and turns to me. 'I leave at 4.25,' she says, 'do you think you'll be done by then?'

'I hope so,' I say.

'It would be terrible,' she jokes, 'to leave you locked up here overnight.'

It sure would. This place seems to have been designed on the same one-size-fits-all architectural principle as everything else: the Runden Ecke in Leipzig and Stasi HQ at Normannenstrasse; the same as prisons and hospitals and schools and administrative buildings all over this country, and probably the same as inside the brown Palast der Republik only it's behind bars and I can't get in. From here to Vladivostok this was Communism's gift to the built environment—linoleum and grey cement, asbestos and prefabricated concrete and, always, long long corridors with all-purpose rooms. Behind these doors anything could be happening: inter-rogations, imprisonment, examinations, education, administration, hiding out from nuclear catastrophe or, in this case, propaganda.

Inside, the room has the proportions of a prison cell, but is decorated like a trailer-home from the 1960s. There are brown curtains for the small high-up window, and brown wallpaper on the walls in a flower pattern. There's an ancient reel-to-reel film-cutting machine, an office chair, and a tourist poster for the Gobi Desert with text in Russian and German. In the corner there's a television set and a video player.

Frau Anderson leaves me with some tapes they found. I put one in the machine and turn the lights out. It's von Schnitzler's first program from March 1960. The titles come on: a mean-looking cartoon eagle, the West German emblem, wearing the red-white-and-black of fascism alights onto a television antenna. Then the words come up: THE BLACK CHANNEL. Suddenly, a man in a suit with boxy black glasses fills the screen. He addresses me directly, as if he were sitting here in the room:

> The Black Channel, my dear ladies and gentlemen, carries filth and sewage. But instead of carrying it to a sewage farm as it ought, it pours, day after day, into hundreds of thousands of West German and West Berlin homes. This channel is the channel broadcasting West German television programs: The Black Channel. And every Monday at this time, we are going to devote ourselves to, as you might say, a hygiene operation.

The next tape was from 1965 after two people had been shot trying to flee over the Wall.

Dear viewers

You all know why I'm here today, returned from my holiday especially to appear before you tonight. Our border guards have, in accordance with their duty, had to shoot at two men. They were breaking the law and seeking to breach our national border. They stopped neither when called, nor when warning shots were fired. One of them was fatally wounded...

People should listen to us when we say, again and again: *we* determine the order at our border! And *we* ensure that it is maintained, for good reasons. Whosoever wants to traverse the GDR border needs permission. Otherwise: stay away from our border! He who puts himself in danger will die. I know, ladies and gentlemen, it sounds hard. And will perhaps even be interpreted by some of you as 'inhumane'... But what is 'humane' and what is 'inhumane'?

Humane it is, to make peace for all men on earth. That is not done by prayer! It is done by fighting. And if, as history teaches us, wars are made by man and not God, then peace too, is a work of man. And for the first time on German soil, here in the German Democratic Republic, peace has been elevated to a governing principle of the state. Whoever seeks to weaken or damage the GDR, whether consciously or unconsciously, weakens or damages the prospects of peace in Germany. It is humane to have created and built this state! It is humane to strengthen and protect it! It is humane to guard the German Democratic Republic against these people who would most like to eat it for breakfast...

He goes on and on, but I wind the tape back and take notes. I want to be able to see exactly how this man turned inhumanity into humanity, these deaths into symbols of salvation. I want more urgently to meet him, and see what he thinks now that the bulwark is down and his world is gone.

It's nearly 4 pm, and I'm doing well for time. I'm not going to be locked up in here, no way. I start packing my things together. The tape is still running. It switches to another program called 'In the Mood' (*Gut*

Aufgelegt) with cheery introductory music. A beautiful blue-eyed brunette in a 1960s pinched-waisted dress is in a record shop. She approaches the camera.

'Record sellers have been getting strange requests from customers lately,' she says, 'for "Lipsi" music. I have a question: just what is "Lipsi"? Brockhaus [the music encyclopaedist] would say, "I have no idea and if it isn't in any of my twenty volumes, it doesn't exist." But the record seller would tell you, "Lipsi—that's all my customers are asking for! It's an epidemic!" A young couple might say, "Lipsi—it's the simplest thing. The dance itself is in 6/4 time and you just take her in your left arm like this"'— she extends her arm—'well…it's easy, look.' She pretends to get stuck for words, and then finds her slogan:

> If you really want to know, simply dance away,
> All the young people dance the Lipsi today!

I'm curious and stop packing. The screen shows a couple in a dance hall: he clean-cut in a suit, and she in a dress and stilettos. And, together, they do the strangest dance that I have ever seen.

At first the man and the woman face the same way like Greek dancers, he behind her, her hand in his. They move from side to side with one another, then raise their forearms and bend apart, alarmingly, like teapots. The camera cuts to their feet, which, without warning, break into the complex footsies of an Irish jig. Then the pair turn to one another in a waltz grip before separating again and giving a little jump in the air. This is followed by a Russian-type movement with hands on hips. All the while they smile huge fixed smiles as if they needn't give a single thought to what their feet are doing. Then they start with the Greek teapot manoeuvre again. Over the top a Doris Day voice sings to a bossa nova beat:

> Today, all young people dance
> The Lipsi step, only in lipsistep,

Today, all young people like to learn
The Lipsistep: it is modern!
Rhumba, boogie and Cha cha cha
These dances are all passé
Now out of nowhere and overnight
This new beat is here to stay!

I wind the tape back. I want to pinpoint, in all these movements, what it is that makes the dance so curious. 'Lipsi' is colloquial for 'Leipzig' but it wasn't just the regime's overt attempt to manufacture a trend for the masses, as if it had come from that hip city. I watch the stiff couple closely. The woman seems to be missing an incisor—an odd choice for a dance model. Then I concentrate on their movements, and I get it: in not one of this panoply of gestures do the dancers' hips move. Their torsos remain straight—neither bending towards one another, nor swivelling from side to side. The makers of this dance had plundered every tradition they could find and painstakingly extracted only the sexless moves. Just as 'The Black Channel' was the antidote for western television, the Lipsi step was the East's answer to Elvis and decadent foreign rock'n'roll. And here it was: a dance invented by a committee, a bizarre hipless camel of a thing.

I throw my things together and hightail it out of the room down the corridor. The fluorescent is still on, but there's no light coming from the counter. I'm halfway there when I remember I've left the video in the machine. I run back to the room and pull it out so I can return it to Frau Anderson, if she's still here. If anyone's still here. Running down the corridor for the second time, I wonder if I need to know a code to get out.

My watch says 4.27 and the Cardigans are gone. I stand in front of the counter, my bag in one hand, the tape in the other. To each side of me the corridor stretches to infinity, its doors all shut. I turn and face the exit, and see, to the left of it, an old keypad security system. How many attempts at getting the combination before I'm trapped? Or an alarm goes off? I don't want a scene. But I don't want to spend the night here either.

I need to find a phone. As I turn back, I hear a sound. It's a door opening. Frau Anderson is coming out, in a fake fur hat and carrying a green mock-crocodile handbag.

'I was just coming to fetch you,' she says. 'Thought I'd give you a bit more time.' She takes the tape from me. I steady my breath. I don't know whether she can tell I've panicked and is having a bit of fun with me. Perhaps I've started to take deadlines, train times and closing hours too seriously in this land of merciless punctuality.

A week later an anonymous man calls me. Herr Winz has told him what I want, and he is ringing to check me out before he calls Herr von Schnitzler. In a few minutes he phones back and says that Frau von Schnitzler will take my call. He gives me the number. Frau von Schnitzler answers, and she tells me their address.

13
Von Schni—

It's her maiden name, not his on the doorbell. A fine-faced woman in her sixties lets me in. She has bobbed dark hair, red lips and red fingernails. Frau Marta von Schnitzler was an actress.

'Welcome,' she says extending a lacquered hand. She shows me through to the living room. The apartment is small but light. The accumulated debris of a lifetime rests on bookcases and shelves, hangs on the walls: books, medal boxes, figurines, and plastic cups full of biros.

In the living room a man with square glasses and a carefully contoured beard sits in an easy chair. His right hand, smooth for a seventy-nine-year-old, holds the top of a walking stick. He greets me, nodding in my direction. On the coffee table there's a thermos of hot water, a jar of Nescafé and a medicine bottle. In front of him Herr von Schnitzler has a large wineglass of something that looks like red cordial. I sit down opposite. His head is larger and more wizened, the cheekbones more pronounced than on television but it is unmistakably 'Sudel-Ede' or 'Filthy Ed'. Behind his head I notice another row of other heads at the same level on a picture rail: a bust of Marx, a daguerreotype of Lenin, and, as my eye casts along, even a miniature full-body statue of Stalin.

'Herr von Schnitzler,' I say, 'I'd like to ask you some questions about your biography—'

'Yes, that's important, a) for my life history, and b) because what you will have read about me is 95 per cent false.' His voice comes croaky through a dry old throat.

'You think—'

'I don't think, I know. It is so.' His voice is gaining strength and timbre.

'—but I've been reading books you wrote yourself,' I say. 'They wouldn't be wrong, would they?'

'Well, in that case, it's different,' he says, but he doesn't even crack a smile. 'No, that's good, that's very good.' This is not going to be easy. He looks challengingly in my direction. I can hear him breathing.

Karl-Eduard von Schnitzler was born in 1918 into a wealthy Berlin family. His father Julius Eduard Schnitzler had been Emperor Wilhelm's consul-general in Antwerp, and a lieutenant in the Prussian military. In 1913, the emperor elevated Julius and his two brothers to the nobility, granting them the privilege of using the prefix 'von'. The family remained close to power into the Nazi regime. One of von Schnitzler's cousins was banker to Hitler, another was the sales director of IG-Farben, the company responsible for delivering the poison gas Zyklon B to concentration camps.

Karl-Eduard reacted against the disparities of wealth, and the Nazism around him. At fourteen he became fascinated with Communism. He briefly studied medicine, then switched to an apprenticeship in sales. During World War II he served in Hitler's army. In June 1944 the British took him into custody in their 'anti-fascist' POW camp Ascot, and a few days later he began making broadcasts in German at the BBC for the program 'German Prisoners of War speak to the Homeland'.

Von Schnitzler was released back to Germany in 1945, where he continued to broadcast from the British Occupied Zone in Cologne, but before long his staunchly Communist views brought him into conflict with the British administrators and he was sacked.

In 1947 he left for the Soviet Occupation Zone. When he got there he told its future leader Walter Ulbricht that he wanted to drop the 'von' in front of his name. Ulbricht said, 'Are you crazy? Everyone should know that *all* sorts of people are coming over to us!'

This is how the man with the ridiculously noble name became the media face of the regime. 'The Black Channel' aired until the very end in October 1989.

Von Schnitzler has started talking and is going into a lot of detail about the war.

I interrupt him. 'I'd like to talk about "The Black Channel"—'

'But you're jumping over a very important part of my life—my time as a POW when I broadcast from the BBC—'

'I'm happy to talk about that, but it depends how much time you have.'

'I have time,' he counters. 'How much time do you have?'

'I have the whole day,' I say, 'but presumably we don't want to talk the whole day. I'd like to talk for a couple of hours.'

Frau von Schnitzler has installed herself away from our sight-line but well within earshot. The apartment is smaller than I thought; it is a far cry from the mansion Karl-Eduard was born in. I think Frau von Schnitzler is sewing. She murmurs something about time that I don't quite catch.

'*Nein?*' he says, sort of to her.

'Then maybe one hour,' I say.

But he continues with his full life story anyway. Von Schnitzler spent his career excerpting and critiquing western television and he will not have his life excerpted by me. He has slipped into a practised authoritarian speech rhythm with occasional startling emphases—any one of which could turn into a rebuke to the listener whose attention waned.

I put out my hand, palm up, and cut him off again. 'If we only have an hour, I'd really like to talk about "The Black Channel".'

He's angry now. 'But it is more important to talk about history!' The walking stick slips out of his grasp and falls against the chair. He picks it up again. 'You can read, read, read about "The Black Channel"!' He shakes the stick from side to side. '"The Black Channel" was part of the Cold War. I was one of the leading figures of the GDR during the Cold War—' He runs out of puff, or loses the connection.

'Yes,' I say, 'and it's the GDR I'm most interested in.'

'Aha. Aha,' he says, suddenly calm. I recognise this pattern of unpredictable shouting followed by bouts of quiet reason from other bullies I have known. 'OK,' he says, perfectly politely. 'What is it you want to know about the Channel?'

'How did you start it? Was it your idea or were you given the task?'

'It was my idea,' he says. 'I once saw the western politicians on the television news spouting filthy lies about the GDR and before the program was even over I had prepared a script for a broadcast! I socked it right back to them. Then the question was: how often? I insisted on once a week. Today'—he leans towards me, furious—'Today I could make one every…single…day!' This is a tantrum engineered to frighten me. 'That's how disgusting this, this shitbox television is!' He points with his stick at the set in the room.

All right then, I think, we'll go in his direction. 'What angers you most about the television today?'

'Nothing "angers" me!' he says. He is incandescent with rage. Out of the corner of my eye I see Frau von Schnitzler raise her head. 'That's why I'm a Communist! So nothing can anger me!' Then suddenly he's quiet again. 'What makes me sorry,' he says in a withering tone, 'is what is dished up to people today on that piece-of-filth television. For instance that, that idiotic program—whatsit called?' He addresses no-one in particular, but a murmur comes from across the room.

He ignores it. 'They are all idiots, aren't they?' he says to me. 'Marta, do you have to grimace like that?' Then, as if to himself, 'What was the name of that program? B-Block'?

'B-Block?'

'That one where they locked up ten people—'

'Ah yes,' his wife says loudly, 'now I know what you're talking about. "Big Brozer."'

'Yes,' he says, '"Big Brozer".'

'Big Brother' was a wildly popular 'reality-tv' program screened here recently, where people were locked in a house together and filmed day and night by security cameras. Named for the head of the surveillance regime in Orwell's novel *Nineteen Eighty-Four*, the program offered a cash prize for the person who could survive the longest living with others under such closed and scrutinised circumstances. Orwell was banned in the GDR; I wonder if von Schnitzler has taken particular offence to the program for its Orwellian overtones, or just its general stupidity.

He is looking at me. 'I think that big television tyrant of yours was involved in that—'

'She's Australian,' Frau von Schnitzler corrects him, 'not American.'

'I know what I'm saying,' he says.

'Murdoch,' I say. 'Yes, he was Australian but now he's American.'

'Who cares?' von Schnitzler counters airily. 'He's a global imperialist.'

I open my notebook. I want to quote him back to himself. I am apprehensive. 'Can I read you something?' I ask. 'In November 1965 two easterners tried to get over the border, and one of them was shot to death. And at Christmas time that year you made a program—'

'Escapes were always tried on at Christmas time,' he says. He uses the word *'inszeniert'* which means 'staged', as though escapes were orchestrated deliberately to make the regime look bad.

He is so offhand about it, I feel my apprehension being replaced with something more businesslike. 'I want to read you this text from your program, and ask you whether you still agree with it.' I read from my transcription:

The politics of 'freeing those in the Eastern Bloc' is code for liquidating the GDR, and that means civil war, world war, nuclear war, that means ripping apart families, atomic Armageddon—that is inhumanity! Against that we have founded a state! Against that we have erected a border with strict control measures to stop what went on during the thirteen years that it was left open and abused—that is humane! That is a service to humanity!

When I finish, he's staring at me, chin up. 'And your question, young lady?'

'My question is whether today you are of the same view about the Wall as something humane, and the killings at the border an act of peace.'

He raises his free arm, inhales and screams, 'More! Than! Ever!' He brings his fist down.

I'm startled for an instant. Then I'm concerned that Frau von Schnitzler will stop the interview. 'You considered it necessary?' I ask quickly.

'I did not "consider" it necessary. It *was* absolutely necessary! It was an historical necessity. It was the most useful construction in all of German history! In European history!'

'Why?'

'Because it prevented imperialism from contaminating the east. It walled it in.'

The only people walled-in were his own. It is as if he has followed my thinking.

'Moreover people in the GDR were not "walled-in"! They could go to Hungary, they could go to Poland. They just couldn't go to NATO countries. Because, naturally, you don't travel around in enemy territory. It's as simple as that.'

This is so mad that I can't think of a question immediately. But in the next breath he contradicts himself. It seems to be his *modus operandi* to have a bet each way.

'I do think, though, that in the last few years they should have opened it up earlier,' he says. Then, almost ruefully, 'The people would have come back again.' I wonder if he can truly believe this. The eastern states are still, seven years on, losing people. He shifts in his seat. 'Most of them, most of them would have.'

Von Schnitzler is one of the cadre whose ideas were moulded in the 1920s by the battle against the gross free market injustices of the Weimar Republic and then the outrages of fascism, and who went on to see the birth and then the death of the nation built on those ideas. He is a true believer and for him my questions only serve to demonstrate a sorry lack of faith.

'You lived through the whole GDR, from beginning to end—'

'So I did, so I did.'

'Is there anything in your opinion that could have been done better, or differently?'

'Oh I'm sure there are things that could have been done differently or better, but that is no longer the question to examine.'

'I think it is,' I say, although something stirs uncomfortably in the back of my mind. 'There was a serious attempt to build a socialist state, and we should examine why, at the end, that state no longer exists. It's important.' The something reveals itself to be the memory of the western-ers Scheller and Uwe also having so little interest in the GDR.

'I noticed relatively early,' he says, 'that we would not be able to survive economically. And when we started to get tied up in this ridicu-lous GDR success propaganda—exaggerated harvest results and production levels and so on—I withdrew from that altogether and confined myself to my specialist area: the work against imperialism. Exclusively. And for that reason today I am so be-lov-ed,' he says, heavy with sarcasm.

'What do you mean "beloved"—by whom?' I ask.

'That's why I'm so beloved by all those who think imperialistically and act imperialistically and bring up their children imperialistically!' Each time he says 'imperialistically' he thrusts his fist on the stick forward towards me. This man, who could turn inhumanity into humanity, faces now perhaps his greatest challenge: to turn the fact that he is hated into the fact that he is, in the face of all available evidence, right.

'Your program was based on exposing the lies of the western media. When you noticed the false success propaganda at home, didn't you feel a responsibility to do the same?'

'No. I focused in my program quite deliberately and exclusively on anti-imperialism, not on GDR propaganda.'

'But you understand my question, Herr von Schnitzler. The success propaganda in the GDR media was also lies—'

'It did distance the people from us, because it was in such stark contrast to the reality.' He can switch from one view to another with frightening ease. I think it is a sign of being accustomed to such power that the truth does not matter because you cannot be contradicted.

'Why didn't you comment then on these lies?'

'I wouldn't even consider it!' He frowns and pulls his neck in like a turtle in disgust. 'I'm not about to criticise my own republic!'

'Why not?'

'The critique of imperialism is quite enough!'

'I criticise my own country—' I say.

He doesn't miss a beat. 'You've a lot more reason to.'

There's nothing for it but to laugh. 'That may be,' I say.

We switch to the present. He starts to talk about 'my very good friend Erich Mielke'.

'Did he have a file on you?'

'I don't know.'

'You haven't applied to have a look at it?'

'Why should I?'

'Out of curiosity.'

'My curiosity is directed solely towards the machinations of imperialism and how they can be countered.'

Checkmate. So I start another question. 'The internal observation of the GDR population, with the apparatus of official and unofficial collaborators—'

He cuts me off. 'You can throw 90 per cent of what you know about that out.' He's angry again. 'It's all lies. Mind you, in my opinion even 10 per cent of what they're saying would have been too much.'

'Are you saying that there was only 10 per cent of the number claimed of Stasi employees assigned to work on the East German population?'

'Yes. It's all been exaggerated immeasurably. In any case I am exceptionally sceptical about numbers.'

He changes tack, back to his friend Mielke. 'The Wall was necessary to defend a threatened nation. And there was Erich Mielke at the top, a living example of the most humane human being.'

I have never heard Mielke referred to in this way. He was too fierce and feared to be referred to with anything like affection. I look away to the shelves on the wall close behind him. They are full of books and small objects of memory, a row of pill bottles and a cheap tape deck. The words 'the most humane human being' hang in the air. He starts to cough, hacking and deep, into a handkerchief, then raises the pink drink to his lips.

'And how are you finding it now after 1989, now that you are living in capitalism or, as you say, in imperialism? Is it what you expected,' I hold his gaze, 'or is it not as bad as you thought?'

'I live,' he says fiercely, 'among the enemy. And not for the first time in my life. I lived among the enemy during the Nazi time as well.' He works himself into another little fury. I see Marta watching him, and I wonder whether the medicine is to deal with this, or with its effects. 'What I can tell you,' he says, 'is that as long as the GDR existed no swine in Bonn would have dared start a war!' He gasps for breath. His hand has formed a fist, but he keeps it in his lap. 'The GDR would have prevented that by its very existence!' He means that so long as the Iron Curtain was up, the NATO countries would not have bombed the former Yugoslavia for fear the Russians would have retaliated on behalf of the Serbs.

He's puffing and cross and, I think, finally stuck. He looks at me and I can see the tiny red veins filigreed across his eyeballs. 'Full Stop!' he screams. 'This…conversation…is…now…over!'

There's a brief pause.

'Thank you very much.' I say.

'What?' He shouts back.

'I said thank you.'

'Oh. You're welcome.'

I start collecting my things, and then remember that I have brought him a small gift from Australia. It is an enamel pin of the German and Australian flags crossed over one another.

'What's this?' he asks, taking it from me and holding it far away from his eyes.

'That's our flag—for Australia,' I start, 'I'm sorry I couldn't find—'

'Just a moment. Just a moment,' he says, getting a fix on it. 'That is not my flag. That's the Federal Republic's.'

I think he might scream at me again. 'I know,' I say quickly, 'but I couldn't find one with the GDR flag at home.'

'OK,' he says, suddenly happy enough, 'I think I have room for that over there,' and he gestures behind him, to Marx and Lenin and even Stalin.

14

The Worse You Feel

I call Julia and ask her over for lunch. I make salmon pasta with mascarpone, egg yolks and cream—I'm putting as many calories into something as I know how. She rings about the time she's due, and asks whether it's OK to be late.

'Sure,' I say, 'About how late?'

'Half an hour.'

'See you then.'

I stand at the kitchen window. A man wearing gloves comes into the yard from one of the side wings, carrying a metal bucket of orange coal dust. He opens the hopper and pours it in, particles the consistency of talc, or something cremated. The hopper clangs shut in a burst of orange cloud. This dust is everywhere. When you can't smell it, it's still there, in the orange winter air.

When Julia arrives she's oddly polite, like a person in someone else's house. I guess she's used to slipping in when I'm not here. We sit down in the kitchen and I open a beer.

'Mind if I smoke?' she asks.

'Not at all. I didn't know you smoked.'

'I just started again,' she says. She lights a cigarette and smokes half of it before she stubs it out.

We eat and afterwards she lights another, holding it in a practised way in the cleft of her index and middle fingers, moving it around as she talks. She is in the same chair as before, the one with the blind tethered to it. Her back is to the window and her face is in shadow, her eyes shiny and dark. Behind her the sky is the colour of wet wool. I have invited her here for a meal, but we both know there is more of her story to tell.

I begin by asking whether she saw her life unfolding differently after the Wall came down. I wonder what it would have been like to watch the barrier that had held you in disappear and the whole world open up like some strange and new dreamt-of thing.

'Well, it's complicated,' she says, running a hand through her hair. Static from her sleeve raises single strands into the air. 'I think...I am perhaps.' She pauses. 'I notice that I still.' She breathes in. 'There are some things for instance...' She stops. 'The whole thing really threw me,' she says, exhaling. 'Not only that but also afterwards. Lots of things, personal things. I think that the whole *Wende* in 1989 and everything I went through around it—I think that I experienced it more intensely than others.'

She's found the old place where the lino is leaving the tabletop and starts to worry it with a fingernail. 'I've been talking about it with my therapist, and she keeps coming back to a theme—one that is quite uncomfortable for me. It has to do with how I can't subject myself to any sort of authority. It's now to the point where I can't commit myself to coming anywhere on time'—she smiles—'as you saw. I just can't have structure imposed on me.'

I pour more beer. It's the second, or maybe the third, and it is loosening up the afternoon. For a moment I am an eye in the ceiling corner. I see two women, like reflections of one another, at an old table in an old kitchen in East Berlin. One has her sleeves rolled up, the other draws her black jumper over her fists, bringing them out only to smoke. This room seems small shelter from the outside world because the colours of the yard have seeped in here, grey and brown—apart from the tiny blue pilot light above the sink, and the remains of a pink sauce in a pan.

'It's hard to live in society if you can't subordinate yourself to authority,' Julia says, 'particularly German society. I think the reason why I can't has to do with a lot of things. Being trapped by the Wall before, and then working in jobs which were way under my capacities and where I had no choice—in the hotel, and then afterwards. I just can't stand the sort of structures that keep you in, I guess.' Her voice has gone very soft. 'And as well as that,' she says, 'I was raped. That happened to me just after the Wall fell. It was in the east, and it was really the last straw.'

Now I am cold and sober and scared of what I am about to hear. I didn't know then what it cost Julia to tell me what had happened to her, and maybe she didn't either. A week later she rang and said that afterwards she had felt sick for three days.

Shortly after the Wall came down, prisoners held in the GDR, mostly political prisoners, were amnestied. Julia went back to Thüringen for a wedding. She was spending the night in the bride's apartment, a one-roomer at the top of a high-rise, and her friend was going to stay the night at the groom's. Julia accompanied her downstairs to a taxi. 'You never know what can happen on those housing estates,' she says. 'Often there's no-one around and it can be a bit creepy.'

When she got back inside the building, there was a man waiting for the lift. It came and they both entered and turned to face the closing doors. Julia says, 'I knew then—there was a moment when I thought something was wrong and I should run back out through those doors. But you are taught to say to yourself, "Don't be ridiculous," so I stayed put.'

The man looked at the floor number she had pressed. He didn't press one himself. The lift moved. Then he jammed it with the emergency button.

Some time later the janitor noticed that one of the lifts was stuck. He went to the roof and called down the shaft to see if anyone was inside or needed help. No answer came.

The man was huge. He bashed Julia and held his hands over her face. She thought he was wearing a black wig. He threatened to kill her if she screamed, to kill her if she called the police. When it was over she crawled from the lift to the apartment door. He ran down the stairs into the darkness.

Julia spent the night alone, terrified, in the apartment. There was no telephone. The man was at large, and he knew where to find her. The next day she managed to get herself to the police station. She received no counselling, no medical care, and no sympathetic treatment there. 'Rape was taboo in the GDR,' she says. The female police officer on duty declined to examine her and went outside for a cigarette instead, so a male colleague conducted a complete physical, Julia naked on a table. Then they took her straight back to where it happened and made her go through everything step by step, pressing the emergency button herself and re-enacting the attack. 'It was as if they didn't believe me,' she says. He was at large, and they were offering her no protection.

Then she went to the wedding. 'I couldn't tell anyone. It would have ruined their day,' she says. 'I wore a lot of makeup, and somehow I got through it.'

We sit in the kitchen all afternoon. At one point it begins to hail, pieces of shattered sky falling against the window. Julia half-smokes cigarettes and tells her story. There are no tears; it is as if she has no self-pity at all.

She tells me her parents didn't know how to help her. The authorities quickly caught the man, a serial rapist with a string of previous convictions. Julia became unable to continue her studies, afraid of the slightest things. She felt separated from everybody, again. At one point before the trial she took up an offer to be a teaching assistant for a semester in San Francisco, where she found people who talked about rape in ways that helped her. When she returned, she had to face him again.

'I almost think the trial was the worst thing of all. If it happened to me again I would never bring charges,' she says solemnly. 'I would kill the man.' Julia had trouble finding legal representation, and trouble affording it. While she was in America the man was convicted of another rape committed during the same spree, 'an even worse one—that girl was hospitalised'. At Julia's trial his lawyer argued diminished responsibility on the grounds of drunkenness, and attacked her credibility as a witness: 'If this man's hands were over your face,' he said, 'how could you not see what colour hair was on them?' She said she didn't know. The man's wife testified he had been at home all evening. But his mother lived with them too. She said her son had dyed his hair black that day and gone out. He hadn't come home till late at night, when he had burnt his clothes in the incinerator out the back. She looked across at Julia in the court and said, 'I'm sorry.' The rapist was convicted, but Julia felt violated all over again.

After the trial she lived on her own in Lichtenberg in East Berlin. It was difficult for her to leave the apartment. 'If I had to buy something at the shops,' she says, 'I would get up in the morning and put on all the loosest clothes I had, layers and layers of them to cover my body. Then I'd drink beer—in the morning!—until I was numb enough to be able to get out the door.' Her mother Irene did not understand why she didn't just get on with things. Julia was distressed, dropped out and suicidal, but once a week she dressed and drank and went to the station to call Irene from a phone booth and tell her everything was fine.

A cigarette sits forgotten in the ashtray. Its pale string of smoke responds to unseen currents in the room.

'I wanted to die,' Julia says. 'I could not see how I could go on and live a life in this world, let alone a normal life.' She considered throwing herself under a train at Lichtenberg station, but the idea of her sisters reading about it in the paper horrified her. Instead, she stopped eating. 'It seemed like the course of least resistance,' she says. 'I was so disturbed, so right at the end of what I could manage,' Her sister came over and watched what she ate. 'I owe her my life really,' Julia says. 'I would tell her I'd had enough, but she counted the mouthfuls, and wouldn't let me stop.'

Julia has been able to study, in fits and bursts, over the last six years. She's had odd jobs to make ends meet, 'whatever I could find and whatever came along'—some translation, work in a second-hand clothes shop, private tutoring, the work at the rental agency.

She is convinced that, in the amnesties of 1990, mistakes were made and the serial rapist was released. 'It was terrible that this happened to me right at that time,' she says. 'It meant that before the good things about the west got to us, this negative thing—the letting loose of the criminals— affected me.' She saw a documentary which claimed hardened criminals had been let loose in the scramble to free the political prisoners. Whether the man who raped her was among them, or whether he was just due for release (as he will be again soon) doesn't change Julia's experience: the end of the security state meant the end, too, of her personal security. The system which had imprisoned her had also, somehow, protected her. 'They were much quicker in the east to find and convict people,' she says. Deep down, and for so far indelible reasons, she associates the fall of the Wall with the end of what had remained of her private sphere after the Stasi had finished with it.

Julia says she must go, she's meeting her sister.

'Yes, of course,' I say, but I can't think of anything else. She sees I'm stuck.

'I think it's important, what you're doing,' she says, as if to comfort me, and I am ashamed. 'For anyone to understand a regime like the GDR, the stories of ordinary people must be told. Not just the activists or the famous writers.' Her eyes, grey-green, have a dark shape in them. When it moves, I see that it is me. 'You have to look at how normal people manage with such things in their pasts.'

'I think I'm losing track of normal.'

'Yes,' she says, smiling, 'I know it's relative. We easterners have an advantage, perhaps, in that we can remember and compare two kinds of systems.' Her mouth twists into a smile as she collects her cigarettes and lighter and puts them in her pocket. 'But I don't know if that's an advantage. I mean you see the mistakes of one system—the surveillance— and the mistakes of the other—the inequality—but there's nothing you could have done in the one, and nothing you can do now about the other.' She laughs wryly. 'And the clearer you see that, the worse you feel.'

She leaves, and I move to the front windows to watch over her when she reaches the front of the building. I see the crown of her head, messy blond and vulnerable as a child's as she bends to tuck one leg of her jeans into her sock. Then she puts the other foot on the pedal and pushes off, Tiresias on a bike.

I call Klaus. 'Wanna get drunk?'

'Sure. You OK?'

'Yep.' He doesn't believe me, but he is a co-operative soul, and we meet down the pub.

I wake up and my head hurts if I move it. I need water. I look at the withered palms in the living room (I've crashed on the couch). They reflect my inner state of being. More awful though than my head, my mouth and my poor wretched lungs, is a vague feeling of regret. What did I say? I try to think back and try to remember who else was in the pub besides Klaus, and how drunk they were. I can't. In some kind of cosmic penance, I spend the day in bed.

Late in the afternoon I decide to go for a swim. At my local pool you pay an entry price determined by how long you would like to spend there, starting at an hour and a half. This made no sense to me (who can swim laps for that long?) until I realised that people use the pool as a bath.

I want to do laps. There are bodies everywhere, swimming or paddling or what looks like actually washing themselves in the pool. There are no lanes. There is no agreed direction. People are breaststroking diagonally across, heads out like ducks. One man still has his glasses on. Kids jump in off the sides and an old fellow resting in a corner is fiddling with the hair on a mole under his arm.

I need to swing my limbs around and get some air in my lungs. It must be possible to do a lap or two. Perhaps there is a system of passing one another that I don't yet know, like boat rules. I choose a part of the pool that seems less crowded and begin with some freestyle. But it's not quite the stroke I'm used to because I have to keep a lookout ahead for obstacles. Not only ahead: a teenager swiming cross-wise through the pool is headed my way. As I turn to the other side to breathe, a kid with floaties on her arms jumps in and narrowly misses me. I look up. A woman in a yellow bikini has set off in my direction, dog-paddling to keep her make-up dry. There is no way out.

I stop and tread water and consider my next move. Whilst I'm plotting a course, I am visited by a blinding question: what am I doing in this chaos anyway? In this chaotic city?

The woman in the yellow bikini is pretending she has not seen me. What is this? Swimming chicken? I've had it with this place. I decide to plough on. I think brute force may just win through and I beat my arms fast. I'm no great swimmer and I know this is eastern Germany, home of the drugged and the huge, the men-women and the girl wonders, but for one instant I'm our Dawnie, I'm Shane Gould, I'm Susie O'Neill, I'm the human eggbeater churning up water. Yellow schmellow. I haven't seen her either. *What is the matter with me?*

A whistle sounds. What? The chicken woman looks smug; the round is over and she's been declared a winner. A pool warden in too-small trunks comes to the edge to address me, and provide a diversion for the other paddlers. 'There's no swimming here,' he says, 'only bathing.'

Oh, God. 'So when can I swim then, in this swimming pool?'

'Let's see,' he says, 'warm bathing is Tuesdays, women only Wednesday mornings, women with children Wednesday afternoons, hydrotherapy Friday mornings and, oh yes, there are lanes for swimming between 4 pm and 6 pm on Monday, Thursday and Fridays. Weekends are free bathing, like this.'

I see. I get out. So this is orderly chaos. We will have 'free bathing' between this time and that, which is now. We will allow unusual headgear and bombs, mole picking and washing and babies, but no swimming. There's order everywhere else in German life—even the handicapped are labelled with yellow (yellow!) armbands. (These are meant to alert others that they might need help, but are shocking to outsiders: three yellow dots pinned on the clothing.) This pool must be the subconscious of the country: the mess that gives rise to all that order.

What am I doing here? People are looking at me. I walk away, and see that the diving pool is utterly empty. I will obey. I won't swim in the non-swimming time. I slip into the diving pool and sit in the corner. No-one can see me here, and there cannot be rules that I am breaking. What am I doing here?

My body is weightless and my legs out of perspective. They are both foreshortened, and far away. And then it comes. I'm making portraits of people, East Germans, of whom there will be none left in a generation. And I'm painting a picture of a city on the old fault-line of east and west. This is working against forgetting, and against time.

Another whistle sounds, very loud. I look up and the warden is standing over me, so close he could have whispered to get my attention. 'This is a diving pool,' he says. 'It is only for diving.' I'm speechless, so he adds for good measure, 'You are not diving.'

He's got me there. Then again, no-one else is diving either. But I can't argue with a man armed with a whistle and prepared to use it, so I get out again.

In the changing room a rotund woman in some kind of uniform tells me my bathers are dripping on the floor.

'That's because they are wet,' I say. She comes towards me, about to say something else, but I pick up my bag and go. Too many rules.

15
Herr Christian

Several days pass in which my main activity seems to be feeding and emptying the heater. Now I'm rugged up and off to the station. Near the entrance there's a photographer's studio. I always look in the window at the prints on display to see the locals as they want to be seen. There are bald babies with ribbons around their heads; there's a wedding shot with the bride on a motorbike like a package deal; there's a young man with a mullet haircut holding proudly onto his girlfriend as if he just caught her. The photos change from time to time but today, as always, there is one of a woman of staggering beauty, beauty so fine I stare at it as if it were a puzzle, or an answer.

On the train another beautiful woman sits opposite me. She has a baby in a halter on her chest. I wonder whether others notice the loveliness of the women here, or are used to it. The Turkish man next to me is otherwise absorbed. He can see his own reflection in the window next to the woman, so he pulls a comb from his pocket and draws it lovingly through his moustache. The young mother is looking down at her baby and I can't take my gaze away from them. When she raises her head I see she has a pierced nose and that her blue eyes are crossed, just slightly, drawn to the stud as to a magnet.

I stand at the edge of the carpark at Potsdam station. All the other passengers stream ahead past me, to cars and trams and places they know. When they're gone I am alone, except for a man in jeans leaning on the bonnet of the biggest, blackest BMW I have ever seen. He waves at me. This is my lift. This is my latest Stasi man.

Herr Christian shakes my hand warmly. He has a big crooked smile. 'I thought a tour would be a good idea,' he says, his voice airy and smoky, 'to show you some of the places we operated.'

'Great.'

He opens the car door for me, springs around the other side and jumps in.

I look across. It's quite a long way. Herr Christian is in his mid-forties, with a young flat face and a nose that has been broken several times. His hair is bunched in wiry blond curls close to his head, his eyes are small and blue and sparkly. He looks straight at me, smiling his lopsided smile like a gangster, or an angel.

'Let's go,' he says and I notice he lisps. He puts his sunglasses on, and turns the ignition.

The machine coasts the roads like a cruiser. He handles it lightly, more like a boy with a toy than a man with a vast black asset. We drive through the streets of Potsdam, over cobbles we don't feel and past grand buildings in various states of disrepair. The windows are dark and no-one can see us in here.

We pull up in front of a well-kept yellow mansion with white lintels and a hedge garden. 'This,' he says, 'was the "Coding Villa".' Herr Christian used to work here, encoding transcripts of telephone conversations intercepted from carphones and police walkie-talkies in the west. 'They'd come in by telex, and we'd turn them into code and send them on to

Berlin.' He chuckles. 'We'd encode every last thing that was said, including *Ja, Guten Tag* and what they had for lunch. In Berlin, they had to know *everything*. Mind you, we did catch a lot of western politicians talking among themselves too.'

We depart from the kerb. The plane trees along the streets are bare, with mottled trunks and limbs ending in clotted stumps. They make spirit patterns of light and dark over the bonnet. Herr Christian is chatty and at ease. He has a sense of fun about what he did with the Stasi. He talks to me like a co-conspirator. 'I was never very ideological,' he says. We leave Potsdam city behind us, and sail down a freeway. We are gaining on a frog-green Trabi, with black-tinted windows and a smoking exhaust. Written across the boot in crinkle-cut neon-pink letters is the message, 'I am your worst nightmare.' We laugh as we pass it.

When Herr Christian was nineteen and doing his military service, he was summoned to a special room for an interview. 'I wondered what I'd done wrong,' he says. The man inside was wearing a suit and smoking western cigarettes, and he asked Herr Christian what he wanted to do with his life.

'Box with the Club Dynamo,' Herr Christian said. Dynamo was the sporting club of the armed forces, and the Stasi. The man got him to sign an undertaking to work for the Stasi. 'It wasn't a problem for me,' he says. 'I thought it might lead to a bit of adventure.' A car accident later ended his boxing career, but he stayed with the Firm. 'I've always had an acute sense of duty to obey the law,' he says, 'and I thought it was the right thing to do.'

We pull off the freeway, down a disused road. The forest on either side is tall dark pines, all the same height and planted in rows. The car dips up and over the road like a boat, until we reach a fence with a 'Keep Out' sign on it. Herr Christian drives straight in. We come to what looks like a mound of earth. There are outbuildings scattered around.

He turns to me and his leather jacket makes a sticky noise on the leather seats. 'This was the bunker for the leading cadre of the Potsdam

Stasi in the event of a nuclear catastrophe,' he says. 'I guarded it for a while. The entrance was in one of those buildings'—he points to a grey fibro-cement hut—'and you walked down steps to a huge concrete complex under the ground. When they built it, they had to move tonnes and tonnes of earth in trucks disguised as animal transports, and dump it far away. The bunker had everything you can imagine inside it—food and medicine and sleeping quarters, communications equipment, table tennis, the lot.' There were many bunkers in the GDR, for the Stasi to save themselves in and repopulate the earth—if they remembered to take any women with them.

A policeman in green uniform comes towards us. He is young and clean-shaven and has an alsatian dog on a lead. 'What business do you have here?' he asks.

Herr Christian tells him he used to guard this place when it was a Stasi bunker.

'I wouldn't know anything about that,' he says. 'This is federal property and I must ask you to leave.'

In the car Herr Christian asks, 'I wonder what they are using it for now?'

Instead of going back the way we came to the freeway, he manoeu-vres the car along a series of muddy tracks through the pines. At several points there's a break in the trees and I see where the Wall used to be, a strip which is now a sandy gash in the forest with earth-moving equip-ment on it, and old guard towers covered in graffiti. I ask him what he does for a living these days.

'I'm a, uh, private detective,' he says self-consciously. 'Yep. I'm pretty much doing the same job as I did back then. In this, my second life.'

'How's business?'

'Not so great actually,' he says. 'The jobs don't come in as regularly as I'd like, and many of them are the kinds of jobs,' he coughs a little, 'that I don't take.' He looks across at me under his eyebrows.

'What kind is that?'

'Marriage work,' he says, turning back to the track. 'I won't touch it.'

Where one spouse suspects another of having an affair and wants them tailed.' He lights a cigarette from a softpack of Stuyvesants and drags deeply. 'When I was first with the Stasi I was married, but we weren't happy, and I fell in love with one of my son's teachers. We began an affair. I confided in my best friend, but he turned out to have what you might call an overdeveloped sense of loyalty—and he told them at work. They locked me up in solitary for three days. Then they demoted me to working on a building site for a year. My supervisor said, "Anyone can have an affair, but *everything* must be reported."'

The Stasi could not bear it that one of their own had something in his life that they didn't know about. But Herr Christian, it seems, has always known that some things are private. He exhales two streams of smoke from his nostrils into the blackness of the car. 'I was scared, you know, when I worked on that building site. I knew so much from having been in the coding centre that I thought they'd come after me. I was scared I'd suffer some traffic accident or a mishap at work or that in some other way a sentence would be carried out.' He shakes his head. 'I just won't do marriage work. It's beneath my dignity.'

After his stint on the building site, and after he had married his new love, Herr Christian was accepted back into the fold and put on duty as a covert security officer on Stasi buildings. 'Now we should be right near where I did most of my work,' he says, 'the Rest Stop Michendorf.' We emerge from the neat sad forest, and travel along the freeway to an ordinary-looking truck stop. The main building is two storeys of grey concrete, with a café underneath. It was the last stop on the freeway before cars from the west entered West Berlin. It is still in use, the old bowsers standing bent-elbowed out the front, beside two new pink phone-boxes from Deutsche Telekom.

We get out and walk around on the gravel. Herr Christian pushes his glasses on top of his head and lights another cigarette. 'In my day, we had this place completely under surveillance. That room over the top there,' he says, pointing to some dark dormer windows, 'was occupied day and night. And from it we had an overview of everything that happened here—of all the vehicles passing from east to west. It was top secret. The petrol-station attendants were mainly informers, but not even they knew what went on up there.

'We always had at least two people in civilian clothes around, for observations on the ground. That was my job. I'd have a recording device in my pocket, or if I was in a car, it would have cameras in the headlights. We had eavesdropping equipment that could catch the conversations in the vehicles. There was a camera in that bowser there,' he points to the petrol pump, 'which I could operate remotely to get a close-up shot of someone if I was standing in the background. We had it pretty much covered.'

Herr Christian's job here was to hunt out the cars which might have stowaway East Germans in them trying to escape. We walk around the rest stop to the other side. The sky is the same colour as the concrete; we are sandwiched in grey. The tip of my nose and my earlobes are starting to pulse with cold. 'People-smuggling to the west was a business, run by criminals really—they'd take huge sums of money from the poor souls they were smuggling after they got them through, something like 20,000 westmarks. Or, they'd make them pay earlier, with family heirlooms or stamp collections. The western car would pull off at a spot along the transit route and the easterners would meet it, pay over and get in. I saw some terrible things. People would drug their children and put them in the boot. I opened a boot once and found a woman with her child inside. Because I was in civilian clothes they thought that I was with the smuggling organisation. I remember the joy on their faces for the instant they thought they were in freedom.' He stubs out his cigarette and puts his hands in the pockets of his jacket, shoulders hunched against the grey air. 'I have to say that was bitter, because I am a sensitive man. But I am also a stickler for the law, and I thought that what they were doing was wrong, and I'd been brought up to think that from my earliest kindergarten days.'

'What would have happened to them?'

'We took them to remand at Potsdam. Then they would have been convicted. They usually got one and a half to two years. That was the law.

'There were parts of it that were fun though,' he says, his breath like more smoke in this cold. 'I think I had the only job in the world where I got to go into a warehouse each morning and decide, "Who will I be today?"' He laughs. 'I got to choose a disguise. Sometimes I'd be a park ranger—that was a green uniform, sometimes a garbage collector in overalls, or someone come to repair the wiring. I really liked being a western tourist because the clothes were much better quality—real leather gloves—and I got to drive a Mercedes, or at least a VW Golf.'

We walk back to the BMW and he clicks it awake. 'But do you know what was best?' he asks, turning to me. 'Best of all'—he gives me a mock punch on the shoulder—'was when I'd dress up as a blind man: I'd have the cane, the glasses, the armband with three dots. Sometimes I'd even get a girl as a guide on my arm. I'd have to remember to take my watch off though!' He looks around this barren place, enjoying the memory of work well done. A car passes; we are just two small figures climbing into a large car at a petrol station. 'Yes,' he says, 'being a blind man is the best way to observe people.' He chortles, pushes his dark glasses over his eyes and starts the engine of his huge black machine.

16

Socialist Man

In August 1961, a fresh Stasi recruit named Hagen Koch walked the streets of Berlin with a tin of paint and a brush, and painted the line where the Wall would go. He was twenty-one years old, and he was Secretary-General Honecker's personal cartographer. Unlike most heads of state, Honecker needed a personal cartographer, because he was redrawing the limits of the free world.

Koch's apartment is a cell in a honeycomb of high-rises where a lot of other former Stasi officers and their families lived before the Wall fell, and live still. The balconies have all been painted a pinkish colour. On some of them sun umbrellas are furled in hibernation.

The man who opens the door has a sort of glow about him—a bright face, receding hair and soft brown eyes. Koch smiles broadly, and shakes my hand. He gestures around himself exuberantly, like a ringmaster. 'Welcome to the Wall Archive,' he says.

All along the corridor hang framed colour photocopies of what were once top secret Stasi maps. They show various parts of the Wall in aerial view, with a colour-coded key for the guard towers, mine traps, dogs and trip-wires. Black-yellow-red East German pennants are pinned on the walls and the bodice of a uniform of the leaders' elite guard, the Felix Dzerzhinski regiment, hangs from hooks, deflated as a scarecrow. More obscure mementos of the regime sit in glass-fronted cupboards. As we walk along the corridor, I think I see a crocheted doily in the national colours.

Koch talks as we walk, and by the time we reach his study he is listing off on his fingers the VIPs who have been to see him and his archive. Behind his desk a large gold plate bearing the East German hammer and compass shines out from just above head height. The room is lined with framed newspaper articles. The pictures show Koch with his visitors. He looks straight into the camera, clean-featured and moon-faced and beaming: Koch with the Queen of Sweden, Koch with an actor from 'Star Trek', Koch with Christo the wrap artist.

He is more than comfortable with the tiny microphone on my tape recorder. When I ask if I might clip it to his shirt he takes it from me and wields it like a rock star. His forearms are honey-brown and lightly haired.

I ask him how he had applied to join the Stasi.

'No, no, no, no. It didn't work like that. You had to be chosen.' Apparently this was one of the fundamentals of the system: don't call us, we'll call you.

'Who chose you then?'

'Just a moment,' he says. 'It is hard for you to understand. Without understanding my childhood, you can't see why anyone would want to join the Stasi.'

This isn't quite true. I have given a lot of thought to why people would want to join. In a society riven into 'us' and 'them', an ambitious young person might well want to be one of the group in the know, one of the unmolested. If there was never going to be an end to your country, and you could never leave, why wouldn't you opt for a peaceful life and a satisfying career? What interests me is the process of dealing with that decision now that it is all over. Can you rework your past, the grit that rubs in you, until it is shiny and smooth as a pearl?

'My upbringing was so...' he searches for the words, 'so... GDR.' His eyebrows move up and down. 'Everything that was GDR-positive, that was me.' Koch turns to a large cardboard box on the floor beside his desk. 'My father put me on this track.' He reaches into the box and pulls out a brownish photograph of his father in army uniform, with the expression men in armed services pictures often have, as if they are already elsewhere. Then he goes back to the box and produces a school report. He flashes it at me and I see the old-style gothic handwriting. Koch starts to read: 'Hagen was a diligent and orderly pupil...' And then he reads on through the report. We are right back at the beginning of his life. I look at the box, and the box is deep. It seems this afternoon we are going to go through it piece by plastic-wrapped piece.

'You have to understand,' he says, 'in the context of my father, and of the propaganda of the Cold War—the GDR was like a religion. It was something I was brought up to believe in...'

He speaks passionately and loudly, although I am sitting close to him and the room is small. I watch him waving his arms and my microphone. He brings out more photographs and more documents and I hear him say, 'You can see here after the war we had no mattresses, holes in our socks...'

But I am mulling over the idea of the GDR as an article of faith. Communism, at least of the East German variety, was a closed system of belief. It was a universe in a vacuum, complete with its own self-created hells and heavens, its punishments and redemptions meted out right here on earth. Many of the punishments were simply for lack of belief, or even suspected lack of belief. Disloyalty was calibrated in the minutest of signs: the antenna turned to receive western television, the red flag not hung out on May Day, someone telling an off-colour joke about Honecker just to stay sane.

I remember Sister Eugenia at school, with her tight sausage-fingers, explaining the 'leap of faith' that was required before the closed universe of Catholicism would make any sense. Her fingers made the leap, pink and unlikely, as we children drew the 'fruits of the holy spirit'—a banana for redemption, as I recall—and all I could think of was a sausage-person walking off a clifftop, believing all the time the hand of God would scoop him up. The sense of having someone examine your inner worth, the violence of the idea that it can in fact be measured, was the same. God could see inside you to reckon whether your faith was enough to save you. The Stasi could see inside your life too, only they had a lot more sons on earth to help.

The GDR, in its forty years, tried strenuously both to create Socialist German Man and to get the people to believe in him. Socialist German Man was to be different from Nazi German Man, and different from western (Capitalist Imperialist) German Man. History was taught as a series of inevitable evolutionary leaps towards Communism: from a feudal state through capitalism and then—in the greatest leap forward to date—socialism. The Communist nirvana was the world to come. Darwinian diagrams flash into my mind showing man on a scale of increasing uprightness and lack of body hair: from monkey to Neanderthal to Cro-Magnon to Modern. Here now in front of me is Socialist Man, smooth and keen and very, very verbal.

As Koch dips into the carton once more, I wonder whether he ever wished he had been a disruptive and disorderly pupil, instead of a diligent and orderly one; whether it would have saved him from carrying his explanatory box through life.

'My story comes directly out of my father's story.' Hagen Koch passes me the photograph of his father again, and Heinz Koch looks out from early in the century. He had the same brown eyes as his son, but in a narrower, more doubtful face.

Heinz Koch was born in a village in Saxony on 5 August 1912, and was brought up as the son of the village tailor. One day when he was sixteen years old he ran home from school, distraught, with his report card in his hand. In the space for 'Name' was written: 'Koch, Heinz, Grandson of the Master Tailor.' Koch pulls a yellowing report from the box. 'This occurred on the twenty-third of the third, 1929,' he says, shaking the document. 'On that day my father learnt of his illegitimacy—his big sister was his mother!' Heinz was stunned by the realisation that everyone had lied to him: You all hid this from me for so long?

'Who was his real father?' I ask.

'I'll get to that,' Hagen says.

'According to the German moral code of that time, illegitimacy was terrible, shameful.' Heinz was immediately ostracised by his friends and left school. He decided to join the army, hoping that a uniform would hide the stigma of his birth. In September 1929 he signed up for a twelve-year term of duty.

Heinz Koch got more than he bargained for. By the time his term was due to expire in October 1941, he found himself stationed in France as part of the Nazi occupation force and could not be discharged. In May 1945, after Berlin surrendered, Master Sergeant Koch somehow made it back to Dessau, to his wife and two small children. He travelled over a landscape pockmarked with craters, through towns of rubble with pipes and plumbing exposed in the streets. People were crazy with pain and secrets. In the woods and on the roads were refugees, war criminals, rogue bomber groups and Allied forces who had started the Cold War between them before the hot one had ended. In Dresden he thought he smelt rotting flesh. But, one week after the war ended, Heinz Koch was home. At the Potsdam conference, Dessau was given to the Russians. They released him from active duty.

Koch is talking, dipping into his document box, talking. Then he leans forward as if to tell me a weighty piece of information. I smell his aftershave. 'On 1 September 1945,' he says, 'the Soviet command issued Heinz with a Permission to Ride a Bicycle.'

'Why did people need a permit to ride a bike?' I ask.

'Because they could bring messages! Pass on news!' Koch cries. 'There was no other transport. People on bikes could evade checkpoints, they could have secret meetings.' Clearly the atmosphere of paranoid control had set in early under the Russians. All the same, I have started to worry about the level of detail we are sinking into. I steal a look towards his bottomless box, wondering whether we are descending into the morass for the sake of it, or whether there was some point to the bicycle tale. Then, as he turns away from me to put the document back in his box, he says, 'But beforehand, you realise, they had to vet his record to check that he wasn't an evil person.'

Was this the point? Was Koch using the available evidence—in this case a bicycle permit—to construct or confirm a story of his father's innocence during the war? There's clearly a portion of the past here that cannot be pinned down with facts, or documents. All that exists is permission to ride a bike.

Immediately after the war ended the Allies divided up their conquered enemy. The English, Americans and French took over the western parts of Germany and the Russians took the eastern states of Thuringia, Saxony, Saxony-Anhalt, Mecklenburg-West Pomerania and Brandenburg. Berlin was divided among the victors in the same way: its western suburbs to the English, French and Americans, its eastern ones to the USSR. But, because the city lay deep in the eastern zone, its western suburbs became an odd island of democratic administration and market economy in a Communist landscape.

In their zones, the western powers set about catching prominent Nazis and establishing democratic systems of governance: a federated system of states, the division of political, administrative and judicial power, and guarantees of private property. In 1948 they handed over these institutions to the newly created Federal Republic of Germany (West Germany) together with massive injections of funds from the Americans' Marshall Plan.

The Russians ran the eastern parts of Germany directly until the German Democratic Republic was established as a satellite state of the USSR in 1949. Production was nationalised, factories and property turned over to the state, health care, rent and food were subsidised. One-party rule was established with an all-powerful secret service to back it up. And the Russians, having refused the offer of American capital, plundered East German production for themselves.

They stripped factories of plant and equipment which they sent back to the USSR. At the same time, they required a rhetoric of 'Communist brotherhood' from the East Germans whom they had 'liberated' from fascism. Whatever their personal histories and private allegiances, the people living in this zone had to switch from being (rhetorically, at the very least) Nazis one day to being Communists and brothers with their former enemies the next.

And almost overnight the Germans in the eastern states were made, or made themselves, innocent of Nazism. It seemed as if they actually believed that Nazis had come from and returned to the western parts of Germany, and were somehow separate from them—which was in no way true. History was so quickly remade, and so successfully, that it can truly be said that the easterners did not feel then, and do not feel now, that they were the same Germans as those responsible for Hitler's regime. This sleight-of-history must rank as one of the most extraordinary innocence manoeuvres of the century.

In Dresden once, on a blue bridge over the river Elbe, I saw a plaque commemorating the liberation of the East Germans from their Nazi oppressors by their brothers the Russians. I looked at it for a long time, a small thing dulled by grime from the air. I wondered whether it had been put there immediately after the Russians came into a vanquished Germany, or whether a certain time had been allowed to elapse before things could begin to be rewritten.

To start a new country, with new values and newly minted socialist citizens, it is necessary to begin at the beginning: with children. Schoolteachers in the eastern regions were immediately dismissed because their job had been to educate children in the values of the Nazi regime. Socialist teachers had to be created. The authorities established six-month training schemes for 'People's Teachers', who then went into the schools. By February 1946 Heinz Koch, who hadn't finished school himself, was a fully qualified teacher in the village of Lindau, thirty kilometres from Dessau.

In October of that year, the first 'free democratic' elections were held in East Germany. In fact, throughout the life of East Germany, elections were regularly held. On the ballot paper there were representatives of all the major parties: mirror-image replicas of the parties that existed in West Germany. There were centre-right Christian Democrats (CDU), Liberal Democrats (later the FDP), and Communists (SED). Election after election for forty years, the results would be broadcast on television: and always, overwhelmingly, the Communists were voted in. The majorities stretched credibility: 98.1 per cent; 95.4 per cent; 97.6 per cent.

None of this, though, was evident in 1946. At that time, it was possible, just possible, that somehow a socialist state would emerge which lived up to the 'democratic' of its name. They'd all been through hell on earth; didn't they deserve heaven? People's dreams had been honed by suffering, whittled into sharp and definite shapes.

Heinz Koch founded the Lindau branch of the Liberal Democrats and stood for election as mayor. September there is a month of long sunsets, late light falling through the leaves, still on the trees. Even in this land of rubble and dust there was room for hope. This was, after all, an election: there were parties, there were candidates, there were local campaigns and there were polling stations.

And there was a ballot paper on which the Communist Party candidate's name was top of the list. It might have been a coincidence, except that next to this candidate's name, 'Paul Enke', was written not 'SED Candidate', but, already, 'Mayor'.

Nevertheless, when the vote came in, it was clear Heinz Koch had won the election. Lindau was a tiny place: the Liberal Democrats got 363 votes, the SED 289 and the CDU 131. People no longer wanted right or left—they wanted middle-of-the-road. 'But Enke the Communist,' Koch says, 'was chairman of the Electoral Commission.' Enke immediately called a meeting in the town hall, 'for the evaluation of the vote'.

Koch tells me that the hall was full of women, some with children. There were several old men, but there were scarcely any young or middle-aged ones. Enke welcomed them, and then addressed the room: 'So where are all your men?'

There was a silence, shuffling.

'Fallen in war,' came one answer.

'Missing in action,' said another voice.

One woman said quietly, 'I don't know.'

Then a voice came from the back of the hall. 'My husband is a prisoner of war in Russia.'

Enke seized his moment. 'How many of your men are in POW camps?' he asked. The hands started to go up, at first slowly, but then there were many. 'So how long did your husband serve in the forces?' Enke asked a woman sitting near the front.

'One year,' she said. The answers started to come from all over the room: five years, three years, seven years.

'And for that they were taken prisoners of war?'

'That's the way it happened,' said the women.

'Well, I ask you,' said Enke, 'do you think it right that your men, who served three years, five years, seven years in the armed forces, are in prison, when Master Sergeant Koch on my right here, who served that fascist imperialist army for sixteen years, gets off scot-free? Not one single day's punishment?'

'So in this way,' Koch says, 'my father was sentenced to seven years in a prisoner-of-war camp.'

'What? Just like that?' I ask.

Koch is agitated now. 'The Russians came and took him into custody. That was just the way it worked. And the people said that it's right that it should be so. If my husband is sitting it out over there, then so should he.'

Between 1945 and 1950 the Russian secret police imprisoned POWs, Nazis, and others like infantryman Heinz Koch who might have got in their way. They re-used the Nazi concentration camps of Sachsenhausen and Buchenwald and other places, and when they were full they built new prisons, or sent people to Russia. It is estimated that some 43,000 of these people died from illness, starvation or violence after the war. In Lindau, the people helped the victors punish their fellows and called it fair.

After nearly a month in custody, on 22 October 1946, Enke came to visit his prisoner. Heinz thought his time was up. Enke started in on an unusual tack.

'It's your wife's birthday today, I gather,' he said.

'Yes.'

'Wouldn't it be a nice birthday surprise for her if you came home? What would you say to that?'

Heinz was confused. He had been steeling himself for transportation. 'Is that...possible?' he asked.

'Sure it is. I am mayor, after all, and what I say goes.'

There was a pause, then it became clear. 'What are the conditions?' Heinz asked.

'Relax, comrade, relax. It's simple, really. All you need to do is quit the Liberal Democrats and come over to us. Become a member of the Socialist Unity Party. Just as soon as that happens I can take you home. In fact, I could take you home today.'

Koch is looking at me closely. 'What would you do?' he asks. 'How should my father decide?'

'For the wife and life, of course,' I say.

Koch is pleased, smiling and nodding and waving the mike. 'So,' he says, 'on his wife's birthday Heinz changed parties and went home.'

In this way the Lindau Communist Party annihilated its opposition and at the same time installed one of their own as the local primary school teacher, under threat of deportation to a POW camp. They had him where they could keep an eye on him: there was only one school, and the children of all the Party members were there.

Later that same year Hagen started school. Heinz taught all his pupils the doctrine of Communism, including his little boy. He found himself educating good socialist citizens for a regime that had tried to ruin his family, and his life.

In late 1946 the Communists founded the *Pioniere*, a youth organisation designed to instil in young children a love of Marx and country. For the older ones the Free German Youth was established. The scheme mirrored exactly the Nazis' *Pimpfe* for small children and the Hitler Youth for adolescents. People joked that the Free German Youth and the Hitler Youth were so similar that only the colour of the neckerchiefs distinguished them. In both, there were meetings, torches, oaths of allegiance and a confirmation ceremony for thirteen-year-olds, complete with candles and prayer-like incantations.

All small children were required to join the *Pioniere*. But this came too soon for the villagers of Lindau. They baulked at seeing their children once more in line and marching and refused to put them in uniform again for the powers that be. Heinz Koch was arrested and taken into custody.

Enke said, 'Why should the other children join up if the teacher's own son does not?' It was necessary for Heinz Koch to set an example through his son. He was released and given one more chance to show why he should not be deported.

Koch turns to his box and pulls out a small blue scarf. 'So, as a result, on 13 December 1946 I was the first child to wear this kerchief around my neck.'

This is how Hagen Koch became a *Musterknabe*, a poster boy for the new regime.

My gaze has wandered to the wall behind him. Next to the gold plate hangs a girly calendar displaying a naked woman's torso in a forest. The photographer has cut off her head and her legs below the knee. The caption reads, 'Wilderness Area'.

Hagen Koch turns back to his box, his collection of strange talismans from a bygone world. 'Let me show you this beetle,' he says, pulling out a poster. He unrolls it: 'STOP THE AMERICAN BEETLE!' is written in large capitals across the top. Below there's a drawing of a child holding a magnifying glass to the ground. Under it is a beetle with a human face and big human teeth. The beetle wears a jacket in the colours of the American flag, and its face is the face of President Truman. 'These were all over our school,' he says, and explains why.

In 1948 the Russians decided they had had enough of the small island of capitalist imperialism that was West Berlin. It seethed with the spies of enemy countries. It was a toehold for the Allies on socialist soil. In a modern siege, Stalin's forces cut off the land supply routes through East Germany to West Berlin. On the night of 24 June 1948, they switched off the eastern power plant that supplied the city. The West Berliners were to be starved out in the dark.

But the Allies would not give up the two million West Berliners. For almost a year, from June 1948 to October 1949, they kept the city alive by plane. In that time American and British planes made some 277,728 flights through Soviet airspace to drop bundles of food, clothing, cigarettes, medicine, fuel and equipment, including components for a new power station, to the people of West Berlin.

In the west, the aircraft came to be known as the '*Rosinenbomber*', or 'raisin bombers', because they brought food. But in the east, Koch and his classmates were told the enemy planes sprayed potato beetles over East German crops as they flew over, in order to spoil the harvest. 'Lindau was virtually under the flight path—the planes flew day and night,' Koch says. 'This is how they gave us a picture of the enemy: in a place where people get no news from outside, they have nothing else to believe.'

'Why was it credible that the Americans would do this?' I ask. It seemed improbable that a nuclear superpower would be loading up planes full of live beetles on leaves and setting out across the Atlantic with them.

'Because they had just bombed Dresden flat!' he cried. 'That beautiful centre of German culture! Senselessly! And they even dropped two atom bombs on Japan! They were clearly truly evil! What more proof do you need?'

Bombs, atomic weapons, and now a biblical pestilence.

'I am telling you how propaganda works!' he continues. 'That is how I grew up.'

At this time, there was still rationing. Sugar was scarce and boiled sweets were a luxury. But there was an incentive scheme for the children. 'For every beetle we collected we could redeem a penny. For a larva, a halfpenny. And for every hundred, we got ten ration cards for sugar! So we children went into the fields every spare minute we had, collecting beetles and larvae, beetles and larvae. We handed them in and we got more sweets than we could eat!'

In Koch's mind, the sweet taste of reward is connected with foiling the American plot to spoil the potato crop and starve his people. This story—of insects and sweets and the making of an enemy—is the story of the making of a patriot.

17

Drawing the Line

'So it was that I came on 5 April 1960 to the Ministry of State Security.' Hagen Koch nearly swallows the words. 'Four days later,' he says, 'this photo was taken.' The photo shows a young man in his grey Stasi uniform spruced and tense behind a huge lectern. Koch was giving his maiden speech: why I want to protect and defend my homeland. He took the oath: 'By order of the workers' and farmers' state, I promise if necessary to lay down my life...to protect against the enemy...obediently and every-where...' All the top brass were there. Mielke was there.

Afterwards, Koch stood in a loose group with his commandant. The other recruits were pretending to relax and trying to be noticed at the same time. Suddenly Koch felt all eyes on him, a hand on his shoulder. He turned around. It was Mielke.

'What is your training, young man?'

'Technical draftsman.'

Mielke addressed Koch's commandant. 'I want you to look after this one. His career. This is the kind we need.'

'And so,' Koch says, 'that is how I was lifted out from the great grey mass.' He was immediately made director of the Drafting Office for Cartographics and Topography. 'I didn't have a clue,' he tells me. 'My training was as a technical draftsman for machines. I knew nothing about maps.'

In the summer of 1960, shortly after joining the Stasi, Koch fell in love with a girl from Berlin. She hadn't been in the *Pioniere* or the Free German Youth, and she certainly wasn't in the Party, but she wasn't radical either. Koch smiles and sort of half-winks. 'I chose my wife by her outside, not her political convictions.' I find myself looking away, and the girly calendar catches my eye. It can't meet my gaze because its head is cut off. I look at its map of Tasmania in the forest.

The Stasi knew everything. Koch's boss called him in and told him, 'That girl is inappropriate. We have plans for you, and that little one, she is GDR-negative.'

For their part, her parents were horrified: he was one of *them*. As soon as she turned eighteen they eloped. It was 21 July 1961.

Koch turns around and flicks a hand at the calendar. 'You noticed that did you?' he chuckles.

'Hmm.'

'Do you know what it is?'

'What do you mean?' I ask.

'That is the calendar for the border troops of the GDR,' he said. 'Do you know what is special about it?'

'No.'

'That calendar was printed in mid-1990. *After* the Wall came down. It was printed because, even at that late stage, people here could not believe that the nation would simply cease to exist. Despite all the evidence, they thought the GDR would go on as an independent country, with an army and a border guard of its own. And that border guard would need its own girly calendar.'

'When the Wall was built in 1961 I thought it was something we had to do because they were robbing us blind,' Koch says. 'The GDR was compelled to protect itself from the swindlers and parasites and black marketeers of the west.'

Because of subsidisation, prices were lower in the east, but so were wages. 'Before there was a Wall,' he says, 'people thought: why should I work in the east when I could earn more in the west? So they went across to them each day and offered them their labour, when we so badly needed it here to rebuild.

'And then at the checkpoints on their way home they'd change their west marks for eastern ones at a rate of five to one! Can you imagine?' He says this as if rates of exchange were some kind of money voodoo. 'They'd come back here able to buy up everything of ours. Not only that, but they'd buy up for friends in the west as well—in the mornings we used to see these people on their way to work with rucksacks full of our bread, our butter, our milk, eggs and meat. Something had to be done to stop people fleeing through this mousehole in the GDR.'

As well as leaving to work in the western sector each day, hundreds and later thousands of refugees started leaving the eastern sector for good. By 1961 about 2000 people were leaving the east each day through West Berlin.

Koch says his thinking was orthodox for the time. 'These people were shirking the hard work that had to be done here in order to build a better future for themselves—they wanted to enjoy their lives right here, right now.' It was as if that were a moral failure, a religious falling off the branch—who are these people who will reap where they have not sown?

The GDR was haemorrhaging. 'And it wasn't just the ordinary workers who were leaving! It was the doctors, the engineers, the educated people. The GDR had paid for their education and then they allowed themselves to be seduced by the lure of the west.'

So, according to Koch, Ulbricht, the head of state, decided he needed to build an 'anti-fascist protective measure'. I have always been fond of this term which has something of the prophylactic about it, protecting easterners from the western disease of shallow materialism. It obeys all the logic of locking up free people to keep them safe from criminals.

On the night of Sunday 12 August 1961 the East German army rolled out barbed wire along the streets bordering the eastern sector, and stationed sentries at regular intervals. At daylight people woke to find themselves cut off from relatives, from work, from school. Some made a dash through the wire. Others who lived in apartments overlooking the borderline started to jump from the windows into blankets held out by westerners on the footpath below. Then the troops made residents brick up their own windows. They started with the lower floors, forcing people to jump from higher and higher windows.

Koch was called to the garrison on 13 August, the day the Wall went up. It was a state of emergency and they were to stay on alert. 'Two days later, I was called in to the commandant. He looked at my boots and pronounced them too shoddy for the mission. He ordered me to accompany a group, including Honecker, along where they had rolled out all the barbed wire, where the Wall was starting to be. And he ordered me to get new boots.

'It was an ordinary summer day. When we got to where Checkpoint Charlie was to be, there were crowds of protesters on the western side shouting at us. I had my left leg in the east, my right leg in the west, and I drew my white line across the street. I concentrated on the line, and not on what was happening around me. I thought to myself that those in the west were enemies, looters and profiteers.' Koch then walked with Honecker and the others the length of the border through the city, nearly fifty kilometres. I'm surprised he doesn't have more to say about this day, which one might consider the beginning of his life's obsession. 'I was only twenty-one years old,' he says, 'I just concentrated on my job of drawing the line.' Then he adds, 'The next day I could hardly stand. You know how it is with new boots.'

He leans forward. 'People ask me why I didn't cross the line when I was drawing it along the streets? Why didn't I just step over to the west and keep on walking? Because I was in love! I'd been married three weeks. So of course I went back to my young wife, it's only natural. Just like my father: he went back to his wife, and I went back to mine.'

But his father went back to his family under threat of deportation to a POW camp. Koch didn't need to be threatened: trained by his father, he had become Socialist Man.

Koch says he is the only person alive who can represent, in his documents and photocopies and photographs, the Wall from the eastern side. Perhaps this is because most people on that side want to forget it. In fact, it seems now most people on both sides want to pretend it was never there. The Wall has been erased so quickly that there is hardly a trace of it in the streets. Only a small part of the most colourful section remains, like a gaudy headstone.

In 1966 Heinz Koch traced his biological father, who lived in Holland. The grandfather came to the GDR on a day visa to meet his son. He came as an ordinary tourist. 'And because I was with the Stasi,' Hagen says, 'my dad, aged fifty-four, was thrown out of his job.'

'Because he was a close relative to you, so he was not allowed to have *Westkontakte*?'

'Because I hadn't told them about the visit.' The Stasi had to know everything about the extended families of everyone, but most particularly about their own. 'That was when my father first told me about his illegitimacy, about running for mayor, and about the threats to him if he didn't make me into a good socialist.'

I wondered what it would feel like to find out that you had been brought up by your parents as a paragon of a regime they did not believe in.

Koch said to his father, 'Dad, if that's the way it is, I've had it. I want out.' He thought: if my working here is a reason my father can't meet with his father, I don't want to be here any more. 'I handed in my letter of resignation,' he says.

The same day he was arrested and put into a cell. Criminal charges were laid. They were: 'Preparation and Reproduction of Pornographic Material.'

'What?'

He enjoys my surprise, and reaches once more into his box. He pulls out a stapled handmade pamphlet. It has roneo-purple handwriting on it, and cartoon pictures. Koch made a dozen copies of the booklet to celebrate a friend's wedding. In traditional German style, it sent up the groom, the bride and the in-laws. It showed caricatures of them (fully clothed) with speech balloons, and was very far from being pornography. It was, however, illegal. In this country any kind of printing was forbidden unless authorised. The Stasi had even developed a science of connecting individual typewriters to the print they made, as if to fingerprint thought. Koch had used the machines at his office.

They kept him in the cell for two nights and didn't tell his wife where he was. He was permitted no outside contact, no lawyer, no phone calls. Standard procedure. On the third day, the Stasi and the DA searched his apartment for more 'pornographic' material as evidence. They didn't find any. They questioned Mrs Koch, who experienced a strange mixture of relief and focused terror: so that's where he is.

'They asked her'—Koch's voice goes soft with distaste—'they asked her about our sex life. They told her that, if there was something wrong in that department, they would understand and "it might account for why your husband has taken up as a pornographer".'

'No, no,' she started to cry. She said there was nothing wrong.

The DA said, 'Well, then, in that case, Frau Koch, I put it to you that your husband would only have prepared this pornography—'

'What pornography?' She was desperate.

'—this pornography,' he ignored her, 'at your instigation.' The only sound was of the other men rifling through the apartment. 'It seems you have nothing to say,' he went on. 'Let me ask you something. Is there anyone who could look after your little boy for the next five years or so?'

'What? Why?'

'Because I'm afraid, Frau Koch, that, as the instigator of a pornographic scheme, the penalties for you are severe.'

She started to cry. 'I don't understand! What do you want from us? What do you want from me? Don't take my child from me, please!'

'Frau Koch,' the DA said, 'the way I see it, the only chance for you would be if you credibly, and I mean credibly, distance yourself from your husband and what he has done. Only then would it be possible for me to recommend lenience to the judge in your case.'

'What do you mean? What is it you want me to do?'

'It's quite simple,' he said, opening his briefcase. 'All you need to do is sign this application for divorce.'

I feel a mild physical shock.

Koch says an application for divorce was put on the table, and it was already filled out with each of their names in full, their dates of birth, identity numbers and address. 'She signed it,' he says quietly. 'She signed it out of fear they'd take the child away. Then they came to me in prison with this—this thing.' He is disgusted again even in the telling. 'They said, "Have a look at this here. It would appear your wife wants nothing more to do with you."' Koch lowers his voice. 'At that moment my world broke apart.'

'Three days later my Party secretary came to see me in the lock-up. He was a man in his fifties with yellow hair and a red face. He said, "Koch my friend, I haven't been able to sleep for three nights! For God's sake what is going on here? You were always so punctual and reliable. So diligent and orderly. We have got to get you out of this mess." He walked up and down in the cell. "The thing is, if you leave, knowledge leaves with you. Operational knowledge goes with you! And knowledge must stay! Either you understand you have made an error in thinking by trying to resign, or you will be locked up for four and a half years so that your knowledge stays here anyway." He spread his hands in a gesture of sympathy. "You know Koch, you've really only got one chance left: you have to take back your resignation, and, as proof that you have understood the error in thinking you have made, you will renew your pledge to lifelong service." He put two documents on the table, already filled out: a retraction and another pledge. "Oh, and what's this I hear about your wife leaving you? Terrible. You know, it's times like these that we, the Party, we will stick by you, comrade."'

'Did you believe your wife would leave you?' I ask Koch.

'I had it in writing!' he shouts. 'I had it in writing!'

'Yes, but did you believe it?'

'I had it in writing!' This is a man who believes in documents. 'Oh, and another thing,' he says, 'they said to me: when you've got rid of this wife, this negative influence—then you can probably be promoted.

'I was sitting in the prison. There was no-one to talk it over with. So I said, "Can I go into the cultural division then?" and he said "Yes."'

I wonder how it worked inside the Stasi: who thought up these blackmail schemes? Did they send them up the line for approval? Did pieces of paper come back initialled and stamped 'Approved': the ruining of a marriage, the destruction of a career, the imprisonment of a wife, the abandonment of a child? Did they circulate internal updates: 'Five new and different ways to break a heart'?

When Koch came out of the lock-up he was deaf to everything but his distress. It clearly upsets him to be telling me. 'I wanted nothing more to do with that woman,' he says. 'She thinks she can just leave me in the lurch like that! And then come back and be my wife?

'We were divorced. Our boy Frank was five and he went to live with her.'

I try to think myself into his place. I think what I would most want to hear would be an explanation from my beloved that it was all a terrible mistake. I ask him why he didn't ask—

'Because I wouldn't hear it! I wouldn't hear it!' He shouts, imitating how he cut off his wife. 'How dare you tell me to listen after what you've done?'

But he did listen to his son. Months later, taking Frank for an ice-cream, the story came out. Frank had been in the apartment and heard the officers threaten to take him away. Koch spoke with his ex-wife. A year after his imprisonment and six months after their divorce, Mr and Mrs Koch remarried.

The Stasi subjected him to disciplinary proceedings on account of 'inconstancy', and in their files attributed the remarriage to 'the repeated negative influence of Frau Koch'.

18
The Plate

In 1985 Heinz Koch died. His sister, who lived in Hamburg, West Germany, received permission to attend the funeral. Because she was coming, Hagen was forbidden to attend. This was more than he could take.

He applied to leave his regiment. He would have liked this to be a final small defiance, a little signal of 'up yours' at a time when no harm could come to his father, and he didn't have much to lose. But it was merely a transfer out of the Stasi and into the regular army, under condition of maintaining Stasi secrecy. They were going to let him leave, and it made him feel empty.

He sat in his office. There are strange moments where the present already belongs to your past—your last day at work, for instance, when problems and politics there become a tale told in the third person. Koch looked around his office as if it belonged to someone else.

Everything in the room was to stay there. His replacement would come in, and no-one would know the difference. He was interchangeable with any other uniform and bad crewcut. It made him angry to think he would leave no mark here, and it made him angrier still that, even if he had his time again, he suspected he wouldn't have had the guts.

The wall opposite him had an unhealthy sheen of old paint, and so did the plate pinned on it. It was an award for cultural work by his unit, third place. It shone like gold but it was made of plastic, covered in metallic paint like a cheap toy. It was not something he could say he himself had won. Nevertheless, Koch closed his office door, got up on his chair and slid the plate from its hooks. He was surprised how light it was. His briefcase wouldn't close over it, so he took off his vest, draped it over the bag and held the handles together. He walked out of his office, said goodbye to the assistant and didn't come back.

'My little private revenge,' he says. 'That plate'—he looks straight at me—'was all I had the courage for.'

Three weeks later, there was a knock at his apartment door. The head of Koch's old Stasi section stood in the passageway. He was still being collegial. 'The plate is gone.'

'What?'

'You heard me, comrade, the plate is gone. The commandant wants the plate back.'

'What do you know?' Koch said to him, leaning on the open door. 'As soon as I'm gone, the whole place falls apart. As long as *I* sat in that chair, that plate hung on the wall.'

'Come on, Koch, it can't have just disappeared. At the Ministry for State Security nothing just disappears!'

'I'm afraid I can't help you.' Koch closed the door.

The commandant established a 'Working Group on Plate Re-Procurement'. Koch was summoned back to headquarters for interviews and required to give a statement. He hid the plate in his kitchen.

A short time later they sent in bigger guns. The district attorney came by. 'Where's this plate?'

'I don't know.'

'I'll need a sworn affidavit to that effect.'

'Fine by me.'

Nothing further happened. Nineteen eighty-nine came, the Wall came down, and Koch started to build up his archive. He retrieved the plate from behind the sink pipe and pinned it up in his study. Now, it was a real trophy.

In 1993 a television crew came to interview him. Germany was reunited, and East Germany was a place in the past. The interviewer went through his questions before they started to shoot, so Koch would be prepared. But he was already prepared, because they were all the usual questions: Do your regret your time with the Stasi? What is your connection to the Wall? Is that what made you establish this 'Wall Archive'?

Koch could see the strapline already: 'Stasi man keeps Wall alive at home…' He thought how easy it is for an interviewer to assume moral superiority by virtue of the fact he gets to ask the questions. Even in this new Germany, these weren't really questions about how the regime possessed people, and his weren't really answers. Koch would dutifully tell the story of his upbringing.

The interviewer was ready to roll and had started the cue-in when the cameraman called, 'Stop!' The crew relaxed their shoulders.

'What's up?' asked the interviewer.

'I need that plate down. It's reflecting in my lens.'

The interviewer motioned for an offsider to step around Koch and take it down, but Koch stood up. He tells it to me as a moment of glory. 'No,' he said. The room fell silent. 'I don't care what you want from me,' he continued slowly. 'I will do whatever you ask—I will turn everything in this apartment upside down, I will sing the national anthem if you want. But that…plate…stays…there.'

The interviewer was puzzled. Here was a man who had worked for the Firm for twenty-five years and who now had the gall to try to make a living talking about it; a shameless moral gymnast re-performing his capitulations for the camera. And he was drawing the line at a plate?

Koch remained standing. 'That plate,' he said again, 'stays there.'

'OK, OK.'

Koch sat down. The interviewer knew when to say nothing. Koch started to tell the whole story: his theft, the establishment of the Working Group on Plate Re-Procurement, the interviews and statements, the threats and fuss. Koch says he didn't realise that the camera was rolling. The way he tells it, he didn't mind that it was.

The program was made and broadcast. Several days later, the doorbell rang at Koch's apartment. Two men showed their wallet passes: Treuhand. This was the body set up after the regime collapsed to oversee the fire sale of East German state-owned enterprises to the private sector. 'Herr Koch, we've come for the plate,' said one of them.

'*What?*' This was unified Germany, westernised and democratic Germany, and still someone wanted that plate.

'Pursuant to the Treaty of Reunification between the Federal Republic of Germany and the former German Democratic Republic, all property belonging to the latter is vested in the former. That plate was rightfully property of the GDR and is now property of the Federal Republic of Germany. We are charged with its collection.'

'Get out.'

'We are willing to turn a blind eye to the manner in which that plate came into your possession, Herr Koch, provided you return it immediately.'

Koch was incensed. 'Get out of my apartment. If you want the plate, go get a court order for it. Without an order, you're not coming in. No-one takes the plate.'

So it came in the mail. Criminal proceedings were issued against him. The indictment charged him with theft of GDR property. Still Koch did nothing.

Not long afterwards there was another knock at the door. It was the same men again. 'Excuse us, Herr Koch. I am pleased to inform you that the allegation of theft has been withdrawn.'

'Mmmhh.'

'In the first place on account of triviality: the plate was worth only sixteen eastern marks. In the second place because of the Statute of Limitations for such crimes: the allegations concerned an act which took place eight years ago and are therefore barred.'

Koch looks at me closely.

'However,' the officer said, 'new proceedings have been issued against you.'

'Oh?'

'For perjury.'

'Get out.'

The official put his foot in the door. 'I'm afraid, Herr Koch, that it is alleged that on 14 June 1985 you swore in an affidavit to the Ministry of State Security of the former German Democratic Republic that you did not know the whereabouts of the plate in question. That is an offence against the law then in force in the GDR, and it is the responsibility of the new Germany to ensure prosecution of crimes which occurred in the former GDR.'

I am laughing by now. Koch goes on.

'I said, "Bravo. Terrific. Well done. Can't you people make up your minds? Do you want to see me punished because I worked for the Firm, or do you want to see me punished because I worked against the Firm? What is it, exactly, you want?"' He's laughing now too. This is his moment. The man who drew the line, and who sat on the fence, pulls some right-eousness from the post-Wall rubble.

'Did the trial come about?' I ask him.

'No. But all these allegations did quite a bit of damage. My wife lost her job because of them. The rumours were pretty bad, and they took on a life of their own—you know, Koch is a thief, a liar, a perjurer.' He pauses, and leans towards me. I can smell him again, warm and piny. He says,

'You know though, it was worth it. All the courage I had is in that plate. The whole shitty little skerrick of it. That's all I had. That plate,' he says pointing behind him, 'stays there.'

Beep. 'Hi Miriam, it's Anna.' I'm keeping this upbeat. 'Just thought I'd call to say hello. I'd love to catch up. I've been having some odd adventures in your old country! Curiouser and curiouser—I've a lot to tell. Anyway, I'll call, or you can reach me.' I leave my number. 'See you.'

Herr Koch gave me Stasi diagrams and photographs of the 'border installation' at Bornholmer Strasse. 'Top Secret!' he cried gleefully, as he made copies of them on the machine in his hallway.

A day or two later I have them rolled in my pocket as I walk from my apartment to where Miriam climbed over. I also have the sketch she drew; the place where she was caught is marked with a gash of blue ink. I want to see what it looked like to her; I want to place these pictures over what's there now, as if to bring the past into some kind of focus.

It is muggy today. Everyone has been burning their heaters without pause for weeks and the clouds are low and tinted with coal dust. I take breaths of this orange sky as I walk.

The first thing I reach is the garden colony. A path leads through the plots, each one fenced off from its neighbour with cyclone mesh. There are small huts on them—for garden tools and seeds, for barbecue grills and folding chairs and ladders. There are a few larger trees, but mostly there is just sodden black earth arranged into rectangles, waiting for a lick of sun to bring up vegetables and flowers. These are squared-off places for contained fantasies—in one plot I find Snow White and her dwarves, two fawns and two portly gnomes all cohabiting peacefully with an almost life-size sow and her three fat piglets.

Between the garden plots and where the Wall was there's a wider stretch of grass and then an embankment. I climb up to another cyclone fence and look through at the mess of railway lines and small walls. This fence is old and rusted. I wonder whether it was the same one Miriam climbed. To my left is the bridge where she thought the guards were watching her, and where, twenty years later, ten thousand people thronged on a single night to get through to the west.

I hold up a black and white photograph with one hand and the Stasi diagram with the other, 'Technical Improvements on the National Border to Berlin (West)'. I want to see where the second fence, the sand strip, the tank traps, the guard towers, the light-pylons, the dog run and the trip-wires were. They are all gone. Then I remember that they were *in front* of the railway lines—they must have been in the stretch of grass I walked over between the garden plots and where I am now standing.

I take out Miriam's sketch. It is a few lines on a page—for walls, for the kink in the wall where she stopped to breathe and lock eyes with the dog, for the trip-wire where she was caught. My hands are blue as I hold the paper up to the rusted diamonds of wire. I wonder if I am in the right place. Miriam said the bridge was about one hundred and fifty metres away from where she crossed. I move to my right till I think I'm in the same spot. Two trains cross; the rhythm of their wheels fuses and then parts again. When they are gone I peer at the railway lines. There are at least six of them, shunting trains from north to south and back. Then there's an earth retaining wall, not particularly high, but the ground behind it is at another level. Is this where she climbed? I look for a kink, and I find one. Was that where she crouched?

It starts to get dark. The streetlights on the bridge glow their sick yellow light. I roll up the photo and the diagram and Miriam's drawing and crumple them into my pocket. I put my fingers through the wire, and hang onto the fence for a while.

19

Klaus

'Can I come over?'

'Wuffor?'

I think I've woken him up. It's one o'clock in the afternoon. 'A visit, Klaus, I need to get out of the house.' What I need, in fact, is becoming a habit: an act of hops-and-malt chemistry. I need to feel good, temporarily, about plates and walls, old men and rules, bakeries and rug-work and corridor after corridor of rooms sealed with secret purpose. I need to see a survivor.

'OK,' he says, 'not now though. Later.'

'All right, see you later then.'

We're onto our third beer and it's only 6 pm. Klaus's tremor has stopped, and he's changed out of the dressing gown he was in when I arrived, to black jeans and a black windcheater. His hair is motley on his head, and motley in his beard. He has a crumpled face with brown teeth and squinty, smiley eyes. His hands are large and purplish, the hands of a dedicated smoker. He is grumpy and friendly at the same time, just warming up.

Like most people, I know a little about his life, but I wouldn't mind hearing it from him, a night-time story. He grumbles at first—what self-respecting icon needs to say how they got that way? But we crack open more cans and he obliges me, relaxing into it. He sits soft-bodied in the chair; he assumes the shape of the furniture.

We face a coffee table with matches and tins on it and ashtrays already full of butts and papers and clumps of tobacco like hair. Behind that there's a massive television set with stereo speakers. This room is also Klaus's bedroom and office—there's a mattress on the mezzanine to my left, and underneath it a fax machine, a computer and synthesizer.

The walls are lined with photographs and posters, and Klaus's dark oil paintings. The one nearest my eyeline has a series of pictures etched into it; it's the evolution of the breast, from pointy to pendulous. This room is Klaus's life; it's the inside of his head.

The early photographs show Klaus Jentzsch, before he took his mother's maiden name as a stage-name: a clean-cut young man in 1958 wearing a suit and pencil tie, looking down modestly at his double bass. They track his development into a long-haired star with a sheepskin coat and a bass guitar. The most recent ones are tour posters: a group of six middle-aged men in an assortment of headbands, beards and sunglasses, with raised fists and sweat on their chests. Klaus, though, seems to have become, if anything, more himself: no headband, no glasses, just jeans and a T-shirt and a guitar.

Klaus Renft is the bad boy of East German rock'n'roll. The Klaus Renft Combo became the wildest and the most popular rock band in the GDR.

Klaus started off playing Chuck Berry and Bill Haley covers in the fifties, and then moved on in the sixties to the Animals, the Beatles and the Rolling Stones, and in the seventies to Steppenwolf, Led Zeppelin and

Pink Floyd. Often these records were banned outright so Klaus and his friends listened illegally to western RIAS radio, and recorded the songs on huge tape decks in order to work out the music. They sang, screaming, 'A ken't get nö, zetizfektion.'

I'm amazed that the authorities let them get away with the Stones' 'Satisfaction', a song which, if it became an anthem for desire of all kinds in the west, was bound to be a rallying cry against the whole system in the east. 'Did they know what it meant?' I ask.

'We didn't know what it meant,' Klaus laughs, prodding down tobacco and small burnt beads of hash into a white-handled pipe. His laugh is deep and innocent, he is a man with the gift of pleasure. His smile heats the room.

Over time, the Klaus Renft Combo played more and more of their own songs, and when Gerulf Pannach joined in 1969 the lyrics suggested rebellion, poignancy and hope, or, as one magazine put it, 'soul, frailty and pain'. In the ersatz world of the Lipsi, Renft was something authentic and unauthorised. But there was only one record company, AMIGA, and Klaus says that the lyrics to every one of their songs were changed before they could be recorded. Renft took, he says, the 'holy things' of the GDR—the army and the Wall—and sang about them, because they wanted to 'scratch the GDR at its marrow'.

Klaus gets up from the chair, his movements quick as a cat, although maybe I'm starting to see things slower. I'm trying to think what it would mean to have all your experience of rock music brought to you live, but second-hand—wondering: did Jagger, Plant and Daltry know of their doppelgängers in the east?

But as soon as Klaus puts the music on, I am a believer. There is something about good rock that defies thought. It is pure and base at the same time, and it moves you inside in ways you can't say. The singer, Christian 'Kuno' Kunert, was trained in a church choir in Leipzig and his voice hits you like the truth. He sings their famous *'Die Ketten werden knapper'* (The Chains Are Getting Tighter) and 'The Ballad of Little Otto', who longed to reach his brother in the west. Klaus sits down again and puffs happily. When the songs are over, he keeps talking.

Renft were not permitted to play in towns, so they played to enormous crowds which came out to the villages. 'Woodstock every day.' He grins. 'You know for us the GDR wasn't just Stasi, Stasi, Stasi. It was "Sex und Drugs und Rock'n'Roll",' he says in English. By drugs he means alcohol and cigarettes which were all the drugs they had, but they made the most of them. 'I mean we really *lived*!' he says. 'And it was fun.'

'Some towns we went to, the main street would have its buildings painted only halfway up! The top part would be bare grey concrete.' He looks at me as if he has posed a riddle, which he has. 'It was because when Honecker came through, that was the level he could see to from the back seat of the limousine. They didn't have enough paint to go further up!' I know about this, and about the butchers' shops full of smallgoods for the drive-by, which would vanish again after Honecker or other officials had been through. Klaus finds all this hysterically funny. Then he says, 'This society, it was built on lies—lie after lie after lie.'

The emperor has no clothes! The buildings are half-naked! Renft might have started off with borrowed western rock songs, but there were so many lies that singing the truth guaranteed them both hero and criminal status. By the mid-seventies the band embodied a lethal combination of rock, anti-establishment message and mass adoration. They were shaggy men with bellbottoms and attitude, they were hot, they were rich by GDR standards, and they were way too explosive for the regime.

Performers needed a licence to work. In September 1975 Renft were called to play for the Ministry of Culture in Leipzig to have theirs renewed. Klaus gets up again to reach for a folder under the mezzanine. 'I can look up the details of my life now in the files,' he smiles, 'which is just as well.' He once referred to the state of his brain as 'dog food'. I like him for his self-knowledge, and smile back. Shortly before the licence-renewal hearing he was offered a passport, hard currency and a smooth ride through life— here or in the west—if he would separate from two of the most politically outspoken band members, Pannach and Kunert. He refused. 'I knew then, that was a death sentence for us,' he says.

'It must have taken guts to turn that down.'

He shrugs. 'It was much worse under Hitler,' he says. 'We would have been whisked off to a concentration camp.'

The smoke is sweet and time is losing its grip on the evening. There is a guilelessness about Klaus, for a rock star; none of his answers come pat. 'It's hard to describe,' he says, 'on the one hand I suppose it shows character or something. But on the other, if you're honest you know you were shitting yourself...' He starts laughing. Then he stops. 'It looked like we'd all go to prison—that would have been the usual thing,' he says soberly. 'And people there were treated worse than animals. Of course we didn't want that.'

Now that he has the documents from his file he can see the sequence of events from the other side. He flicks through the folder, then stops. 'This is funny,' he says. 'This was from Honecker to Mielke.' He reads: 'Dear Erich, Please attend to the case of Jentzsch, Klaus, as speedily as possible. Regards, Erich.' He laughs, 'Get that? From one Erich to another.' But it could have quickly stopped being funny. At one point Mielke asked his officers in Leipzig, 'Why can't you just grab them? Why aren't they liqui-dated?' But Renft members were too famous to handle so directly.

Klaus turns more pages and finds a formal complaint from the administration of the 'Klubhaus Marx Engels' where Renft had performed a fortnight before. It is to Comrade Ruth Oelschlägel, chairperson of the licensing committee they were about to face.

'You'll like this one,' he says, and reads it out. Klaus is the only person I know who gets such distinct pleasure from the story-telling in their file. The clubhouse administration complained about the group's drinking: 'After the end of the concert, approx. forty bottles of wine were found...it is incomprehensible to us that a musical ensemble should require the consumption of such a quantity of alcohol to attain the right mood.' It complained about 'belching into the microphone, use of words such as "shit"'. I start to laugh, harder than this is probably worth, but who cares? Klaus is swinging a leg over the side of the chair and laughing too. He continues, 'We protest the use of inflammatory calls from the stage such as, "It's the society that's decadent, we are the opposite," "Today, I feel free," "There are people sitting in this room reporting on us," or "You are the audience that will experience the group Renft for the last time, because we are about to be banned."' Klaus's laugh moves down to his chest and turns into a cough. He takes a long draught of beer, and then starts rolling a joint.

'I had some western money,' he says, 'so before the licensing hearing I bought a small cassette recorder from an Intershop.' When performing, Klaus holds his guitar idiosyncratically upright, more like a double bass player. He runs the strap over his left shoulder, down his back and between his legs, encircling his body. While they were setting up to play for the committee he turned the cassette recorder on and hid it between his guitar and his groin, held up by the strap.

But they didn't get to play. Comrade Oelschlägel asked them to approach the desk. She said the committee would not be listening to 'the musical version of what you have seen fit to put to us in writing' because 'the lyrics have absolutely nothing to do with our socialist reality…the working class is insulted and the state and defence organisations are defamed'.

Klaus leans in and picks up his tin of tobacco. 'And then she said to us, "We are here to inform you today, that you don't exist any more."'

There was silence. One of the band members signalled to a roadie to stop setting up. Kuno asked, 'Does that mean we're banned?'

'We didn't say you were banned,' Comrade Oelschlägel said. 'We said you don't exist.'

Klaus is flicking his Zippo trying to get the flame to lick his spliff. He sucks and looks over it at me and starts exhaling, laughing. 'Then I said, "But…we're…still…here." She looked me straight in the face. "As a combo," she said, "you no longer exist."'

They were dismissed. Klaus managed to pass the tape to his girlfriend Angelika. 'She didn't know what it was,' he says, 'but she knew it was important.' Angelika hid it in her scarf and took it back to their flat. When he got home after drinking all afternoon in the Ratskeller, Klaus wrote 'Fats Domino' in big letters on the cassette and put it up on the shelf.

Angelika had a Greek passport, which meant she could travel to the west. The next day Klaus asked her to go over to West Berlin for a day trip, 'to get toothpaste or whatever'. He couldn't be sure she wouldn't be strip-searched at the border so she didn't take the tape, but he wanted the authorities to see she'd been over and back. Then he let it be known in Leipzig that he had made a recording of the decree of the licensing committee, that it was now at the RIAS (Radio in the American Sector) radio station in West Berlin, and that if anything happened to them it would be broadcast immediately.

It is hard to say how much protection that gave them, if any. Renft records disappeared from the shops overnight. The band ceased to be written about or played on the radio. The recording company AMIGA reprinted its entire catalogue so it could leave them out. 'In the end it was as they had said: we simply did not exist any more,' he says, 'just like in Orwell.'

Rumours were put about by the state that the band had split up, that it was in difficulties. It was: it couldn't play. Some members wanted to stay in the GDR, others knew they'd have to leave. Pannach and Kunert were arrested and imprisoned until August 1977 when they were bought free by the west. The other two, 'the more unpolitical ones', Klaus says, stayed in the east with their manager. He shifts in his chair. 'Have you heard of the group Karussell?' he asks.

'No.'

Klaus explains that the manager who stayed with the pliable members turned out to be a Stasi man. Under him, Renft regrouped as Karussell and went on to record Renft songs, 'note for note'. 'They copied us so exactly you can't tell,' Klaus says, 'whether it's Renft, or it's Karussell.' The Stasi were satisfying the needs of the people, but with a band it could control.

'Weren't you furious?'

He shrugs. Someone else might have found this a betrayal, reason to dwell on this part of their life. After all it marked, for Klaus, the beginning of a fifteen-year hiatus. But he has the gift of taking things easy. Cushioned by alcohol, his landings are soft. He seems incapable of regret, and anger evaporates off him like sweat.

From the end of 1975, Klaus was left with nothing to do, no-one to do it with. After the usual chicanery from the authorities, he was let out with his girlfriend into West Berlin. It was hard to go from money and fame to nothing. Renft's cachet did not translate over the Wall. He was bewildered. His fans were rebels, and they were not here. Klaus worked for years in the west as a sound-man in the theatre. After the Wall came down, he found out that 'we'd become a cult band in the GDR—our records were more expensive than a Pink Floyd album'. Since then the band members have been getting back together, but the line-up has changed and Pannach, their wordsmith, died.

I've been reading about Pannach's death lately. He died prematurely of an unusual kind of cancer, as did Jürgen Fuchs and Rudolf Bahro, both dissidents and writers. All of them had been in Stasi prisons at around the same time. When a radiation machine was found in one of these prisons, the Stasi File Authority began to investigate the possible use of radiation against dissidents. What it uncovered shocked a people used to bad news.

The Stasi had used radiation to mark people and objects it wanted to track. It developed a range of radioactive tags including irradiated pins it could surreptitiously insert into a person's clothing, radioactive magnets to place on cars, and radioactive pellets to shoot into tyres. It developed hand-pump sprays so Stasi operatives could approach people in a crowd and impregnate them with radiation or secretly spray their floor at home so they would leave radioactive footprints everywhere they went. Rudolf Bahro's manuscript was irradiated so it could be traced to recipients, even in the west. To detect the marked person or object, the Stasi developed personal geiger counters that could be strapped to the body, and would silently vibrate if the officer got a reading. And in the prison and remand centres, the Stasi sometimes used radiation machines as well as cameras where the prisoners' mug shots were taken. The File Authority report was cautious. It found no evidence that radiation was used to kill off marked men and women. But it did find that it was used with reckless disregard for people's health. And it recommended that former prisoners of the Stasi get regular medical check-ups.

Although Pannach died, Kuno is well, and he is now fronting the reformed Klaus Renft Combo. They are on tour again through the old GDR, playing to sell-out crowds hungry for something that was theirs, that was untainted, and that was good. They play a mixture of old and new songs. Their latest album is called *As If Nothing Had Happened*. The cover is a picture of a full ashtray, emtpy beer cans and an open bottle of whisky. Part joke, part revenge, and part explanation for the lost years, the last item on the CD is the authentic 1975 recording of the Oelschlägel interchange, declaring them to no longer exist.

Our conversation is sliding back and forward. Klaus is still thinking about my question of whether it took courage to turn down the initial offers to leave, or to play along with the Stasi. 'I don't know whether it was courage,' he says. 'More like some kind of naivety, that protected me, I think.' I think he's right here, but it is a naivety that is carefully nurtured and maintained, an innocence that he did not let them damage. 'I mean, we didn't all get huge villas on the Mugglesee like the Puhdys, but I can look at myself in the mirror in the morning and say, "Klaus, you did all right." Material things are not what matter to me.'

He leans back. The smoke leaving his mouth obscures it in a haze of grey, and grey beard. 'I think the Stasi people have been punished enough.'

'How do you mean?'

'Well, if they've got any conscience at all…'

'And if not?' I think of Herr Winz and Herr Christian and Herr

Koch and the different kinds of conscience there are.

'I'm not that interested,' he says. 'I didn't let them get to me.'

This, I think, is his victory. This is what stops him being bound to the past and carrying it around like a wound. If there was 'internal emigration' in the GDR, there was also, perhaps, internal victory.

He looks at me. Over the evening he seems to have become more insightful and nimble-minded while I am inert as a sponge. 'Do you want to hear something beautiful?' he asks. I nod. He puts on a video of the band performing a song Pannach wrote shortly before he died. Kuno looks now like a butcher or a bikie, but his voice is mellow and grand, fine as it ever was.

> I sing my blues for a man
> Who could tell you
> How red the dreams were in the ruins
> Where the concrete towers are now
> And do you want to know what's left
> Of that man's dreams? Then ask the walls
> Of Cell 307 in Hohenschönhausen
> I sing the blues in red
> For one who can't hear me
> As a child in the dark
> Sings a song to himself…

For this moment the song soars and nothing else exists; I have no body, and time stops passing. Klaus stretches in his chair. When it finishes he says, 'You can't let it eat you up, you know, make you bitter. You've got to laugh where you can.' He's right, of course. And to drink. By my reckoning, I am pacing him at about 1:3 but I am not so sure of my counting. He picks up a guitar and starts to stroke it absent-mindedly, lovingly across its curved wooden body. I see through the bottom of my glass—the table, the ashtray and the cans of beer. They look weirdly small and far away. I take my face out of the glass in a hurry and realise it's the CD cover I'm looking at. But the table is covered in ashtrays and beer cans—the same scene in two different sizes. It's time to go.

I don't feel the cold, I don't feel much. Rolling stone. Stone rolling home. The cobbles are wet, and the streetlamps make puddles of yellow light on the ground. I think of my friend in his room, singing himself happy.

20

Herr Bock of Golm

The phone calls keep coming.

'Bock.' A quiet voice, an old man's heavy breath on the receiver. 'In response to your notice.'

'Ah. Yes. Herr Bock. Thank you for calling me.' Before I can explain what I'm doing he says, 'I can tell you all there is to know about the Ministry of State Security. Everything you need, young woman, I can give you, because I was a professor at the training academy of the ministry. In fact, I taught *Spezialdisziplin*.'

'Oh,' I say. '*Ja?*'

'*Spezialdisziplin*,' he repeats. 'Do you know what that means?'

'No, I don't.'

'*Spezialdisziplin* is the science of recruiting informers. *Spezialdisziplin* is the art,' he says, 'of the handler.' He pauses. 'You should come to my house. It is directly opposite the academy at Golm. Do you know where that is?'

'No, I don't.' He gives me train and bus directions.

The more prone to getting lost one is, the more one tries to compensate. My grandmother has a small spirex notepad bound discreetly to an undergarment as an *aide memoire*, and I have a lot of maps. I have a 1986 map of Potsdam in which the areas where there were Stasi buildings—anything from bunkers to multi-storey edifices to shooting ranges—are left blank. On another, a 1984 map of East Berlin, entire city blocks and streets in Stasi areas are simply not represented: they are pale orange gaps in the map. Out of curiosity I look up Golm, and find that it is a gap on the map, on the outskirts of Potsdam.

I follow Herr Bock's instructions. I take the train from Berlin to the end of the line, and then I take two buses. His house is one in a street of identical semi-detached dwellings, each with a patch of lawn and a wire gate in front of it. It seems to be the only street that exists here, as though a town planner had an idea for a settlement that was begun before he thought better of it. The houses are covered in rough grey concrete, knobbly all over as if from cold. None of them, including Herr Bock's, looks inhabited.

It is late afternoon. Herr Bock's living room is, overwhelmingly, beige and brown: brown linoleum and dark veneer wall units, a brown couch and Herr Bock sitting camouflaged in it in a beige-and-brown diamond pattern acrylic cardigan. He has thick square glasses that give him underwater eyes, and an overbite. A moustache hangs on his upper lip. His voice is so soft I have to lean in to him.

'You must not use my name,' he says as an opener.

I agree.

He relaxes back into the couch and starts to hold forth. He says that the ministry was divided into two main sections: internal (called 'Defence') and external ('Counter-espionage'). He taught a course for Stasi officers destined to work in Defence. This title is euphemistic. The internal service of the Stasi was designed to spy on and control the citizens of the GDR. The only way to make sense of its name is to understand the Stasi as defending the government against the people. I take notes like a student. Herr Bock outlines each department of the Defence. I write:

Main Departments:
Economy
State Apparatus
Church
Sport
Culture
Counter-terrorism

East Germany was a small country of only seventeen million people, but these Stasi divisions and sub-departments were replicated throughout its territory no fewer than fifteen times. In every corner of the nation, every aspect of your life had its mirror nemesis in a department.

'Let us take,' says Herr Bock, 'as a specific instance the department of the church.' The church—pastors and people—was the only area of society in the GDR where oppositional thought could find a structure and could coalesce into something real. Consequently, theological colleges attracted bright, independent-minded students. 'All our people had to have theological training themselves so they'd pass for members of the churches they infiltrated.' He crosses an ankle onto his knee. 'How did we do it you might ask?' He snaps his fingers. 'Answer: we went into the theological colleges and recruited the students themselves!' He rubs his hands together. They make a papery sound. 'You know,' he says, 'we were supremely effective. It is not widely known that in the end, 65 per cent of the church leaders were informers for us, and the rest of them were under surveillance anyhow.'

I once saw a note on a Stasi file from early 1989 that I would never forget. In it a young lieutenant alerted his superiors to the fact that there were so many informers in church opposition groups at demonstrations that they were making these groups appear stronger than they really were. In one of the most beautiful ironies I have ever seen, he dutifully noted that, by having swelled the ranks of the opposition, the Stasi was giving the people heart to keep demonstrating against them.

Herr Bock uncrosses his legs and spreads his knees. His feet, in socks and sandals, barely touch the floor. Outside, the light is leaving us. He is on a roll. 'Now to our working methods. These were set out in Directives. There were four main areas.' I write:

Working Methods:
Exposing of Moles (*Enttarnung*)
Recruitment of Informers
Operational Control of Persons (Surveillance)
Security Checks

Herr Bock's passion is for recruitment. 'Directive 1/79!' he cries. 'One seventy-nine! On the Conversion of and Collaboration with Informers!' He takes out a handkerchief and wipes the corners of his mouth. 'There was nothing willy-nilly about it. We had to decide where in society, on *objective* principles, there was a need for an informer. For example, we might need one in an apartment block, a factory, or a supermarket. Then a rational evaluation would be made: what sort of person do we need here? What qualities should they have? We would find three or four people who fitted the bill. Without their knowledge, they would be comprehensively observed and evaluated in order to determine whether they could be approached or not.

'Most often,' he says, 'people we approached would inform for us. It was very rare that they would not. However, sometimes we felt that we might need to know where their weak points were, just in case. For instance, if we wanted a pastor, we'd find out if he'd had an affair, or had a drinking problem—things that we could use as leverage. Mostly though, people just said yes.'

It is dark now, but Herr Bock seems to be brightening right up. 'The third method was "Operational Control of Persons".'

'What does that mean?' I ask.

'Well,' he says, 'they were controlled using means and methods, all the means and methods allowable could be used to control them.' He puts his palms together, then closes them up between his legs. 'It got pretty tough for some people, you'd have to say,' he says.

These were the allowable means and methods:

Telephone tapping
Mobilisation of Informers
Shadow surveillance by Observational Forces
Use of Investigative Forces
Use of Technical Forces (including the installation of technology—bugs—in living quarters of the subject)
Post and parcel interception

That leaves only one thing I can think of. 'Did you use smell sampling?'

'Oh, no, no, no,' he says, 'that was for criminals.'

'Well who were the people you were doing the "Operational Control" on?'

'They were enemies.'

'Oh. How did you know they were enemies?'

'Well,' he says in his soft voice, 'once an investigation was started into someone, that meant there was suspicion of enemy activity.' This was perfect dictator-logic: we investigate you, therefore you are an enemy. 'We searched for enemies in all the areas I mentioned: in the factories, in the state apparatus, the church, the schools and so on. In fact,' he says, 'as time went on there was more and more work to do because the definition of "enemy" became wider and wider.'

I put my pen in the crease of my notebook and peer into the gloom in his direction. Herr Bock says other professors at the academy spent their careers expanding the reach of the paragraphs of the law so as to be able to encompass more enemies in them. 'In fact, their promotions depended on it,' he says. 'We talked about it among ourselves up on the sixth floor over there,' an arm gestures towards the building opposite. 'And I don't mind telling you that some of us actually thought the paragraphs became a little too wide.' I nod. If, by the mere fact of investigating someone you turn them into an Enemy of the State, you could potentially busy yourself with the entire population.

'Too wide,' he continues, 'to be properly carried out. Within available resources I mean.'

'What qualities did you look for in an informer?' I ask Herr Bock.

'Well,' he says, leaning back and clasping both hands behind his head, 'he had to be able to adapt to new situations quickly and make himself belong wherever we put him. And at the same time he had to have a stable enough character to keep it clear in his mind that he was reporting to us. And above all else,' he says, looking straight at me, his eyes distorted and magnified through the glasses, 'he needed to be honest, faithful and trustworthy.'

I look back at him. I feel my eyes too, getting wider.

'I mean only towards the ministry, of course,' he corrects himself. 'We weren't interested if he betrayed anyone else...' He leans his head to one side, in thought. 'In point of the fact he had to, didn't he?' he says. 'Perhaps,' he continues, 'this ability is not a great quality in a human being. But it was vital for our work. I have to say that it is the same in all secret services.'

But it is not. Few secret services have informers reporting meticulously on activities at kindergartens and dinner parties and sporting events across the nation.

'What was in it for the informers?' I want to know how much they were paid.

'It was pitiful actually,' Bock admits. 'They were hardly paid at all. Every week they had to meet with their handlers, and they were not paid for that. Every now and then they might have been given some money as a reward for a specific piece of information. Sometimes they were given a birthday present.'

'So why did they do it?'

'Well, some of them were convinced of the cause,' he says. 'But I think it was mainly because informers got the feeling that, doing it, they were somebody. You know—someone was listening to them for a couple of hours a week, taking notes. They felt they had it over other people.'

To my mind, there is something warmer and more human about the carnality of other dictatorships, say in Latin America. One can more easily understand a desire for cases stuffed with money and drugs, for women and weapons and blood. These obedient grey men doing it with their underpaid informers on a weekly basis seem at once more stupid and more sinister. Betrayal clearly has its own reward: the small deep human satisfaction of having one up on someone else. It is the psychology of the mistress, and this regime used it as fuel.

Herr Bock is still talking, and I am still taking notes. Every meeting with an informer had to take place in a covert location. 'In fact,' he says proudly, twisting his neck towards the stairs, 'I have a covert location here upstairs in my house.' His upstairs bedroom is still fitted out for the purpose, with a round table and brown vinyl-covered chairs. 'Every informer,' he says, 'knew exactly what he or she was doing.' He reaches behind himself to switch on a small lamp.

I look at my watch. It's nine o'clock. 'If you don't mind me asking,' I say. 'What is it you do now, Herr Bock?'

'I am a business adviser.'

I don't say anything.

'You look surprised,' he says. 'You are wondering what I could possibly know about business.'

'Yes, I am.'

'I work for West German firms who come here to buy up East German assets. I mediate between them and the East Germans, because the westerners don't speak their language. The easterners are wary because of their fancy clothes, their Mercedes Benzes, and so on.'

Terrific. Here he is once more getting the trust of his people and selling them cheap. Stasi men are by and large less affected by the unemployment that has consumed East Germany since the Wall came down. Many of them have found work in insurance, telemarketing and real estate. None of these businesses existed in the GDR. But the Stasi were, in effect, trained for them, schooled in the art of convincing people to do things against their own self-interest.

'We never thought, no-one ever thought, that it would all come to an end,' he says. 'It would not have occurred to anyone that our country could somehow cease to be. Just like that! Up on the sixth floor over there'—he gestures again with his head in the direction of the academy across the road—'at the end of 1989 we used to joke around. We'd say, "Last one here turn the lights out" because, at the end there'd be no-one left in the GDR.'

I think I should leave too. I thank Herr Bock and pack up and walk to the bus stop. There is only one street lamp along this road, and it is right here. So that the bus will stop for me, I have to stand in its cone of light. I can't see much beyond it; there are no lights on in any of the buildings around. Here I am, standing in a blank on the map, lit up for all to see. According to the timetable, it is forty-five minutes until the next bus comes. In ten minutes' time, the cold will be through to my bones.

I pick up my little pack and walk back to Herr Bock's. There are no lights on, but where could he have gone? No cars passed. The gate is stuck and it rattles. A piece of wire I can't see bites into my palm. I imagine Herr Bock looking through his curtains, and in fact the moment the gate springs wide he opens the door. He is chewing.

'I think I might call a taxi, if you don't mind,' I say. 'It's three-quarters of an hour till the next bus comes, and I'll miss the connection for the Berlin train. May I come in?'

It is dim inside. He has turned off the lamp to watch television, and now he switches that off too. He swallows and says, 'I don't know anything about taxis. I don't think they come here.'

'Let's try calling one, shall we?' I say.

He is enjoying himself, here in the dark. 'It might be a while,' he answers, 'they probably have to come from Potsdam.' But he finds a phone book in the gloom anyway, and calls a cab company. We sit down. My eyes are adjusting. He takes something off a plate.

'You are not afraid of the dark, are you?' he says, mouth full.

'It *is* very dark.'

'This way we can see the taxi come,' he says.

I don't see how. All his curtains are drawn and, even if there were any light in here, no chink of it could escape to the street. I start to fiddle around in my bag, looking for I don't know what. I am buying time to think and avoiding peering at him. I am tired and hungry and this language is not coming easily any more. This man with his brown cocoon and his conspiratorial room is unlikely to touch me, but I resent his enjoyment in having me at his mercy. I am worried the taxi will see a dark house in a dark street and turn around and leave. And I am thinking of ways out of here when he gets up and peeks through the curtains. He does this in a way so as not to let any movement be seen. But he turns from the window, disappointed.

'That was quick,' he says.

I grab my things and I leave him there, all lights out in the GDR.

21

Frau Paul

I know very little about this woman. The guide at Stasi HQ was so adamant I needed to speak with her that I just called and made a time. I take the train from Mitte to the end of the line at Elsterwerdaer Platz, in the southern part of East Berlin. Then I wait for a bus to Frau Paul's.

At the bus stop there's a Vietnamese flower-seller with a stall of sad and frostbitten flowers. The GDR imported North Vietnamese 'socialist brothers' as workers, and treated them badly. They lived in camps, and were bussed to work in factories each day so as to avoid contact with the locals. Now, they manage as best they can.

I buy the least tired-looking arrangement I can see. It's baby's breath with carnations. For some reason it looks funereal. The vendor is a tiny man with a face stretched like a mummy and teeth that don't fit in his mouth. He gives me change from a leather pocket in his apron and offers me a cigarette. I take it and we smile at one another. Then he bends down under the counter, and pulls out a carton of Marlboro Reds. 'Cigarette?'

he asks again, grinning widely.

'No, thanks,' I say. So this wilted flower stall is a front for black-market cigarettes. Truckloads of them are smuggled in from Poland to avoid duties and taxes and are sold, largely by Vietnamese, on street corners, at the entrance to the underground, or, more poetically, at flower stalls. I like this man's cover, and his generous style.

A large woman in her early sixties opens the door. She has a cap of dark hair and very blue eyes in a soft face. I follow her into the living room, filled with a pair of vinyl couches and hanging potted plants. Everything here is, as my mother would say, 'spic and span', and so is Sigrid Paul. Her clothes and hair are neat and she has the tapered plump fingers of a mournful magdalene. In them she is already holding a pressed handkerchief. She has made exquisite open sandwiches of mashed egg, and pink meat with stripes of gherkin.

Frau Paul apologises to me in advance. 'I lose my track,' she says. 'It might use up lots of tape. I have written a short biographical note'—she picks it up from the coffee table—'so I don't depart from the theme.' She seems wobbly, a woman holding onto notes on her own life. She hands me the two-page account. The heading reads, 'The Wall Went Straight through My Heart'.

Frau Paul doesn't, however, use the notes. It is true that she loses her thread, and sometimes repeats herself. But she tells her story well.

In January 1961, Frau Paul—who then went by her married name of Rührdanz—a dental technician, gave birth to her first child. The labour was difficult—a breech birth. The doctors were changing shifts and there was a delay in attending to her. By the time they did, she says, 'one leg was already out' but they performed an emergency caesarean anyway.

For the first few days after he was born Torsten Rührdanz spat blood. He couldn't feed at all. The doctors thought it might be some kind of stomach trouble and tried to give him tea. Six days after the birth Frau

Paul was sent home from hospital, but her baby was keeping very little nourishment down. And he was still spitting up blood. She took him to a hospital in the eastern part of the city but they could not find what was wrong. 'This made me very nervous,' she says. 'For my husband and me he was the child of our dreams.'

Then she took him to the Westend Hospital in the western sector of the city, where they gave her a diagnosis within twenty-four hours: Torsten had suffered a ruptured diaphragm during delivery. His stomach and oesophagus were damaged; there was inflammation and internal bleeding. The condition was life-threatening, so they operated immediately. Torsten recuperated in hospital.

By early July 1961 he was well enough to be taken home, with strict instructions for his feeding and medication. Frau Paul and her husband Hartmut were to collect special formula and medicines regularly from the Westend Hospital. Although there was no wall, the sector border was controlled, and they needed permission to bring over the medicines. Frau Paul applied to the Ministry of Health for the authority each time before she went across to fetch them.

Over the next weeks, Torsten made slow but undeniable progress. 'We were told that with this special nourishment and the medicine, he was likely to be able to develop normally,' she says. She starts to cry, so silently it is more like leaking. Tears roll down her face and she mops them up. 'Please,' she says, 'eat something.' I put something in my mouth. I look around for family photographs, but there are none on the walls, and none that I can see in the cabinets.

On the night of 12–13 August the Berlin Wall was rolled out in barbed wire. Frau Paul lived then with her husband in this same half-house deep in the eastern sector. They didn't see or hear anything of what was going on to divide the city but they woke to a changed world.

The next time Frau Paul went to the ministry for permission to collect the formula and medicines, it was refused. She remembers pleading with the official, telling him how sick her baby was, and how without these provisions he might die. 'If your son is as sick as all that,' the official told to her, 'it would be better if he did.' Frau Paul's tears have stopped now, and her broad face is hot with anger. The couple had no choice but to switch Torsten to ordinary formula. He started spitting up blood again. They took him one midnight to the Charité, the big eastern hospital. The doctors kept him under observation and told Frau Paul to go home.

'The next morning when I went to the hospital again to see my son he wasn't there. No-one had spoken with me about it. There was no time to speak with me about it.' When they realised they couldn't help him, the eastern doctors managed to have the baby spirited across the new border, back to the Westend Hospital. Frau Paul doesn't know how they did it, but she thinks that it saved his life. 'I hold absolutely nothing against the doctors at the Charité. What it would mean for him, what would come of it for all of us, was not possible to foresee.'

Her baby was now on the other side of the Wall. Frau Paul and her husband went back to the health ministry to get permission to visit him. But crossing the 'anti-fascist protective measure' was now a matter for the Ministry of the Interior.

Frau Paul reaches down and passes me an old photograph. It is of her, smoother-faced, and with stiff, 1960s hair. She is holding a baby and smiling uncertainly. The child sucks his bottom lip and looks straight at the camera. His body is not visible. A man in a pastor's black cassock and white collar stands next to them and they are flanked by nurses in hospital uniforms and wimples. 'That was October 1961,' Frau Paul says, 'the emergency christening.'

After nine and a half weeks of separation from their baby, who once more seemed likely to die, Frau Paul alone had been issued a day pass and a visa to attend his christening. The authorities would not let her husband visit in case, together, they decided to remain in the west. She is weeping again, as if she is overflowing. Everything is silent here, there's not even traffic noise. The only sound is her breath.

Each morning for an instant Sigrid Paul would wake up like her old self, before the image of Torsten's small sick body flooded into her mind. His condition was not improving. He was operated on four times in the Westend Hospital. He had to have an artificial oesophagus, an artificial diaphragm, and an artificial pylorus inserted. He had to be artificially fed. His parents were told, again, he might die. 'I went to see him that time and of course I wanted more,' she says. 'I wanted more.'

As Frau Paul puts it, in the language of the authorities, 'My husband and I decided to attempt illegally to leave the territory of the GDR.' She holds the handkerchief with both hands in her lap. 'I am not your classic resistance fighter,' she says. 'I was not even part of the opposition. To this day I am not a member of a political party.' She blows her nose. 'And I am not a criminal.'

She takes a deep breath and sits up straight. 'I did used to listen to RIAS, western radio. It was illegal, but everyone did it. It was important to me to get news from outside. And, in the end, it was RIAS that saved me.'

Frau Paul and her husband, a boat builder, began to look for ways to be with their son. In 1961 and 1962 countless small communities of inter- est were forming in East Germany; people united by nothing more than a tenuous acquaintance and a desire to get out. A Dr Hinze and his wife lived in the town of Rathenow in Brandenburg, and they wanted to join their son Michael in the west. Michael Hinze had been studying sociology at the Free University when the Wall went up, and he'd decided to stay. Dr Hinze had spoken a few times with Frau Paul's husband about building a yacht and sailing around the world. Clearly, that was not going to happen now, but it meant he knew of their plight. And his son Michael, along with some other young western students, was involved in a scheme to get people out.

Michael Hinze lives in West Germany, where I called him up. He's softly spoken and humble. He doesn't speak of what he did as if it were risking his own freedom to free others. He doesn't even sound like a modest man uncomfortable with suggestions of heroism. His tone is more that of someone recalling how he once, step by step, and in the usual manner, repaired his car. 'In 1961,' he says, 'I was twenty-three years old, inexperienced in these things.' After the Wall went up Michael contacted a human rights group in West Berlin. 'Someone there told me about a way to get people out.'

When the Wall was built, the GDR tried to block every avenue of escape. It altered bus routes, prevented its trains from stopping at stations in the western sector, set up road blocks along the border and stepped up patrols in the waters of the Baltic Sea. But it is impossible to seal off a country from the outside world altogether, and certainly impossible to do it in all places and for all methods of transport at once. Trains travelling from western Europe to Denmark and Sweden passed through East Germany, and they stopped at the Ostbahnhof in East Berlin on the way. With valid transit visas in their passports, West German citizens could travel through East German territory on their journey to Warnemünde on the Baltic Sea coast to catch the ferry to Malmö or Copenhagen. And at the station in East Berlin there was as yet no wall, no checkpoint between the local train platforms and the long distance ones. As it always had been, and as it is today, the check for tickets, passports and visas was on the train. A person with a West German passport and transit visa could board a train in East Berlin and ride out of there.

'There were maybe eight or ten of us,' Michael Hinze says, 'students who were doing this. I'd say all up we managed to get about fifty people out in this way.' Then he adds, 'I was really no big wheel.'

The scheme was clever and simple. It consisted of turning an East German into a West German for a day. The students asked West German citizens to give up their passports for the cause. 'We had no trouble getting hold of the papers. People were more than willing to help others get out of there.' They chose those who resembled, in age and height and eye colour, the East Germans they were going to smuggle out. The passport-holder would send off to the East Berlin authorities for a transit visa. At the same time, passport-sized photographs of the East Germans were conveyed across the border into West Berlin. When the passports came back to their owners with the visas stamped into them, the students took them to a graphic artist who inserted the photograph of the person trying to escape. The complete passports were then smuggled back to the East Germans wanting to leave.

'We would wrap five or six passports up in newspaper and stick them in the airvents of my VW beetle.' Michael could travel to the east on a day pass. Along with the passports he would take over articles necessary to complete the East Germans' transformation into West German tourists. 'We brought them things like western brand-name toothpaste to put in their luggage, and the driver's licences of the passport-holders. Western cigarettes too, of course—Marlboros or whatever. And we'd tell them to remove the labels from their clothes so that they didn't read 'People's Own Manufacture'.

In an alley near the station Michael handed over the passports and supplies. The East Germans, with a case no bigger than for a holiday, prepared to leave for their new lives. By Christmas 1961, Michael Hinze's father and stepmother were safely in West Berlin.

Over the winter of 1961 Frau Paul had permission to visit Torsten four times. Once, an envelope was waiting for her at the hospital. It was a brief note from Dr Hinze, with his telephone number and some small change. When she phoned, Dr Hinze told Frau Paul his son would help get them out. The next time she was over at the Westend Hospital she brought passport-sized photos of herself and her husband. Michael had them inserted into West German passports.

'So in February 1962,' Frau Paul says, 'we planned to get out using the transit route from Berlin Ostbahnhof through Denmark in order to reach West Berlin. It was a very roundabout route.' Frau Paul is a woman utterly without irony. She seems to have, in fact, very little distance from what happened to her. Things remain close, and hard.

Three eastern students were going to escape with them: a young man called Werner Coch and another couple. Frau Paul and her husband gave their car away to a friend and sold, discreetly, some of their belongings. They left their home intact, full of furniture. 'It was a terrible, uncertain time,' she says.

Werner Coch is a chemical engineer in his late fifties. Soft spoken and exact, he has dark hair, and dark eyes in a calm face. He is dressed neatly in pale clothes and light-coloured shoes. We sit in the living room of the spacious and comfortable house he built himself and he tells me about the escape route. A small grandfather clock strikes the half-hours of the afternoon.

'We got the passports and the train tickets,' he says, 'and we learned the appropriate story by heart: who we were—name, date of birth, where we were going on our holiday and so on.' They also had to learn where they had been. Coch's passport had belonged to someone who once travelled to Togo. 'Togo!' he laughs, 'I can't say I'm an expert on the history of Togo or anything, but I did bone up on the name of the capital— Lomé—and the language they spoke—French.'

On the appointed day the five of them went to the railway station. They were to stay in the waiting hall until the signal came from a western student, visiting on a day pass, that all was in order to proceed. Then they were to go up to the long-distance platform and board the train. The student would phone Copenhagen to make sure the group before them had arrived safely. Then he would give the signal to go ahead. Coch doesn't remember the signal exactly. He says it was 'something with a newspaper. Something about how it was held.'

Frau Paul seems to have forgotten or repressed details like this altogether. She says only, 'There came a sign from a student that meant that we shouldn't get on the train. If we did, we would be arrested. We went straight home.'

Coch elaborates. He says when the signal came, 'It was a shock. But I have to say that at the same time there was a sense of relief. I knew there were things in my luggage that still looked like eastern goods.'

Frau Paul now knows that the group before them were all arrested and jailed. The western student with them was arrested and served a two-year sentence in an eastern prison. The Stasi had become suspicious and overnight instituted a new stamp as part of the transit visa. In the time it took for the visas to be applied for, and the doctored passports to be smuggled back to the east, this stamp had, unknown to the little group, become necessary.

'We took all the passports home,' Frau Paul says, 'and we burnt them. Here in this apartment.' She says this with exaggerated finality, as though the little fire washed them clean of the crime. 'Then we just hoped that our son would get better, and that he could come home to us. We thought: we've tried it once and it didn't work. We'll not try that again.' Failure had at least brought an end to that particular anxiety, and it felt like a reprieve. She is adamant that she and her husband Hartmut, then and there, gave up trying to get out. 'That was it for us. But through this whole business, we had got to know the three students who lived here in the east.' Frau Paul and her husband corresponded with them a bit over the next year. 'So it is in life that similarly-minded people find each other and we stayed in contact.'

In February 1963, a year after the passport attempt, the three students asked if they might come to stay for a few nights in Berlin. Torsten was still in the west, still in hospital. 'We said yes,' Frau Paul says. From then on her conversation becomes muddled, peppered with statements of what she 'didn't know at the time' or 'couldn't have suspected'. She trusted the students, and gave them keys to her home. 'I was working full-time in my job as a dental technician,' she says, 'so I could not know what went on in this apartment during the day. I simply wasn't here.' She fiddles with her collar. 'My husband was here,' she says.

'Frau Paul and Hartmut were nervous,' Coch says of his stay in their house, 'it was a tense atmosphere.' The students were back to try again. A tunnel had been built from West Berlin under the Wall, to the cellar of an apartment block on Brunnenstrasse in East Berlin. Twenty-nine people had made it through several months earlier. But then the tunnel flooded, leaving others stranded on the eastern side. Now, the groundwater had frozen and a new escape was being planned.

The Deal

'I wanted to go,' Coch tells me, 'because I had the feeling it was all perfectly organised. I thought if the danger was too great we'd get a signal, just as we had with the false passports scheme.'

The students waited at Frau Paul's apartment for word to come from a courier. As before, this attempt was being organised by western students who would tell the easterners where the tunnel was, and when and how they could enter.

The courier came with the information. 'The instructions were to go to a particular street near the Rosa Luxemburg Theatre,' Coch says. 'There, a car would be parked with a small sign on its back dash. From that sign we'd be able to decipher the address of the building where the tunnel could be entered.' Then they were to go to a telephone booth nearby. If everything was in order to proceed, there would be a sticking plaster under the receiver. 'If the plaster wasn't there, it meant that someone had ripped it off as a warning. Then, it was just a matter of proceeding to the address and uttering the code words.' They were to enter the building at intervals of half an hour, and they would be shown through the tunnel. If all went well, a signal would come from the window of a building on the western side: a white flag for success. If there were problems, they would see a red ball instead.

'Hartmut Rührdanz and I went to check it out the afternoon beforehand. We took the underground to Rosa Luxemburg station, and had a look around.' They saw the car, and the telephone booth, and they worked out how long it would take to get there from the Pauls' apartment that evening. 'I set out by myself, and Hartmut came after me at a safe interval. He was about a hundred metres behind me or so.' Coch went to the car and read the sign on the back dash. 'It was some kind of riddle to do with springs, I can't remember exactly,' he says, 'and the number forty-five.' *Brunnen* means spring, or creek. Coch worked out he was to go to 45 Brunnenstrasse. Then he went to the phone booth to find the sticking plaster under the receiver.

Forty-five Brunnenstrasse was a short way from the booth. It's also right around the corner from my place. I wandered there one morning. The sky was pale blue and high, and the sun shone like a small light in a freezer. Brunnenstrasse hits Bernauer Strasse, which is where the Wall ran, and where the famous pictures of people jumping out of their apartments onto mattresses on the western side were taken on 13 August 1961. Now, there's just a stretch of overgrown grass here. If you didn't know that the Wall had been in this place, you'd find it hard to imagine. Eventually, there will be new apartment buildings built over it in the same style as the older ones, and in less than one generation this scar will be invisible. For the moment though, there is something strange about this stretch: it's not a park, it's not even an empty lot. It's just a hole in the city.

I hunched my collar up high as I walked. I was watching the street numbers closely looking for number forty-five when I passed a shop and read its sign. I retraced my steps. I had read it right. The sign said: 'Digging Equipment for Hire or Sale: Spring Diggers; Electrical Percussion-

Hammers, Augers, Hand-Borers, Pumps.' Two young men walked past. They were tough, both of them wearing their jackets open in the cold. One's T-shirt read, in English, 'Too Drunk to Fuck', and the other's, in German, 'Out of the Way—an Arsehole Is Coming'. They stared hard at me then at the shop, then back at me again, as if to figure out what I might find so fascinating about a pump-and-drill place.

Forty-five Brunnenstrasse is an ordinary five-storey apartment block. Nothing distinguishes it from any other building in the street. There are no plaques on it, no footpath inlay commemorating the tunnel. And, like so many buildings in the former east, it is being renovated. As I entered, two Turkish workmen were coming out carrying tools and pails of plaster dust. I nodded a greeting as if I knew what I was doing, and walked straight in. The cellar door was on the right. I stood there for a moment. Then I opened the door onto darkness, the smell of dust and damp. I started down the steps when I heard a call.

'Excuse me! Excuse me! Can I help you?' The foreman, also Turkish, stood at the top of the steps. I explained I was looking for a tunnel that had been accessible from the cellar of this building.

'Wait here,' he said. He fetched a torch on a long lead. We went down the steps. The cellar had a vaulted roof and wooden partitions for each apartment's section. I don't think either of us thought we'd find a tunnel. He swung the light along the dirt-floored passage right to the end. And there, in the wall, was a manhole-sized area where the bricks were newer than all the others. We shone the torch at it and stood there, and I thought of the twenty-nine people who left their country from here, and of Werner Coch and the others.

When he got to the building, Coch says, 'I went to the door of the cellar in the hall, and I said the code words. They were, "Does Herr Lindemann live here?" There was no answer, so I repeated, "Does Herr Lindemann live here?" It was meant to be for the people—the helpers—behind the door. I was meant to wait for the reaction. I expected someone to appear with a torch, or perhaps to speak to me, and lead me out of there.' Nothing happened. Nothing at all. 'I thought: something's not right here. Please God, just let me get out in one piece. I turned around and walked out of the building.

'And that's when they got me—Stasi in civilian clothes. I think there were three of them waiting on the street for me to come out again. I know now they had the building surrounded—there was one on the stairs inside too.'

They asked him what he was doing there, and he told them he was visiting Herr Lindemann. 'There's no Herr Lindemann here,' they said. They took him away, first to the police station, then into custody at the Stasi headquarters in Berlin, and finally to prison at Hohenschönhausen.

'Hartmut Rührdanz watched the whole thing from the other side of the street,' Coch says, 'then he went home, terrified.' The Rührdanzes would stay in the east. They would wait till their baby was well enough to come home. And they hoped he would survive.

Memory, like so much else, is unreliable. Not only for what it hides and what it alters, but also for what it reveals. Frau Paul must have known why the three students had come to stay, and she probably knew that the tunnel attempt had failed. If she does not admit to having known, it is because for this knowledge she was made a criminal in the GDR, and because, saddest of all, she still feels like one.

Frau Paul showed me a Stasi report on the tunnel. Its outlet had been under our feet at Brunnenstrasse, and not in the wall, as this document shows, in its excruciating bureaucratese:

GOVERNMENT OF THE GERMAN DEMOCRATIC REPUBLIC

Ministry for State Security

ATTESTATION

On the existence of a tunnel from West Berlin into the Capital of the German Democratic Republic.

In the course of a cellar check by members of the National People's Army on 18.02.1963 at 45 Brunnen

Street in Berlin Mitte it was established that there was a hole in the floor of the cellar that gave rise to the supposition that a tunnel was to be found here.

A widening of the hole and subsequent examination gave rise to the confirmation that in this building at 45 Brunnen Street was the end of a tunnel built across from West Berlin territory.

The tunnel began on West Berlin territory, went under Bernauer Street in West Berlin and under several occupied houses in the capital of the German Democratic Republic to the cellar of 45 Brunnen Street.

From the cellar of 45 Brunnen Street to the national border the tunnel measured 130 metres and extended after that under Bernauer Street which is approximately 30 metres wide.

The dimensions of the passage amounted to 75cm width and 70-80cm in height. At the examination of the passage 4 torches of western make, 1 folding spade of American origin, 1 hand spade, 2 hatchets, 1 rock drill as well as several screwdrivers were confiscated.

Further to this a range of light-cables, several light globes and rubber mats were found at the site of the tunnel and confiscated.

By means of comparisons with material already gathered to date it was deduced that the student [name] of the Technical University in West Berlin was definitely involved in the organisation of the building of the tunnel to the cellar of 45 Brunnen Street.

From that time on, Frau Paul and her husband were followed. 'In the morning when I went to work, there'd be someone close behind me,' she says. 'If I went in to Alexanderplatz to do some shopping a man would come with me from my door onto the bus and train and then home again.

They changed the personnel, but there was always someone there. They wanted us to feel it.' Feel what? A simmering, non-specific anxiety? Apart from the fact that they were being followed, there was nothing they could have anticipated. Like most things, until it happens to you, you don't think it will. This continued for a fortnight.

One morning on her way to the bus stop two men in civilian clothes asked Frau Paul for her ID. 'This was quite common. You had to carry your ID at all times.' Before she could reach into her bag to find it a 'big black limousine' pulled up to the kerb. The men grabbed her above the elbows, and shoved her in. 'I was kidnapped right off the street,' she says.

She didn't know where she was taken, 'but I knew I was at the Stasi'. She now has the record of her interrogation and it shows that she was at Magdalenenstrasse, part of Normannenstrasse at Stasi HQ. She was interrogated from 8 am on the morning of 28 February 1963 until the following day at 6 am. 'That was how long it lasted,' she says, passing the document across to me. 'I always said it lasted twenty-two hours and when I got access to my file there it was: twenty-two hours.' It is as if the things that happened to Frau Paul are so extreme to her way of thinking and to her sense of what life should be like, that she wants to make sure she does not, on any account, exaggerate. It is also as if she just can't believe it happened to her.

Frau Paul remembers her interrogator clearly. He was young, portly and snide. 'In the beginning I denied everything, but then I noticed that they already knew a great deal. They wanted to get information about the students who had stayed with us.' At the end of her interrogation she was taken back to her cell. 'I could hardly speak any more. I was finished. But they didn't leave me there long. They came and took me in a paddy wagon to another place. Then they continued the interrogation day and night— they liked to do it when one was sleep-deprived. They didn't give me any rest.'

It was during one of these sessions that they offered Frau Paul the deal.

She was seated low on a backless stool, in the corner of the room. When the door opened, it concealed her. I think of Frau Paul's ample body on that small stool, designed for indignity. The lieutenant interrogating her was behind a large desk. 'I understand your son finds himself in enemy territory,' he said.

'Yes, sir.'

'From our information, it appears he is very ill.'

'Yes, sir.' Where was this going? Had something happened to Torsten that she didn't know about? Surely they wouldn't do anything to a tiny, sick baby?

'Would you like to see your son?'

What sort of a question was that? 'Yes, sir.'

'That can be arranged.'

I imagine the huge hope in her then, swelling her heart as she sat on that stool. But she says, 'That's when I got suspicious. Here I was sitting in the slammer—I mean prison, sorry—and they were offering for me to go into enemy territory—that's what the west was then. I couldn't make any sense of it at all.'

'How is that possible?' she asked.

'It is not at all complicated,' he said. 'In fact, it's a simple matter. If you would like to visit your son in enemy territory, we would ask only that, while you are there, you arrange to meet up with your young friend Michael Hinze. The two of you could go for a stroll. For instance, in the grounds of Charlottenburg Castle.'

She was confused. And then he said, 'You can leave the rest to us.'

'"You can leave the rest to us!"' she cries. 'Then he added, "One good turn deserves another." "One good turn deserves another!"' Her tone is a mixture of horror and triumph. I am clearly missing something here. I wonder whether in German there is a sticklebrick noun for this strange combined emotion.

'At that moment,' she explains, 'Karl Wilhelm Fricke shot through my head. I had heard him years before on the radio from the west tell of his kidnapping and imprisonment, and I had never forgotten it. In a flash I knew: they were going to use me as bait in a trap to kidnap Michael.'

Karl Wilhelm Fricke is well known in Germany as a broadcaster and journalist, and as a phenomenon: 'the case of Fricke.' He has always been an agitator against the German Democratic Republic. On April Fools' Day 1955, at a meeting in West Berlin, Stasi agents drugged his cognac and then shunted him, unconscious, over the sector border. He was convicted of 'war and boycott instigation against the GDR' and sentenced to four years in solitary confinement, which he served until the last day. There was nothing the west could do to get him out. When he was released into West Berlin, he immediately, and at some risk to himself, broadcast over the airwaves the story of his abduction. At the end of an afternoon spent with him he said to me, 'Frau Paul—then Rührdanz—is a *very* brave woman.'

Frau Paul knew Michael would trust her to come to a meeting in the park, and when they came to bundle him into a vehicle she would have to turn her back and walk away. She doesn't know whether the offer would have meant more than one visit to Torsten, or staying out of prison. She knew only that, if she accepted, they would have her then, her soul bought with a visit to her critically ill son. She would be theirs forever: a stool pigeon and a tame little rat.

'Me—bait in a trap for Michael! And of course that was an absolute no. I couldn't.' Her back is straight, and her hands are clenched into fists on her thighs. 'Karl Wilhelm Fricke,' she says, 'was my guardian angel.' She starts to crumble and break. At this moment, she does not look like a woman who was saved from anything. 'I had to decide against my son, but I couldn't let myself be used in this way.' Her back slumps and she is crying again. She holds one hand in the other, and from time to time swaps them around, as if to give herself some kind of comfort.

'At that time it was the right decision,' she says through tears. 'And even later too, I could always say to myself, "I did not make myself guilty. I can sleep at night with what I have done."' She doesn't try to cover her face. There was no right answer here, no good outcome. 'It is true that I didn't burden myself with this on my conscience, but I did,' she draws in breath in a spasm of pain, 'decide against my son.'

It is so hard to know what kind of mortgage our acts put on our future. Frau Paul had the courage to do the right thing by her conscience in a situation where most people would decide to see their baby, and tell themselves later they had no choice. Once made though, her decision took a whole new fund of courage to live with. It seems to me that Frau Paul, as one does, may have overestimated her own strength, her resistance to damage, and that she is now, for her principles, a lonely, teary guilt-wracked wreck. 'The result of this was that I was never interrogated again.' She learnt that her husband and the three students had also been arrested, as well as some thirty others from all over the GDR who had been planning to leave through the tunnel.

Hohenschönhausen

Frau Paul and her husband were held at Hohenschönhausen prison for five months, and then, along with the three students, transported to Rostock on the Baltic Sea coast for trial. Frau Paul thinks this was because the western media knew of the plight of Torsten on one side of the Wall and of his parents on the other, and the authorities wanted to make sure there was no chance of publicity.

The couple never saw the charges against them, nor the judgment. They were offered the services of Dr Vogel, the lawyer with close government connections who became famous for negotiating the trade in people between east and west. But they mistrusted the arrangement and turned it down, insisting on their own family solicitor. He couldn't do much to help them though, because he was handed the charges against his clients only five minutes before the trial began.

The prosecutor alleged:

Rührdanz, Sigrid, is accused of inducing or, at the least aiding and abetting citizens of the German Democratic Republic to illegally leave the GDR.

The accused maintains connections with members of a West Berlin people smuggling and terrorist organisation which lures people out of the GDR and facilitates their illegal leaving of the GDR either with illegal papers, or through the violation of the national border… [She] had custody of forged passports in her flat, organised meetings and conveyed information about planned people smuggling operations and accommodated persons to be smuggled in her flat. There exists the urgent suspicion that she herself will illegally leave the GDR.

Frau Paul reads this to me, and maintains, at each point, her innocence. 'We'd long since, as I told you, given up trying to get out,' she says, and, 'I did not know what the students were doing at our flat.' In 1992, twenty-nine years after the trial, Frau Paul saw in her file the judgment for the first time. There was no mention of Torsten. The judges wrote that her 'attitude of rejection towards our State' had been 'exacerbated through the fact that the accused has been a constant listener to NATO smear-radio'.

'They put that in about the NATO smear-radio because I would not let myself be misused as bait in their trap.' Frau Paul and her husband were each given four years hard labour. She was put in a paddy wagon and taken from Rostock back to Hohenschönhausen to serve her time. Werner Coch got one year and nine months in ordinary prison, because the penalties for being an accessory to the attempt to flee the country were greater than the crime of trying to flee itself.

Hohenschönhausen prison is not far from the centre of East Berlin, but its existence was unknown even to people in neighbouring suburbs. Every street that leads in or out of the area around it was blocked off by a boom gate and a sentry. Hohenschönhausen was a prison for political prisoners—it was the innermost security installation in a secured area within a walled-off country; it was another blank on the map.

Frau Paul took me there one day. It was an ordinarily cold day, and we were in an ordinarily grey residential street. As we walked along she nodded and said, 'That's where the boom gates were.' All that remained was a hip-height bollard on the pavement. We passed it into what had been the secure Stasi zone. 'That building there was Department M, Postal Surveillance,' Frau Paul said, walking slightly ahead of me and pointing with an open hand. 'That one over there was the Forgery Workshop for the Stasi. That one was a special Stasi hospital.' These were plain concrete buildings. They looked empty. 'Those high-rises over there are Stasi housing,' she continued. I followed her hand and saw a cluster of grey and white multi-storey towers. From one of them emerged a middle-aged man with a dachshund on a retractable lead. The man ignored us, but the dog eyed me warily as it pissed on the kerb.

Further inside the zone we reached a building with high concrete walls topped by barbed wire. The walls seemed to stretch on and on, enclosing an area as big as a city block. At the corners were octagonal guard towers, and underneath them, along the outside, an empty dog-run. Hohenschönhausen has been closed for several years. People are now fighting to preserve it as a museum of the regime. Frau Paul is involved with them, and she has a key.

We approached the towering grey steel entry gates. There was a man-sized door next to them. Her eyes were clear, her clothes made the rustle of nylon. She moved ahead of me in a businesslike way that said, 'I hate this place, but I'm still here.' We slipped into the empty prison, into a huge yard surrounded by buildings, with a squat building in the centre. The ground was asphalt and gravel, cracking like the top of a cake. A truck was parked in the yard. It was painted grey, and had a solid steel cage on the back with no windows or apparent ventilation of any kind. 'This is the same as the paddy wagon I was transported in for five hours from Rostock,' she said. And then to my surprise she added, 'Get in.' I did. Inside, instead of two benches for the prisoners as I had expected, it had a tiny corridor and six internal cells each with a lockable door. These were not big enough to stand upright in, and contained only a crossboard to sit on. She followed me into the truck. 'Get in,' she said again, pointing at the furthest tiny cell, 'it'll give you a feel for what it was like.' I climbed into one and she closed the heavy steel door. The key turned in the lock. I sat on the bench and everything was pitch black and horrible. Outside the door she said, loudly, 'You have to imagine that someone is sitting here with a machine gun.' I imagined it, then she let me out.

Later, I learned that these trucks were sometimes disguised as linen service vehicles, or refrigerated fish transports, or bakers' vans, when all the time they were ferrying prisoners and dissidents at gunpoint around the Republic.

We walked across the yard to the building in the middle and entered it via a truck bay with giant doors. 'This is where I was brought,' she said. 'I had no idea where I was. For all I knew, I could have been taken from Rostock to any place in the GDR. I certainly didn't know I was right in the heart of Berlin.' The paddy wagon and the truck bay were designed so that the prisoners could be let out one at a time, and never see each other, or daylight, or a street, or the entrance to the building.

We walked up the steps. A huge studded metal door slid sideways to reveal a long linoleum corridor. Frau Paul pointed out a primitive cable-and-hook system that ran along the walls at head height. When a new prisoner was coming, it operated as an alarm system, turning on red lights at intervals. That was the signal for all other prisoners to be locked in their cells, and guards to be out of sight. The prisoner was not to know who else was here, or have any human contact which was not strictly monitored, for psychological purposes, by her captors.

We walked along the corridor. Some of the cells were open, some shut. The only sound was our footfalls on the floor. Grey paint peeled off the walls. It is not the first time Frau Paul has been back, but I don't imagine this is easy for her. I know there are places that I don't visit, some even that I prefer not to drive past, where bad things have happened. But here she is in the place that broke her, and she is telling me about it. It is part bravery, like the bravery that made her refuse the Stasi deal, and it is part, perhaps, obsession, caused by what they did to her after that.

She took me to the room where she was interrogated. In this complex 120 rooms were available for simultaneous interrogations. Hers had brown patterned wallpaper reaching halfway up the walls, a dun-coloured linoleum floor, and a large desk and chair. Behind the door was a small, four-legged stool like a milking stool. 'Twenty-two hours on that,' Frau Paul said.

Then we went to another building, the 'U-Boat'. From the ground it looked ordinary enough. We entered down some steps. Frau Paul was telling me it had been purpose-built by the Russians in 1946 as a series of torture chambers. I was sort of listening, but mainly I was adjusting to the strange smell. Some smells are hard to unravel. I remember the university library around exam time. It smelt of sweat and damp coats and bad breath. It was a mongrel smell, but it was the smell of pure fear. This U-Boat smelt of damp and old urine and vomit and earth: the smell of misery.

The tunnel-corridor was long and stark. Single bulbs hung on cords. Frau Paul started opening doors. First, a compartment so small a person could only stand. It was designed to be filled with icy water up to the neck. There were sixty-eight of these, she told me. Then there were concrete cells with nothing in them where prisoners would be kept in the dark amid their own excrement. There was a cell lined entirely with padded black rubber. Frau Paul was held nearby. She remembers hearing the prisoner inside the rubber cell gradually lose his mind. At the end the only words he had left were: 'Never…Get…Out!' Once when he was taken away she was ordered in to mop up his vomit and blood.

The strangest cell contained a wooden yoke arrangement, something like an apparatus at a county fair. The prisoner would be nearly bent double, head and hands through the slots and the yoke closed over them. In front of his head hung a metal bucket of water like a nosebag. The floor and walls were black, and lined with spiky ridges. Frau Paul explained that the prisoner would be barefoot, yoked into position. The ridges would bite into the soles of his feet. Then water dripped from a pipe hanging through the ceiling, onto his head. Eventually, the prisoner would be in such pain that he would lose consciousness, and his head would slump. It would hit the water in the bucket in front of him, and he would either revive into pain again, or drown.

There was nothing funny about this cell and there was nothing funny about standing in it with Frau Paul, feeling the spiky floor through my boots and touching the coarse yoke and imagining being bent nearly double in the dark, in pain and drifting between consciousness and drowning. But there was something barnyard about it. It seemed too primitive for the mid-twentieth century and too primitive for here. This contraption belonged further east and further back in time, in some Pythonesque sideshow of history.

But there was something even more chilling about the office with the little stool Frau Paul was made to sit on, and the ordinary administrative desk and chair where the interrogator sat over her. It was in offices that the Stasi truly came into their own: as innovators, story-makers, and Faustian bargain-hunters. That room was where a deal was offered and refused, and a soul buckled out of shape, forever.

Not one of the torturers at Hohenschönhausen has been brought to justice.

Four times a year Frau Paul received permission to have a visitor (mostly her mother) but she'd be transported elsewhere for it so that neither she nor her visitor would know where in the GDR she was being kept. Mail was sent to another Stasi address, and brought to her opened. She had been taken out of time, and out of place.

Torsten remained over the years at the Westend Hospital. The nurses and doctors fed him through tubes and gave him medicine and changed his nappies. They sang him songs, they taught him to speak, and they tried to teach him to walk. The hospital was the only home and its staff the only people Torsten Rührdanz knew. This is one of the letters that got through to his parents. It was written in November 1963 when Torsten was nearly three years old:

> Dear Mr and Mrs Rührdanz,
> I learnt that you would like to be informed as to Torsten's health, which I can very well understand. Generally he is cheerful, making progress with his walking, and happy. He has become the darling of the ward. Of course from time to time we still have difficulties to overcome, which means that, unfortunately, discharge from hospital is not possible in the foreseeable future. We cannot manage to feed him without a stomach tube, because as soon as he eats normally he is in pain. His weight is still unsatisfactory, at 7670 g. His height is also significantly less than the norm for his age. His diarrhoea has virtually ceased though. There is nothing left for us but to continue as we have been, and in the hope that his stomach will gradually widen and that the problems at the end of his diaphragm will mend.
> You can be assured that everything possible will continue to be done for your child. I will write again before Christmas.
> Yours sincerely,
> Prof. Dr L.

Michael Hinze has always lived in the west. He was never kidnapped by the Stasi; he didn't even know that they were after him. And, until recently, he had no idea that Frau Paul was in any way connected with his continuing freedom. 'I found out about it a couple of years ago, after the Wall fell. For years I'd heard nothing from the Rührdanzes. Then they called me,' he says. 'All this story with the blackmailing and the plans to kidnap me—I knew nothing about that at all.' He is slightly uncomfortable with the whole idea. 'I mean I always saw myself as small fry. I just put people together, got passports. I knew it was illegal under GDR law, but...' he trails off. He didn't really think it through. Even if he had, how could he have imagined that someone else was being asked to pay a price for his liberty? 'She's a very courageous woman,' Hinze continues, 'I have a great deal of respect for her. I'm also grateful to her. But at the same time I don't think I need to feel guilty—I don't feel guilty, I mean, I was just lucky that I didn't fall into the clutches of the Stasi. That way, or by other means.' He thinks that if they had really wanted him they could have got him, and this is probably true.

'She was very active in the whole thing,' Hinze says admiringly. 'The Rührdanzes used to marshal the people from Halle or Dresden or wherever who wanted to get out, and help them. They were very committed people.'

Frau Paul has told me none of this, although it might be something another person would be proud of. The picture we make of ourselves, with all its congruences and fantastical edges, sustains us. Frau Paul does not picture herself as a hero, or a dissident. She is a dental technician and a mother with a terrible family history. And she is a criminal. This seems to me the sorriest thing; that the picture she has of herself is one that the Stasi made for her.

'I told her that her story moved me deeply,' Hinze says. 'And that I don't know many people who would not have betrayed me. I said that there are not many people who have the courage she did. To behave with'—he's looking for a way to describe it—'with such great humanity, can I say. She behaved with such great humanity.' We are both silent for a moment. 'But unfortunately,' he says, 'at her cost.'

In August 1964 the Rührdanzes were bought free for 40,000 western marks. But instead of being released into the west to be with their baby, they were dumped on the street in East Berlin with no papers. Frau Paul puts this down to their refusal of Dr Vogel as lawyer. Of the estimated 34,000 people bought free between 1963 and 1989 there are at this stage only nine documented cases of such cruelty, where the west paid hard currency and the east did not deliver the people whose freedom had been purchased.

Torsten was still living in the Westend Hospital. On 9 April 1965 when he was four years old Frau Paul had news of him from Sister Gisela, one of the nurses.

We all wish you and your husband a very healthy and happy Easter. Torsten has painted you an Easter picture, all by himself—brown Easter bunnies and a nest with colourful eggs. He said, 'That is for my mummy, she'll like that!' Yesterday we received your lovely card, and we thank you on behalf of Torsten. He was so happy, we had to read it out to him straight away. He never lets it out of his little hands, and keeps looking at the Sandman on it…

My dear Mrs Rührdanz, Torsten is really coming along now. It is such a shame that you can't be here to enjoy his progress. It could drive one to despair, this drama between parts of a single city!! But I don't want to write about that.

Better some more news of Torsten. He weighs 9450g now and is 84cm tall. He speaks and understands everything like a six year old. He doesn't miss a trick! He told me I should write you that he's coming home soon to Kaulsdorf. Torsten can walk 5 m by himself! Apart from that he wheels around all afternoon about the station. Dear Mrs Rührdanz, every best wish from us and one thousand kisses from Torsten—for his Daddy too.

They waited another eight months before Torsten was well enough to be released from the Westend Hospital. When he came home to East Germany he was nearly five, small and bent and very polite.

'Of course he didn't recognise me as his mother,' Frau Paul says. 'He didn't know what a mother was. He only knew the sterile atmosphere of the hospital and the staff there, the doctors, the sisters and the other personnel. Even though they all dealt very lovingly with him and they tried'—she's crying now, hard—'tried to create for him in whatever ways they could something like a family atmosphere, it just wasn't his home. He was frightened. And when I…' She has to stop because she can't get the words out. 'And when I took him in my arms for the first time and held him to me he must have thought, "What does this old lady want with me? She says she is my mother, but what is that, a mother?" He addressed us with the formal "*Sie*". He would say, "Mother, would you kindly be able to make me a sandwich, I'm hungry," or "Father, would you mind lifting me onto the chair, I can't manage," and this, this terrible distance. They made our boy a stranger to us.' She lowers her voice. 'And it was then I fought with myself the most: did I decide right in the interrogation when I refused to be used as bait for a kidnapping? Or should I have come to my son?' She is weeping and weeping.

I'm upset too. It's the small things that make you cry. The idea of nurses and doctors in West Berlin trying to tell a little boy what a family was, to prepare him for one. The idea that in justifying her decision of more than thirty years ago to me here today, there is no peace for Frau Paul. I am scrabbling for tissues which seem to exist only in various embarrassing degrees of decay in the bottom of my backpack. I don't even think about Torsten.

The doorbell sounds, and Frau Paul gets up to answer it. She comes back into the room with a man whose age is hard to tell, but I know immediately it's him. When I stand up to shake hands I tower over him and his hand fits inside mine. His body is small and hunched and his arms and legs seem crooked, spidery. His head seems small too. He has bright deep-set dark eyes and prominent cheekbones. He's wearing a jacket with a couple of badges on the lapel, casual cool. 'Pleased to meet you,' Torsten says genially, and he sinks down lopsided into the couch next to me. He does not seem surprised to see his mother has been crying.

Torsten is not sure whether he remembers meeting his parents for the first time. 'I've seen the photos,' he says, 'and it's hard to distinguish what I remember from what I've since seen. I know from being told that I addressed them with the formal "Sie" because I didn't know what a parent was. Sometimes I have an inkling of the meeting, in the dark past like a *fata morgana*, but not consciously so, no.' His voice is very soft.

I want to know if he thinks his mother made the right decision not to come to him, so I ask him directly. He is relaxed. 'I have never looked at my parents and thought they made the wrong decision,' he says, 'or looked at them like the Stasi did, as criminals or anything like that—quite the opposite: I admire them for what they did.' He seems to have learned to contain both longing and regret. 'It doesn't occur to me,' he says, 'to think that perhaps they might have done things differently and things might have worked out differently.'

'But then again,' I offer, 'I suppose one visit wouldn't have made much difference—' I wasn't trying to take any of her heroism away. I was trying to find a way of thinking about her choice that wasn't such a drastic abandonment of him. But he gently cuts me off and thinks of it from his mother's point of view. 'Well yes,' he says, 'but if you think someone is dying you probably want to see them just one more time before they do. That would make a difference to you, even if it doesn't change anything.'

Torsten supplements his invalid pension by working with bands in the electronic music scene. It is something he has done, in one form or another, since before the Wall fell. Back then, because of his invalid status, he was permitted to travel to the west once a fortnight. He would be commissioned by rock musicians in the GDR to smuggle back spare parts for them. Torsten was well known to the border guards, and was searched 'about 90 per cent of the time', he says, smiling. 'I was frequently caught, but luckily the consequences weren't so bad for me. They did accuse me though, of "dangerous trade with musical instruments and musical electronics,"' he laughs.

Despite his family history, the Stasi went after Torsten to see if he would inform for them. First, they gathered compromising material on his smuggling. Then they brought him in for questioning. Torsten went mum, so the same material that would have been used to pressure him into informing became instead evidence of his unsuitability for it. A final report of 17 June 1985 is two sentences long. 'R. is not suited for an unofficial collaboration with the Ministry. (R. participates in criminal activity).' It was clearly not an option to write, 'R. refuses, on principle, to collaborate.'

I ask Torsten whether he thinks of his life as having been shaped by the Wall.

'I find it hard to tell exactly, in what sense my life has been shaped by the Wall—how it might have been different otherwise,' he says, 'but that it has been, I have no doubt.'

He has learned not to play the 'if only' game: if only there had been no Wall I might not have relapsed; I might have grown up with my parents; they might not have gone to prison; I might have had a healthy body, a job, a partner. He shifts in his seat to look at me straight on. 'There are no people who are whole,' he says. 'Everyone has issues of their own to deal with. Mine might be a little harder, but the main thing is how one deals with them.'

'And how do you?' I am facing him, looking at his twisted body, and listening to him breathe through the tubes they placed inside him.

'Well, it is an issue for me. I think life can end much too quickly, so I have no long-term aspirations. Whatever it is I want, I want it now, to experience it today. I have no patience for saving money, or building up some kind of enterprise. It makes me nervous. Other people say, "You have time, you're still relatively young." But I'm always so afraid that things can come to an end at any time.' He pauses. 'Or that politically, too, it could all change again, and then I'd have no chance to experience certain things.'

I remark that for something so big, that shaped their lives so brutally, it's hard now to find a trace of the Wall. I am about to say I think it's odd to let everyone forget so quickly, when Torsten says, 'I'm happy that it's gone, and I'm happy too that there's so little of it left to see. It would remind me that it could come back. That everything that's happened might be reversed.'

'But that wouldn't be possible!' I laugh.

He looks at me soberly. 'But anything is possible,' he says. 'One can never say that something is not possible.'

His mother agrees. 'Who would have thought that a wall could be built!' she says. 'That was also impossible! And who would have thought at the end that it might ever fall! That was also impossible!'

People here talk of the *Mauer im Kopf* or the Wall in the Head. I thought this was just a shorthand way of referring to how Germans define themselves still as easterners and westerners. But I see now a more literal meaning: the Wall and what it stood for do still exist. The Wall persists in Stasi men's minds as something they hope might one day come again, and in their victims' minds too, as a terrifying possibility.

Torsten offers to give me a lift to the station. Frau Paul kisses him and takes my hand with both of hers. Then she shrugs her shoulders. 'That's it,' she says, as though, when she added up the parts of her life, it was a smallish thing.

Torsten's car is an old-style BMW with a high seat custom-built behind the steering wheel. He puts on some music with a Latin beat, and it keeps strange, syncopated time with the windscreen wipers. We chat and he takes me past the station, nearly all the way to Alexanderplatz. Then he lets me out with a wave and drives on, crooked and crippled and living for the day.

24

Herr Bohnsack

I walk around to pick up my last Stasi man. In his street new tramlines are being laid, lengths of steel are strewn like licorice down the median strip. It's lunchtime and the workers are nowhere to be seen. I ring the buzzer where it says 'Bohnsack'. A man comes out putting on a smart tan overcoat. He's tall and slightly stooped, thickset through the chest. His face is pleasant, with receding hair and full cheeks. He looks me straight in the eye and smiles a warm smile.

'Let's go to my local,' he says.

The pub is a traditional Berlin *Kneipe*. It has a bar in dark wood with mirrors behind it, booth seats and lacy white curtains to shield people from the street. A shaft of light slips past them on an angle, slow afternoon light of lazy particles and beams. Two regulars watch their glasses. There are little pubs like this in both East and West Berlin, where everyone knows everyone else. I have occasionally walked in—for directions, or cigarettes—and each time I felt I had walked into someone's living room uninvited.

When a stranger enters, the hum of conversation breaks while people look up and hunch their shoulders. Here though, when the regulars see Herr Bohnsack, they nod. The publican smiles like a brother. 'How are we?' he asks, rubbing his hands together. 'What it'll be today then?'

'We might go into the side room,' Herr Bohnsack says, 'if that's all right. For a chat.'

'Of course, of course.' He shuffles out from behind the bar in his socks and slippers and shows us in. There are old advertisements for beer on the walls, pictures of glowing-cheeked maidens and horses and hops. I look at Herr Bohnsack. In the light from the windows at his back he seems to have a bit of a glow about him, too.

'What can I get for the lady and the gentleman?'

'I'll have a wheat beer and a *Korn*,' he says, 'and you?' It's early. I order a beer and forgo the schnapps. Günter Bohnsack's voice is deep and slightly slurred, like a person with ill-fitting crowns, or a man who has been drinking. His eyes are bright and he is relaxed with me. He is not, as it turns out, a man with anything to prove. He is fifty-seven years old, and the only Stasi man I have ever met who outed himself. A lieutenant colonel, he worked in one of the most secret divisions of the overseas spy service, the *Hauptverwaltung Aufklärung* (HVA). Herr Bohnsack was in Division X, responsible, as he put it on the phone to me, for 'disinformation and psychological warfare against the west'.

The HVA was the overseas espionage service of the Stasi. Its director, Markus Wolf, the son of a Jewish doctor and playwright, is intelligent and urbane, and was the model, apparently, for John le Carré's spymaster Karla. Wolf's HVA was subject to its minister, Mielke. But Wolf and his men always saw themselves as a breed apart. Although they were organised according to military rank like the rest of the Firm, they wore suits instead of uniforms, were highly educated and enjoyed a privileged existence. 'Because we were responsible for the west,' Herr Bohnsack explained to me, 'we could travel and we were quite different. Our diplomats could speak languages and were cultivated. We all scorned Mielke;

we had our Wolf, the tall slim elegant intellectual.'

Herr Bohnsack trained as a journalist and worked for twenty-six years in disinformation. Much of Division X's work was directed against West Germany. It collected sensitive or secret information from agents in the west and leaked it to cause harm; it manufactured documents and spliced together recordings of conversations that never took place in order to damage persons in the public sphere; and it spread rumours about people in the west, including the devastating rumour that someone worked for them. Division X men fed 'coups' to western journalists about the Nazi past of West German politicians (several major figures were brought down this way); it funded left-wing publications and it managed, at least in one instance, to exert an extraordinary influence over the political process in West Germany itself. In 1972, the Social Democrat head of the West German government Willy Brandt faced a vote of no-confidence in parliament. Division X bribed one and possibly two backbenchers for their votes in order to keep him in power. Colonel Rolf Wagenbreth, the head of Division X, described its work simply as 'an attempt to turn the wheels of history'.

Herr Bohnsack starts with a joke. He told it at lunch back in 1980 to a group of his colleagues at the restaurant reserved for the highest ranks of the Stasi. He leans back and smiles, like an uncle with a secret. 'The USA, the Soviet Union and the GDR want to raise the *Titanic*,' he says, lifting his eyebrows. 'The USA wants the jewels presumed to be in the safe,' he nods, 'the Soviets are after the state-of-the-art technology; and the GDR'—he downs his *Korn* for dramatic pause—'the GDR wants the band that played as it went down.'

We laugh. 'Was it normal to tell jokes like that?' I ask.

'Yes, yes,' he says, 'quite normal, but it depended who was there. As soon as I'd told that one I thought: oh brother, that was a bit foolish of me because there was a general at the table.' He runs a hand over his head. 'After lunch the general took me aside and said, in a quiet voice, "Next time Bohnsack, I wouldn't tell a joke like that." And that was way back in 1980! They were sensitive about the whole thing going down even then.'

'Were there Mielke jokes?'

'Yes, lots,' he says. 'But the worst Mielke ones weren't jokes, they were true.'

Herr Bohnsack was invited to the party the Stasi threw for themselves and their Russian comrades to celebrate the forty years of the GDR. It was 3 October 1989, the height of the demonstrations and unrest. 'There were about two thousand people at the party,' he says. 'Mielke made his entrance'—he raises one arm behind his ear and does a two-fingered walk through the air—'down some stairs in the corner surrounded by his generals. Like a ghost, or the god in the machine.' Mielke made a speech. 'For four hours he spoke, on and on. Every now and then he gave a rallying cry. "And just remember Comrades this one thing: the most important thing you have is power! Hang on to power at all costs! Without it, you are nothing!" He didn't mention the democracy demonstrations and the fact that the Soviets were backing away from us,' Herr Bohnsack says, 'but it was clear he must, at some level, have felt the end coming.'

When Mielke finally finished there was a banquet: there were grapes, and chicken drumsticks and melon and stone fruits, 'things that we never had in the GDR and that were truly exquisite, amazing delicacies to us'. But just as they were about to tuck in, Mielke would quickly pick up the microphone to say 'a few more idiotic words' and everyone would have to put their drumsticks and bunches of grapes back down on their plates until he was done. He would finish up by saying '*Guten Appetit*', and the men would start to eat, but moments later he'd grab the microphone again and they would have to put it all down once more. 'It went on and on,' Herr Bohnsack says. 'The whole occasion was insane.'

At Christmas 1989, from his telling of it, events bloomed into full-scale, fast-forward farce. Herr Bohnsack's entire division was ordered to stay at home so as not to provoke the demonstrators, and to be near the phone. At 3 am they would receive a call ordering them to drive to Normannenstrasse, parking some way away so the demonstrators wouldn't know the buildings were occupied, and to enter by a rear door. When they reached their offices, all the lights would be out. They were ordered to don camouflage combat gear—'like the foreign legion in the jungle'—and then to kit themselves out with cooking equipment and cutlery, a spade, a protective suit in the event of chemical warfare, a blanket, toothpaste and brush, and ammunition. They were each issued with a pistol and a machine gun. The whole operation was timed.

'What would you do then?' I ask.

'We'd lie down on our desks and sleep. The generals upstairs on the ninth floor were simulating a war situation. One would come down and wake us up with a message—say, an American sub has been sighted off Turkey. Or, the American B52s are on stand-by. Then at 5 am we'd get worse news—maybe that a Russian sub had been taken off Norway. They were pretending World War III had broken out.'

'What could you do?'

'Nothing: we slept some more.'

At 7 am they would get an order to go into the field. 'We'd play war for a day, stand around, and shoot the cardboard figures that popped up out of the grass. Everyone was there—highly intelligent specialists who could speak Arabic and goodness knows what—and we were all reduced to playing soldiers.' By the end of 1989 they were doing this every single week. 'And we knew the GDR was lost,' he says, 'so it was a circus.'

Herr Bohnsack's greatest fear was that he and the others would be ordered to shoot the demonstrators outside their building. During the exercises they were told that the enemy had infiltrated the country and was inciting the East Germans against them. At the end Mielke was more direct. He told them that they—he meant the people—were the enemy. He said, 'It's them or us.'

'For me,' Bohnsack says, 'that was the most terrifying thing. That instead of shooting cardboard figures we'd have to shoot our own people. And we knew, just like under Hitler, that if we refused we'd be taken off and shot ourselves.'

There was another fear too. Mielke had also told his men, 'If we lose, they'll string us all up.' The atmosphere was hysterical. Herr Bohnsack had been Markus Wolf's contact man between the Stasi and the secret services in Hungary, Moscow, Prague and Warsaw. 'Our man in Budapest had told me that in the drama of '56 his people were hanged in the trees outside their offices. He said to me, "If someone points you out, five minutes later you'll be swinging."'

Herr Bohnsack runs his hand over his head again. 'Thank God it didn't come to that,' he says. He explains that by the time the demonstrators really got going in Berlin—and it was later there than in Leipzig and elsewhere—Mielke had already stood down. And he had been there so long the generals simply did not know how to give any orders on their own. They could not seize control. 'And this is what saved us,' Bohnsack says, shaking his large head, 'us and the people.'

Somehow, back in September, it became clear to Herr Bohnsack that the files would have to be destroyed. He told his boss he was going to start shredding. 'It is not allowed!' the boss said, 'There is no order to do so!' 'But,' Herr Bohnsack says, 'I just drove my car into the yard and got the files out of the filing cabinets. There were metres and metres of them— agents' key files, films, reports—and I drove to our garden one hundred kilometres away from Berlin.' The family had an old baker's oven on its holiday plot. And then, 'totally privately and personally, without any permission and without any command,' he says, 'I destroyed everything, all day long.' There was so much paper to burn the oven nearly collapsed. A cloud of black smoke hung over him in the sky. Herr Bohnsack stood there for three days, feeding the files into the fire.

The weak afternoon light is fading and the publican comes in to turn on some lamps. He is a man of Herr Bohnsack's age, with a ravaged face, red hands and a tea towel tucked into his apron. 'Everything all right here?' he asks.

Herr Bohnsack orders another beer, another *Korn* and a coffee. I say I'm fine for the moment. Herr Bohnsack smiles gently at me. 'You, no?'

he says. 'You are utterly without need?' I glimpse beneath the genial drinker a man who was the match of anyone east or west.

Herr Bohnsack wanted to stop his files getting into the wrong hands. They concerned the western agents he ran, West German citizens who did things for the Stasi. 'In my section,' he says, 'they were all journalists. We used them to start scandals, or break open political cover-ups. We funded them, and we fed them scoops.'

The smoke attracted attention. Bohnsack's neighbour in the country, he says, was a hopeless soak. 'But of course even he had a suspicion about where I worked. We call it the *Stallgeruch* (the smell of the sty). He used to lean over the fence and slur abuse at me: "Old Shiny Bum" and "SED" and all kinds of insults. He was there again, drunk as usual while I was burning it all up. And as the smoke passed over his house he began singing the anthem of the citizens' rights movement, "*Wir Sind das Volk*". He knew exactly what I was doing. It was grotesque really,' Bohnsack chuckles, 'his aria to accompany my burning pyre.'

I look at Herr Bohnsack in all his clever dishevelment—a strand of his hair has left the rest and sticks out at an angle above his ear. He tilts his head back to drain his shot glass again. His neck is ringed and ridged, the Adam's apple moving up and down like a mouse on a ladder.

Herr Bohnsack looks around him. 'Here,' he says, 'I was always a regular. I had my spot at the bar. I have lived around the corner for thirty-eight years. Before 1989 I was always just Günter—hello how's it going. People didn't know what I did, but of course they had their suspicions. Sometimes I'd come straight from work in a tie and a stylish overcoat with a briefcase and there'd be a rumble through the pub of "doesn't he look fine".' They would have a sniff as much as to say something's not quite right here—'

He pinches his nose between forefinger and thumb. 'The Wall fell on the ninth of November 1989. The first time I came in here afterwards, I think it was the fifteenth.' He pauses, takes a drink, and a breath. 'A drunken man was at the front bar and when he saw me he swivelled around slowly, pointed at me and screamed, "Stasi out!" Everyone shut up and turned to have a look at me. They all thought the same as he, or at least half of them. I couldn't move. I said to the publican, "What do they want from me?" I said, "I can't stand here before you all and undo it, take it all back." After that I sat down. I drank a beer and I just sat there.' He draws his lips into a line and holds his hands out as if to say, 'what could I do?'

Herr Bohnsack kept coming back. It took nearly three years until no-one was aggressive any more. 'But there were no hangings or attempts or anything. In fact I was relieved, really, that the people reacted so sensibly.'

But the drinkers were not the only public. Herr Bohnsack got wind that a magazine, *Die Linke*, had managed to obtain a disk containing the names of the top-paid 20,000 Stasi employees and was about to publish it. He knew everyone would read it, find his name and address on the list and feel whatever they would feel—contempt, hatred, or self-righteousness. He knew there was only one thing for him to do. 'I would out myself before I was outed.'

He called *Der Spiegel*, the famous West German news magazine, and arranged to tell them everything. 'I really pulled my pants down, as they say,' he says. 'When I got the edition in my hand I felt sick. There was a photo and everything. I mean, when you are silent and you lie for twenty-six years and then all of a sudden you see yourself in a magazine, it was really…' He pauses again. 'I have to say it was a bit strange for me here,' he pats his heart.

Hardly any of his former colleagues will talk about what they used to do. It is almost a sort of *omerta*, a code of honour that rules them. He tells me that they still meet in groups according to rank, or at birthdays and funerals. A general who remains on speaking terms with him told him that at a recent seventieth birthday, proceedings were run like a divisional meeting from the old days. There was an agenda and the men went through it item by item. It consisted mainly of passing around clippings or reporting on television programs against the Stasi. It was as if the old Stasi leaders have now found a new enemy: the media.

And Herr Bohnsack is a traitor because he went to them with his story. After he outed himself he got death threats over the phone. 'You arsehole, how low can you go,' and these sorts of things, he says. The calls were anonymous, but sometimes he recognised the voice. A general rang him up from a pub. 'He said, "You motherfucker, that's enough, your time will come." Then he started screaming "Stop it! Stop it!" until people took him away from the phone.'

The calls have stopped now. 'I was never frightened,' Bohnsack says. 'I mean I used to check my car to see if it had been tampered with, but there's not much point doing that because if they're any good they do it so as you can't tell.'

I ask him who his friends are now.

'Well, I have none,' he says, nodding to the publican for more. He looks at me with shiny, anaesthetised eyes. 'I've fallen between two stools, you might say.'

At 3 am there's a phone call. This time it's not Klaus. It's home. They have found four tumours in my young mother's head, secondaries from a cancer we had all dared to hope was gone. She says on the phone, *'Je suis foutu, je suis foutu.'* Later what they did to her affected, for a time, her speech— and she a woman of such elegant and slicing language. But at that moment only the French would do, and she knew she was *foutu*.

Uwe is, unsurprisingly, all kindness. He helps me pack at the apartment, gathering up books and tapes and stray socks covered in dust. I am grateful for his sympathy, and more for the way he ignores, at the right moments, my distress. 'We'll take you to the airport if you like,' he says.

'Thank you.' All my reactions feel unreal, slow and underwater. 'We?'

'Frederica and me. You know Frederica. From the Spanish translation section.'

'Yes,' I lie.

I call Miriam, but I know that it's a formality. I'm not even hoping that I'll get a live voice on the line. 'Hi Miriam. I hope you're well—we seem to be missing each other a lot! My time here is up, and I'm going home.' It strikes me, suddenly, as obscene to be saying that *my* time is up. I think of saying 'I'll be back' but that might be the last thing she wants to hear. The tape is rolling—it will stretch my silence to an embarrassing length. I'd like to say something casual and ironic to cover things here, but my German doesn't reliably stretch to irony. I am forced to say things in a much more direct and heartfelt manner than I would in English. 'Miriam, look after yourself,' I say, 'and good luck.'

The morning I leave I try again and the phone rings out. The answering machine isn't even connected any more.

When they come to collect me I do recognise Frederica—she is a beautiful Venezuelan with a mole at the corner of her mouth and together she and Uwe are electric. He drives calmly to Tegel, solicitous of a world that has, finally, looked after him.

It took nine months for my mother to die, and each day except for the last three she was conscious. Conscious that the days were, as they say, numbered, and that the number was not a big one. And the feeling of being robbed of all the things you were going to do in the future, but seeing at the same time that they were not important, it was simply the future itself, a bigger number, that was.

After she died, grief came down on me like a cage. It was another eighteen months before I could focus on anything outside an immediate small area of sadness, or could imagine myself into anyone else's life. All up it was nearly three years before I came back to Berlin.

Berlin, Spring 2000

Berlin is green, a perfumed city. I realise I have never been here in full spring. Even from my old nightly flying television excursions into summer, I could never have imagined this. The trees are huge and lush, light green. Sunlight filters through them, soft and scented over the pavements and parks, squares and schools and cemeteries. Outside my windows, the chestnuts are magical. They bear white flowers in upright stacks—candelabra produced by a trick of nature. Their heady sweetness floats in the air like the memory of kinder times.

I contacted the rental agency. In a piece of freaky good luck my old apartment had, suddenly, become available. It was about to be renovated, so the students had left. 'Because of its pre-renovation condition,' the agency wrote, 'we make no assurances that the apartment is suitable, or, indeed, liveable.' I'll take my chances, I thought. I bought stationery, bed linen and a coffee maker, and moved in.

I walk through it now, folding and unfolding a copy of the letter. I sent it from Australia to her old address.

Dear Miriam,

It is some time ago now, but you might remember we spent an afternoon and evening together. Afterwards, I tried to write your story, but found I needed to explain other things around it, so the work took a course of its own. I wrote about the GDR and about the Stasi, and then I spoke with other people—some who had been followed by the Stasi, and some who had worked for them. I was trying, I think, to get a perspective on this lost world, and the kinds of courage in it.

I'm coming back to Berlin, and was wondering if we might meet again. I'd like to ask you whether you have got any further with the DA in Dresden, and whether the puzzle women in Nuremberg have discovered any news about Charlie. I want to make sure, too, that I have everything right.

I am sorry I have been such a long time coming back to you. I have been working on this only on and off.

I'm looking forward to summer in Berlin, and, perhaps, to visiting Leipzig…

No reply came, but the letter didn't return to me either. Before I left, I emailed Julia too. She wrote back in English:

Hi Anna

Good to hear from you! I am in San Francisco—I left Berlin 8 months ago for the States. I was just living with too many things from my past that could come find me there.

I am 'doing great' as they say here. I am working in a feminist bookshop near Berkeley, and have made some friends. We went on a 'Reclaim the Night' march recently, something that made me feel real positive, and far away from Thüringen and everything that happened here. They honour their victims here—really, everyone seems to have a story of something that happened to them. I'm sure it could go too far, but for me, now, it is a good thing.

I am foreign here and speak with an accent but am much more at home than in my own country! Funny, no?

If you're ever through San Fran, please let me know.

Julia :)

The apartment is not much changed. Such a rock-bottom flat, it would have been hard to denude it further. In fact, it is the additions that are most noticeable. There is a line of postcards pinned up on the wall and over the ceiling of the living room. They suggest travel, but are souvenirs only of pub crawls through the city—they are the free ones with advertising on them. In the kitchen there is a jar of scrawny but cheery dried lavender. And in the bedroom a large drawing of a mushroom in magic marker has appeared on the wall. The mushroom has two cross-hatched windows on its cap for eyes, and a door in the stem. It also has a wide smile on its face (the door is a big tooth), because this mushroom head is also a penis, and it is coming all up the bedroom wall.

The first morning I get up and take my coffee across the road to the park. It's very early but light already, an exquisite day. The sky is blue-white, the air still and new and the streets are hushed. The park is a sweeping curve of green up to the café, shuttered over like eyelids. At the bottom lies the pond, which I knew before as a black and dead thing. Now, waterlilies float in it, opening up to touch the sun. Somewhere near, a small band of frogs ushers in the day.

I sit on one of the benches and look up at the statue of Heine. I never spent time here before; the seats seemed always to be occupied. Instead of a poet's hands, the East German sculptor has given Heine big workman's paddles. The quote reads:

We don't catch hold of an idea, rather the idea catches hold of us and enslaves us and whips us into the arena so that we, forced to be gladiators, fight for it.

Heine, the free-thinking poet, would be turning in his grave to see the sort of enslaving and forcing and fighting that has gone on here, under his cold black nose and pigeon-shit shoulders.

Shapes catch my eye behind the statue. Two men are shuffling in, one from up the hill and one from the corner below, in suits and slippers with tins of beer in their pockets. Another three appear and take their places on the benches. A couple of them carry cloth shopping bags full of cans; one is wearing a medal on a ribbon around his neck like a lord mayor. Once everyone is settled (am I in someone's place?—they are leaving a whole bench for me) there are polite greetings and handshakes all round, and nods to me. It is as if we were in someone's living room.

One old fellow kneels on his bench to face over the park. He takes out two slices of white bread and breaks them, with shaky hands, into even-sized pieces. Instead of throwing them, he lays out a pattern in crumbs on the concrete rampart behind the seat, each piece equidistant from the others. Some kind of madness, some kind of generosity.

A man jogs past in yellow shorts and a bandana. The drunks greet him in chorus. '*Morgen!*'

'*Morgen!*' he puffs back.

These park men are the gatekeepers here, suited and tracksuited sphinxes.

Sparrows and pigeons start to fly in for the bread and suddenly I understand my companion's ceremonial care. We are now the central focus of the park: nature comes to us in small-winged genuflections at this altar of bread and beer.

A latecomer walks up to the group in black training pants. His legs are stilts inside the synthetic material. He's slightly younger than the others, his hair dark and slicked back. He carries a sports bag full of beer.

'Harry! Mate! Long time no see,' says the man with the medal. The medal rests on his bare belly. He is wearing a suitcoat with no shirt and red braces over his skin to hold his pants up.

'I been away.'

'Where you been?'

'On holiday.'

'You been on holiday? *Mensch!* I need a holiday. Where d'you go?'

'Mexico.'

I feel a laugh forming, but the others are nodding solemnly.

'What you been doing over there then?'

'Huntin'.'

'Ahha,' the lord mayor nods. 'Good huntin' in Mexico?'

'The best.'

'What d'you hunt then, in Mexico?'

'Elephants.'

No-one bats an eye. 'Any luck?'

'Naah…' Harry shakes his head, sits down and zips open his bag to get into the day's drinking. Perhaps this is really a society of poets and priests where all stories are metaphorical. Or perhaps reality has been so strange here that anything else is welcome to take its place.

The man with the medal turns to me and raises his can. 'Cheers,' he says.

'Cheers.' I lift my mug.

'Healthier than beer,' he grins. He is missing two front teeth.

'But not as much fun.' I smile back.

He takes this as an invitation and comes to sit on my bench. 'You're not from around here,' he says, reaching into his pocket for a tin of tobacco.

'No.'

'You from Cologne?'

'No. I'm—'

'Lemme guess. Hamburg?'

'No, I'm from Australia.'

'Oh,' he says. He leans in to me and puts a large hand with curved brown fingernails on my knee. 'Don't worry about it,' he breathes, 'I too have impure blood.'

I'm smiling, astonished. 'How's that?'

'My mother was a Pole.'

'Oh.'

He starts rolling a cigarette. His grey hair is brylcreemed into a neat duck's tail. His moustache is stained brown where he sucks the cigarette. When he puts it in his mouth he can keep talking hands-free, the cigarette clinging mysteriously to his bottom lip.

'You like this park?' he asks.

'Yes, very much.'

'This park is good, but you should come mushrooming with us sometime. That's the best.'

'Really? Where do you go?'

'We all get on the train, me and some of my friends there.' He gestures to the others who have been watching us intently, but now turn quickly back to their business. 'We go out to the end of the line with our baskets and gather mushrooms. It's fantastic!'

I'm wondering whether he's having me on, painting a picture of train-riding drunks springing sprightly through the forests with their baskets and beer, plucking dainty mushrooms as they go, waving at the elephants. But he's not.

'We get,' and he lists the species, '*Steinpilze*, *Pfifferlinge*, *Maron*, *Bergenpilze*, *Butterpilze*, *Sandpilze*—they are yellow underneath and spongy. *Rotkappe*—they look like *Fliegenpilze* but aren't, and—', something I don't quite catch, 'but you mustn't take them, because those you can only eat once!' He laughs, throwing his head back so I see an expanse of gum and ridged palate like an underwater thing. 'We get four kilos in each basket, and we come home and cook them up with a little butter—superb!' He waves a forefinger in front of me. 'You know,' he says, bringing the finger to his chest, 'when it comes to mushrooms, in that field I am a professor!'

Professor Mushroom's medal wobbles a little, blinking in the light on his stomach. A mumbled chorus of approval comes from the other benches; his friends raise their cans to him. I'm glad to be here. It strikes me as absurd to have never spoken with these men before who have been, after all, my neighbours.

He continues with some advice. 'You've got to get outdoors,' he says.

'You know, television is not good for the eyes. Not healthy.' I wonder if he was somehow watching over me that winter, seeing the flickering black and white at my window. Maybe these men, stationed in parks and on street corners, at tramstops and in the underground, are the ones who see everything now. A woman walks past on her way to the lights, and he lifts his hand in greeting, or to let her pass.

'Back in the GDR I was a tailor. Now that's not good for the eyes either. I wanted to be an actor or a cook, but it didn't happen.' I think he has become both, with this performance and his sautéed mushrooms. 'Until 1990 I was in the voluntary fire brigade, but then it all went to hell in a handcart. This *Kapitalismus*, you can't imagine the sort of shit it's building.' He sniffs and spits onto the ground. Then he reaches into his pocket and pulls out a comb. 'It was so much better before. I'm in the same flat—then it cost me 450 marks a month, and now it's 804! So what if we didn't have bananas and mandarins! It doesn't take a banana to turn me on!' He runs the comb carefully through his coiffure. 'I used to be able to get five kilos of potatoes for next to nothing, beer was fifty pfennig a can and now what? Transport was thirty pfennig and twenty on Fridays. I mean we had a social state—you didn't even have to pay for medicine. I tell you I just don't get it. It's all stupid now.' I glimpse past him and see that his friends are nodding in silent, unsteady agreement.

I have heard this kind of thing before, though ex-Stasi men, privileged left-wing intellectuals or former Party members complain more about airfares: 'What good is freedom to travel when I can't afford to go to New York/Las Palmas/New Zealand for my holiday?' Once in Leipzig, an old woman in a pub, drinking her daily schnapps at four in the afternoon, said to me, 'Well, this is better than the Weimar Republic and better than the Nazis but bring back the Communists, is what I say. The pubs were fuller under Honecker. Cheers.' I don't doubt this genuine nostalgia, but I think it has coloured a cheap and nasty world golden; a world where there was nothing to buy, nowhere to go and anyone who wanted to do anything with their lives other than serve the

Party risked persecution, or worse.

The morning has come alive now, insects dance over the grass and pollen hangs in the light as people walk through the park to Rosenthaler Platz station. Professor Mushroom is on a roll. 'Back then when you were drunk the police would just take you under the arms and set you down on a bench. Now, we can't even sleep here any more or we'd get robbed! It's terrible the morals these days. Do you know you can get mugged for one cigarette! It's the Russian mafia and the Romanians and the gypsies. If a gypsy woman came and danced on this bench, I tell you your wallet would be gone in a flash!'

This complaint, too, I have heard before in different versions: an ache for a lost time when things were more secure. In a security state, after all, the least the authorities could do when they were incarcerating so many innocents was to clean up the criminals at the same time.

'Look, 200 metres over there'—Professor Mushroom extends his arm and I see a swathe of grey chest hair between his braces—'was the Wall. Before we had that, the Wessis flocked over here and bought up all our stuff! We put up the Wall so we could go shopping in our own shops! In the end though, they pulled the Wall down and bought us all up anyway, those Wessis with their western money—all the factories and businesses and even the pubs. And they won't let us hold our heads high now—oh no!

'I'll tell you honestly about the border.' He pats my knee again. 'And I am an honest man. We all knew, every GDR citizen knew, that if you went close to it, you'd be shot! That's all there was to it! So we stayed here! I mean they should have all sat here on their arses—then they wouldn't have got them shot full of lead!'

I know this argument as well: if you didn't buck the system, then it wouldn't harm you.

But, from what I have seen, it probably would.

The professor shakes my hand. 'You really should come mushroom-ing with us,' he says. The chorus rumbles and nods and I thank them and go, up to my palace of light and air and lino.

26

The Wall

In this soft spring I have taken to walking everywhere. It's about 10 pm, and the sun has only just set. Cherry trees lining the streets scatter pips and juice stains over the pavement like blood. I walk home past the outdoor cafés at Kollwitzplatz where students, largely from the west, sit eating and laughing. I'm not sure how much they know of what has gone on in this place. I'm dreaming at the kerb as a woman in a jester's cap and short shorts nearly clips my ear as she cycles past.

By the time I turn into my street the sky is black. A man is hunched unsteadily against my building, banging along it like a fly at a window. In the darkness he is more a shape than a person, an outline with a bottle in his hand. He is drunk—very drunk. When I get closer he reaches towards me and speaks, but it's not clear whether he's addressing me or the universe.

'I don't want to be German any more!' he sobs. 'I don't want to be German any more!' His face is tracked with silver tears.

'Why not?' I hold out a hand to steady him.

'We are terrible.' He has hardly looked at me. He couldn't know I'm not German. 'They are terrible. The Germans are terrible.'

He moves off, tapping his way along the buildings.

Which Germans did he mean? Some, or all? For this East German man, long used to thinking the bad Germans were on the other side of the Wall, maybe now it's hard to tell. Are they really so bad? Or are they worse than he thought? And were his people, now broke or drunk, shamed or fled or imprisoned or dead, any good at all?

A friend of mine who works at the File Authority calls me up.

'We had an interesting request here for a personal file yesterday,' he says. 'I thought I'd let you know.'

'Who was it?'

'Mr Mielke.' My friend chuckles. We both know without saying: Mielke must think the apparatus he created was so thorough, with an administrative impetus all of its own, that somewhere, someone was keeping tabs on him.

A few days later I call Frau Paul. We chat for a while. She is active in an organisation for those persecuted by the regime—taking tours of Hohenschönhausen prison ('we're thinking of putting a coffee shop in there,' she tells me), and campaigning for compensation for victims. Then she says, 'There's something else.'

'Yes?'

'I was followed home the other evening, from a public meeting on compensation.'

'What?'

'It's true. A car followed me to the underground at walking pace. I was with friends and I didn't think much about it. But when I got out of the train at Elsterwerdaer Platz I was alone and it was there waiting for me. Then it followed the bus. When I got off the bus it turned its lights off, and drove behind me right to my door.'

'That's horrible.'

'Yes,' she says, 'there are a lot of people who don't want us to raise our voices, to fight for what we deserve.'

'Do you have any idea who it was?'

'No. But it was almost certainly an ex-Stasi man.' She is frightened, but she is steely. 'It was a Volvo,' she says. 'I'm looking for a Volvo driver.'

Mielke died this week. He was ninety-two. The headlines read, 'Most hated man now dead.' I think of the other 'most hated man' and give him a call. His wife answers the phone and passes me to her husband. Karl-Eduard von Schnitzler tells me he's not well, and that things are getting worse. By 'things', he means the world around him. 'People are still spreading lies about my dear friend Erich Mielke and he's under the ground! On Monday the urn was interred and on Tuesday it was desecrated! Right under the noses of the police guarding it! Do you understand? My friend's ashes were scattered and his grave plot was de-se-cra-ted!' His voice is exactly the same: hoarse, old and angry. 'That is capitalism, naked and brutal! An absolute *Unkultur*.'

The desecration of Mielke's grave is unlikely to have been the work of westerners, and it is only a product of capitalism in that capitalism does not protect, or not adequately to his mind, the former leadership of the former GDR from what their people thought of them. I hear fear though in his voice, the flipside of fury. Fear perhaps that his end, soon to come, will also be a desecrated grave. Then I remember his conviction to the cause. I think he may not be so much afraid of death itself but that it will eliminate, finally, his powers of rebuttal.

Today I walk from my place up Brunnenstrasse, past Frau Paul's tunnel to Bernauer Strasse where the Wall was. There is a new museum here. Its greatest exhibit is opposite: a full-size reconstructed section of the Wall, complete with freshly built and neatly raked death strip, for tourists. Right alongside it in Bernauer Strasse there are still some pieces of the real Wall, covered, as they always were on the western side, with bright graffiti. These remnants are behind bushes though, scrappy and crumbling. In some places the steel reinforcements in the concrete are bare as bones.

The new Wall, however, is pristine. It is utterly without grafitti. I can understand why the original has all but disappeared, and why, as Frau Paul and Torsten said, people wanted it to. But this new one is a sanitised Disney version; it is history, airbrushed for effect.

Inside the museum there are displays and touch-screen presentations showing how the Wall was built, recordings of Kennedy's '*Ick bin ein Berliner*' speech, and dramatisations of various escape attempts. 'Yes, yes, yes,' a man with his back to me is saying to another man behind the counter, 'I'll take them from here and bring them back here. I think it'll take about two hours. That's what I'm going to check now.'

'Right then,' the other man says, then he looks over at me. He is wearing fancy eyeglasses that appear to be held together by a row of miniature, multicoloured clothes pegs. 'Can I help you?'

The man standing at the counter turns around to have a look at me. 'Frau Funder!' he cries. It is Hagen Koch. 'Well, well, well! How are you? Yes! You might like to come with me!' He speaks in exclamation marks. It is as if I have hardly been away. For him the past is the Wall, and I am part of the present, whether three years ago or now. His hair has turned white, but his eyes are the same bright and smiley brown.

'Herr Koch, I'm well, thank you. Come where?'

'I'm taking a busload of tourists tomorrow along the route where the Wall was, because you can hardly tell any more. I'm off now to check how long it will take.'

'I'd love to come.'

We are to drive along the municipal boundary where the Wall was built: in a ring around the old city centre in the east, and past the western suburbs of Wedding, Moabit and Tiergarten. Then, he says, we will drive where the Wall went right through the centre of town, down Niederkirchnerstrasse through to the Spree River, and along its bank to the Oberbaum Bridge.

We climb into his small red car and he drives fast and sure. He is happy to have an audience to rehearse his 'tour of the forgotten city' routine. The first stop is just down the street, a stretch of grass maybe a hundred metres wide. Straggly weeds grow to knee-height, sway like sentient things in the warm air. There's a cemetery behind here. A large stone angel on a pedestal is turned this way, her head bent low in prayer. We walk out to the middle. The sky seems wide in this place.

'This was the death strip'—Herr Koch holds his arms out—'but before that the cemetery extended to the street. When they built the Wall they had to dig up the bodies and take away the gravestones.' He raises his eyebrows, 'The guards used to get a bit spooked by that.' Apparently, the border guards working on the death strip preferred no evidence of death in it.

Herr Koch is pleased to be with someone who shares his interest in the Wall. He is also, perhaps, even more obsessed with it than I remember. He seems to have lost the awareness that his is a particular interest. He is, once more, a true believer: the Wall is the thing that defined him, and he will not let it go. I think for a moment of Frau Paul, who will also not let it go. Herr Koch starts to take photographs. I look up at the angel's long face and I think of Miriam and Julia; lives shaped, too, by the Wall. Will they let it go? Or, will it let them go?

Our next stop is the Schiffahrtskanal. Herr Koch is excited, speaking fast. We park outside a new housing development. The apartments are fresh and brightly coloured. They are arranged around a courtyard in the usual Berlin style but, in a startling departure from tradition, there's an original, two-storey East German guard tower in the middle of the yard. Herr Koch gestures towards it. 'This,' he says, proudly, 'is my tower.'

For a moment he's so pleased he's speechless.

I gaze at the thing. It is, unmistakably, an old guard tower from the death strip. It has square cement walls and windows up high to see in all directions. On the top there's a fenced area the guards could shoot from. It is hardly a thing of joy, but Herr Koch's face is shiny with delight.

'Your tower?'

'My tower.'

He explains that at the end of 1989 in his capacity as a cultural officer with the Stasi, he took it upon himself to be responsible for '*Denkmalschutz*' or the preservation of historical monuments. He found a lot of little white-and-blue 'national heritage' enamel plaques, and in the chaos of those last days he went around screwing them into things precious to him like the Wall, the boom gates at Checkpoint Charlie and guard towers. Most of them were pulled down despite his efforts.

This tower here, he says, gave him a lot of trouble, particularly when the developers came in to build the apartments. 'So what did I do?'

I look back at him. I cannot imagine.

'I found a homeless man, and installed him in it! And I gave him money and a job—to renovate the tower! They couldn't pull it down because it was inhabited!'

I see that over the door someone has hand-painted an address: Kieler Strasse 2. We enter and, sure enough, a modern white-tiled bathroom is being installed downstairs. 'Unfortunately,' Herr Koch says, 'my tenant died.' We climb a ladder to the top, where the guards worked. The tower is crumbling and smells of wet concrete, but I enjoy the thought that the previous tenant, an old eastern streetperson, would have lapped up the view from here, where before the guards had watched over him.

Herr Koch says, 'But I think it is saved now. They had to build the apartments around it. The tenants didn't like it at first, but I've been talking to them, and as time goes on they appreciate its historical significance more and more.' He takes a dustpan and brush, and sweeps up proprietorially before we leave.

We drive into town, past the Bundestag, the Reichstag and Potsdamer Platz. At a set of lights I see a bollard with a poster of Renft promoting their current tour of the old East Germany. I enjoy the thought of Klaus strutting his stuff, blossomed once more into his rock star being. We stop in an ordinary street.

'See?' Herr Koch says, opening up his arms. I look around. There's nothing to see.

'You can't see! You can't see where the Wall went at all!' He's right, there's no sign of it left, no bits of concrete, no wasteland.

'Look down here though.' He points to the ground. A narrow strip of granite is inlaid in the pavement, slightly darker grey than the footpath itself. 'That's all there is!' he cries. 'It used to be a red line, but even that was thought too obvious, so they came up with this instead. And what's more, in the places where it does say, "Berliner Mauer 1961–1989" it's written to be read from the western side. For us easterners it's upside down!'

As we get back in the car he says, 'I am the only person who is keeping alive the sense of the Wall from the eastern side. If there is one thing my life has taught me, it is that one must not see things just from one side! People don't like me for it, but it must be done!' Herr Koch is a lone crusader against forgetting.

We drive along Zimmerstrasse away from the centre to Bethaniendamm. It is a scrawny part of town. There are more new brightly painted apartments on one side, and grey cement buildings on the other. In between there's what looks at first like an empty lot, fenced in with wire mesh and boards and sticks. Behind the fence someone has planted potatoes and eggplants in neat rows, and tomatoes on stakes. But I'm still not sure what we're looking at. 'These,' Herr Koch says, 'are the Turkish onions.'

He takes me around the fenced area, a small triangle of land. There is an elaborate three-storey shack at one end made of pieces of fibroboard, crates and a ladder, with a grapevine climbing over it. Outside it there's an old couch and chairs, and at the other end of the plot a child's wooden swing hangs from a tree, painted red and yellow.

Herr Koch says that this land was, strictly speaking, in the eastern zone, but that it was too hard to build a bend in the Wall to include it, so the Wall went straight along the nearest street, leaving this island of land out in the west. No-one in West Berlin knew what to do with it; it could not be resumed for any purpose without antagonising the eastern regime. It was, literally, no-man's land. Eventually, a Turkish family simply fenced it off and planted vegetables. When the Wall came down, no-one seemed to have a claim, so they are gardening here still. I gaze through the fence. There's an apricot tree, and a large oak at the end. I imagine great family working bees; grandma on the couch, the kids on the swing and the smell of coffee from the summer palace at the end.

'But you know what happened,' Koch says. I turn back to him. 'The family eventually fought—it was two brothers, I think. They fought so badly that in the end all they could do was to put a fence down the middle of the garden and split it into two separate zones!' His face is alive with the irony of it. 'Come here, look.' We walk to the middle where a two-metre-high cyclone fence runs right through the little field, separating the part with the hut from the part with the swing, and no way of going between.

Our last stop is at the Oberbaum Bridge. Berlin is a wasteland here, where the tram lines between east and west have only recently been knitted back together. The longest strip of remaining Wall is along this river-bank—more because it was forgotten than deliberately preserved. At the end of it are what look like, at first glance, a small array of circus tents. As we approach I see they are a couple of souvenir stalls, with flags flying atop and signs in English saying 'Souvenirs for You' and 'I Stamp Your Passport'. For one mark you can have your passport stamped with a GDR entry visa, as if you had stepped into this tent and miraculously been admitted to that place in the past. Elderly American tourists are climbing out of a bus. They seem to match—in pressed pale clothes and overly clean running shoes. 'Betty,' one woman asks another in a broad southern accent, 'is that the same jacket you were wearing that day at Auschwitz?'

Herr Koch bounces into the main stall. 'Gerd!' he cries.

'Hagen, my friend!' The stallkeeper jumps up and runs from behind his wares to greet him. Herr Koch introduces me. Gerd is a suntanned man of sixty wearing a blue shirt unbuttoned to the navel and a smile with the wattage of a vaudevillian. Herr Koch later told me he had been a theatre actor in the east.

Gerd's stall is a reliquary of his country's memorabilia. He has Russian and GDR soldiers' caps; Russian medals issued as reward for service in the Berlin invasion of 1945 ('genuine, genuine,' he says winningly); old enamel signs that read, 'You are leaving the American Sector' in English, Russian, French and German and 'Beware—Mines! Closed Area: Danger to Life!' He has matchbox-sized Trabant cars, teddy bears, bottle openers, car stickers and coffee mugs; and on one side of the stall in tiny pigeonholes he has lots and lots of pieces of Wall.

'You must take this as a gift from me,' he says, and he presses a piece of the Wall into my palm. It is in a small plastic bag, complete with a 'Certificate of Authenticity'. It looks like a forensic sample. The two of them are staring at me, grinning and excited. I fear at any moment they will break into song.

'How do you know this is genuine?' I ask.

'Oh, it's genuine,' Gerd says, twinkling like a daytime television host.

There have probably been enough 'genuine' fragments of the Wall sold to build it twice over. Herr Koch leans in, as always, interested in the documents. 'Look,' he says, 'there's a certificate to prove it.'

I thank them both and walk up to the new tramstop at Warschauer Strasse. When I look back, I see Herr Koch has corralled the tourists, and is giving them his side of history.

27

Puzzlers

I catch the train to Nuremberg. When I arrive, I drink an espresso standing up at a bar in the station. A beautiful young woman wearing a fast-food wimple is serving behind the counter. The man next to me orders a *Riesenbockwurst*. The barmaid reaches first for potato salad and a bun, and then the boiled sausage. 'Mustard or ketchup?' She holds the paper plate high for an answer, reaching with her free hand above the bar to where the bottles would normally be, upturned for nips. Instead, there hangs a giant yellow rubber udder. The barmaid does a neat squeeze-and-twist action on one of the teats, milking it for mustard.

Booking my ticket, I thought of Uwe and Scheller and our puzzle women conversation so long ago. I called Uwe at the television station to catch up, and to tell him I've come full circle. A former colleague answered the phone. He said Uwe took a promotion to be roving correspondent in the United States, and that he and Frederica and little Lucas were now happily ensconced in Washington. I asked him to pass on my best.

The Stasi File Authority office where the puzzle women are housed is in Zirndorf, a village outside Nuremberg. The office is in the same walled compound where asylum seekers are being kept. Two Ethiopians, or perhaps Eritreans, men with sad biblical faces and aimless arms, walk about the outdoor area.

The director, Herr Raillard, meets me at the entrance and we go upstairs to his office. It is a plain administrative building that smells of floor wax and wet cardboard. Herr Raillard is a compact man with straight white hair to his shoulders and small glasses. He is an archivist.

I am nervous as a cat. I am in an unaccountable hurry. I have been thinking about this place for so long as the focus of Miriam's hopes; I want there to be stainless steel benches and people wearing hair nets and white cloth gloves. I want security guards on the entrances and cameras in the workrooms. I want the completed puzzle pages to be scanned into computers, correlated to the files they belong to and for the people they affect to be called up by sensitive, trained personnel and informed about the new links in their lives.

I want them to find out what happened to Charlie Weber.

I am sure Herr Raillard has things to do but his desk is uncluttered and he gives me the impression of having cleared the agenda for our meeting today. He is a quiet and unassuming man, who made his career in the West German archives at Koblenz, and he is now looking forward to retirement. 'Yes,' he says, 'I'll be sixty-three shortly,' as if to say, 'and I'm out of here.'

He tells me that this work started in 1995, after the sacks of material had sat around in Berlin for five years. Fifteen thousand sacks were found at Normannenstrasse in January 1990. They contained shredded and hand-ripped files, index cards, photos and unwound tapes and film.

Herr Raillard has arranged for me to take coffee with some of the workers. I am keen to meet the puzzle people. I ask him how many there are, and whether they are all women, as I have heard. 'Oh no,' he says, 'but there are probably more women than men.' He is cautious and exact, and asks his secretary to check the numbers. She comes back with a note: eighteen women and thirteen men.

First, we go down the hall to see the workrooms. On the way, he tells me there has been some controversy because the victims want the work here to go more quickly. A computer program exists that could make this happen; it puts a lot of the pieces together very fast, based on a scan of the exact shape of the ripped edge. But, Herr Raillard says, for the purposes of evidence the documents reconstituted by computer do not count as originals. This doesn't make much sense to me, because generally people don't bring cases, they just want to know what happened in their lives. 'And it would be very expensive,' he adds. That is more likely why it's not in use.

The door opens onto an ordinary office; my eyes take in potted plants and old paint on the walls and a poster of glassy-eyed kittens tangled in wool. There is a large desk with an empty chair behind it. 'Must be on a break,' Herr Raillard says, gesturing towards the chair. But I am only half listening. The window is wide open, a white curtain moves in the breeze and I am panicked, my heart climbing steps up my chest, because on the desk there are masses and masses of tiny pieces of paper—some in small stacks but others spread out all over. There are so many tatters of paper that the desk is not big enough, and the worker has started to lay them out on top of the filing cabinet as well. The pieces are different sizes, from a fifth of an A4 page to only a couple of centimetres square—and there is nothing to stop them flying around the room and out of the window.

Herr Raillard misreads my face. 'Yes, it's a lot of work, as you can see,' he says.

The next room is similar. This person, also on a break, seems to be sorting the material from the sacks first into cut-off cardboard boxes and then all over the desk. A woman's eye from a torn photograph looks out at me from one of the boxes; on the table I glimpse the name of the writer Lutz Rathenow on a shred of paper. There's a roll of double-sided sticky tape near the chair and a partially completed page in front of it: a corner, and the left-hand edge.

In the next room the pieces are even smaller. 'It's painstaking work,' Herr Raillard says, 'the most pieces in one page so far has been ninety-eight.' This person has nearly completed a sheaf of pages that rest in an open manila folder. The pages are all there, piled on top of each other except for a piece or pieces missing in the middle, making a neat hole. 'It takes brute strength to tear that many pages at once.' Herr Raillard shakes his head. 'That Stasi man would have hardly been able to move his fingers the next day.'

On the way to meet the workers, I ask Herr Raillard about security. He tells me that everyone who works here, including the cleaning staff, is checked to make sure they have not had any involvement with the Stasi in the past, even though they are all westerners. He says his workers are told not to speak about the content of the files they piece together. Sometimes this needs to be stressed. 'If they find, say, a file on an important West German politician, then I'll go in and have a word and remind them not to mention it at all,' he says. I ask about electronic surveillance of the rooms, because I imagine there are people out there who would pay a high price to stop some of this information coming to light. 'No, no,' Herr Raillard says, 'sometimes they sit two to a room. But that's more to alleviate boredom than anything else. And I make sure I put the alarm on when I leave of an evening.' This is not what I expected. It is friendly and small and low-key. It is something between a hobby farm for jigsaw enthusiasts and a sheltered workshop for obsessives.

Herr Raillard introduces me and leaves. There are three women and two men sitting at a table with fruit juice, biscuits and a thermos of coffee on it. They have left room for me at the head of the table. The two women on my right are both plump, made-up and middle-aged. On my left there's a young woman with freckles and shoulder-length dark hair, next to her a small brown-haired man with glasses, and at the end a large gentle-looking fellow with fair hair and eyes as blue as marbles. I ask them how they go about their work each day.

The furthest middle-aged woman says, 'It's really just like a puzzle at home. You start with the corners, and fill in the rest from the shape of the edges. We get clues too from the sort of paper it is, the typeface or handwriting and so on.'

'Do you do puzzles at home?' I ask her.

'Yes!' she says, 'I must be crazy.' They all laugh.

The woman next to her started here only two months ago. She has painted nails and a gap between her two front teeth. 'They opened a sack to show me and I saw the really tiny pieces inside and I thought, Oh my God, I can't do that.' The sacks are over a metre tall and paunchy as a person. 'But every sack is different,' she says, 'and I have to say there are things that are interesting.'

The dark man appears to be the most senior person here. He has deep-set eyes and a calm voice. The others listen closely when he speaks. He says, 'Sometimes the satisfaction is in knowing that when people find out what happened to them it might give them some peace of mind—why they lost their place at the university, or what happened to the uncle who disappeared or whatever. It gives those affected an insight into their own lives.'

The others pour coffee and pass long-life milk down the table. I imagine getting more news about myself from a file. You would come to think of your past as a landscape you travelled through without noticing the signs.

'I think at the end the Stasi had so much information,' the fair man says, 'that they thought everyone was an enemy, because everyone was under observation. I don't think they knew who was for them, or against, or whether everyone was just shutting up.' He is shy and looks at his hands, closed around his coffee mug, when he speaks. 'When I find a file where they've been watching a family in their living room for twenty years I ask myself: what sort of people are they who want all this knowledge for themselves?'

'Are you moved by what you find sometimes?' I ask.

The young woman answers, 'When I find love letters I think, good grief, they really opened everything—and how many hands did these pass through? How many times were they copied? I'd hate for that to have happened to me. I don't feel too good about seeing them myself when I piece them together.'

The dark man says he is most shocked by how the Stasi used people's own distress against them. 'When they were in prison, for instance, offering to let them out on condition that they spy for the Stasi.' I think of Koch's father having to change political parties or be exiled to a Russian camp, or Frau Paul, who could have been bait in a trap to catch a westerner, and even of Julia, imprisoned in her country and offered freedom within it only if she would inform on the people in her life. I think of the generational cycles of tragedy the Germans have been inflicting on themselves.

'But this is not about the individuals,' the dark man continues. 'It is about a system that so manipulated people that it drove them to do these things. It shows how people can be used against one another. I'm reluctant to condemn them because the Stasi were also manipulated, they too needed jobs.' The others are nodding. 'On the other hand,' he says, 'there were lots of people who just said no. Not everyone can be bought.' He tells of an engineer who refused to inform, 'And nothing more happened to him. The file was simply closed.'

I am reminded of the story of a factory worker who, after she was approached to inform, announced loudly the next day at the canteen table, 'Guess what! You wouldn't credit it, but *they* think me so reliable that I've been asked to inform!' Her cover blown, she was useless and she was left alone.

The young woman says, 'I think there were advantages over there, that we forget, particularly for mothers and children. I'm a single mum and I know what I'm talking about. I had to work, and it was hard to find a kindergarten place. I have a friend who lived over there and she says she didn't want for anything…'

'And rents were lower,' the gap-toothed woman on my right adds.

'The kindergartens were there,' the dark man says, 'because they wanted to get to the children early to bring them up loyal to the state.'

'Sure,' the young mother says. 'But it all became crudely clear to me just after the Wall came down. I met a couple in the street who'd just come over from the east and had no money and nowhere to go, so I said they could stay with me. They were with me for a weekend and I showed them around. We went to Karstadt department store and looked in the food section. They were beside themselves. "How many kinds of ketchup do you have?" they said as they looked at the shelves. Then I thought to myself, it really is too much—there must be a middle way. Do we really need thirty different kinds of ham and fifteen kinds of ketchup?'

'The mistake the GDR made was to force people into a position,' the dark man says, 'either you are for us or an enemy. And if you then came to think of yourself as an enemy you had to ask yourself: what am I doing here? They wanted to put everything into their narrow schema, but life simply didn't fit into it.' He pauses, and the others wait for him to finish. 'I think we need to remember that they came here for the freedom, not for fifteen kinds of ketchup.'

Herr Raillard sees me out. I check with him what the consequences were when someone who had been approached to inform either told people about it or flatly refused. 'There really were no consequences,' he says. 'That was the thing. The file was just closed, marked "*dekonspiriert*". But of course,' he adds, 'no-one could know at the time that nothing would happen to him. So hardly anyone refused.'

We have reached the door. He says, 'There is something I need to give you.' Without a word he passes me a photocopied sheet of paper with some writing on it. It is a copy of a memo he wrote:

Stasi File Authority—Project Group Reconstruction

Time required for the Reconstruction:
1 worker reconstructs on average 10 pages per day

40 workers reconstruct on average 400 pages per day
40 workers reconstruct on average in a year of 250 working days
    100,000 pages
There are, on average 2,500 pages in one sack
100,000 pages amounts to 40 sacks per year
In all, at the Stasi File Authority there are 15,000 sacks
This means that to reconstruct everything it would take 40 workers
    375 years.

I am speechless. I can only understand this as a small paper protest.
Herr Raillard points at the page. 'These are the figures for forty workers,'
he says. 'As you see, we only have thirty-one.' He is telling me, in his quiet
way, that the resources united Germany is throwing at this part of reconstructing the lives of its former East German citizens are pitiful, some kind
of Sisyphean joke. What he is running here is an almost totally symbolic
act.

Herr Raillard has organised a driver to take me from Zirndorf back
to Nuremberg. The day is a clear sunny blue. Away from the asylum
seekers and scraps of paper, everything is bright and cheerful.

I look out the window, thinking about Miriam and her hopes that the
torn-apart pieces of her life will be put back together in those airy rooms,
some time in the next 375 years.

Miriam and Charlie

The train back to Berlin passes through Leipzig, and I get off.

It's morning, the air is still with a silken warmth that will work itself into something real by midday. Last time the station was being renovated; it is now part of a three-storey shopping mall in a vast atrium. Escalators move people up and down between levels. Near the exit there's a display of photographs of the demonstrations ten years ago. The sign over them reads: 'Leipzig. City of Heroes.' I'm not sure what I'm doing here.

I wander through town. Most of the cranes are gone. New facades of buildings in sun-yellow and dusky pink, some even gilded, have been revealed from behind scaffolding. I walk past the town hall, and past Auerbach's Cellar. Next door a new museum has been inserted into the old streetscape: the Contemporary History Forum Leipzig. The inside is all terrazzo flooring and expensive fittings. This, it turns out, is the federally funded effort to put the history of the separation of Germany behind glass.

There are the famous pictures of the Wall being built: an eastern soldier deciding to make a run for it to the west, parting the barbed wire with his hands; and Peter Fechter, the eighteen-year-old shot trying to escape in 1962 and left to die on the death strip, because each side thought the other would retaliate if they went to help him. Someone has thrown him a roll of bandages, but he lies immobile and bleeding. There are pictures of people coming out of a tunnel in West Berlin—the successful group before Frau Paul tried, and there's a grey paddy wagon parked inside here, exactly the same as the one in which she was transported to her trial. A TV monitor shows Karl-Eduard von Schnitzler in his acidic prime. I come to the seventies, and find a glass case with a display of Renft memorabilia: records, Klaus's old guitar and pictures of the band, its hairy bellbottomed members looking both innocent and louche.

I am the only visitor. The attendants are eager to make eye-contact and chat, bored as bats. Perhaps because of all the money poured into this, the things behind the spanking displays look old and crummy, like articles from a time that has been left behind. I slap down the stairs in my sandals. I am annoyed that this past can look so tawdry and so safe, as if destined from the outset to end up behind glass, securely roped off and under press-button control. And I am annoyed at myself: what's the problem? Isn't a museum the place for things that are over?

It's a fair walk from here but I think I remember the way, so I set off for the Runden Ecke. I hope it's still there, that this slick western-funded version is not all that remains of East Germany. I know that on the outskirts of town there are the usual socialist high-rises, but here the streets are cobbled and the buildings are grand. Carved faces stare down from the archways over arcades, and a row of karyatid creatures holds up the old theatre. I pass a music shop (this was the home of Bach), a bistro and a funeral parlour with a surprising range of offerings available, the sign says, 'day and night': burial, cremation, burial-at-sea and anonymous burials are listed, as well as 'transport of coffins'. A dog walks purpose-fully along the pavement and somewhere, I think, a person is lost. Its high-headed confidence makes me smile. A man in a tobacconist's window sees me and smiles back.

The building is still there, its vastness covering the block and ending in the round corner where the entry is. When I reach it, I see that the citizens' committee's museum still exists, and it's open. Inside me a small stretched thing dissolves with relief. I go up the stone stairs. The entry to the exhibition is on the left, and to the Leipzig branch of the Stasi File Authority on the right. Nothing much has changed. I walk down the corridor past the workroom with the girly calendar, and the cell with its tiny window and bed, to the museum office. There are signs requesting donations for funds to keep the place running.

Frau Hollitzer's not here today, but yes, her young colleague tells me, she still works with the *Bürgerkomitee*. I ask him about the new museum in town, and he shrugs and says something about the incompatibility of funding and autonomy. They had tried to negotiate with the federal authorities about having just one museum of divided Germany in Leipzig, and one run by easterners, but it hadn't worked. This museum has been left a smaller, shabbier outfit than the other, but for all that, it's more authentic: here, in this building where people were held and interrogated, and where, upstairs, their stolen biographies were filed away. I spend some time in the rooms, seeing the piles of file-pulp in one, the moustaches and wigs and glue in another, and the smell sample jars in a third. For me, this is where it all began. I buy a couple of books from the young man and leave. Outside it is hot; since morning the trees have deepened their green, and are making darker shadows. I have nothing more to do here but wander back to the station.

I walk through a small park where people are eating lunch on benches. The air is quiet apart from birdsong and the soughing of trams, and a rolling sound behind me getting louder. I turn and two boys on skateboards are coming towards me, fast. Before I can decide which edge of the path to keep to, they separate around me in graceful formation, one on each side, then join up again. I watch them glide out of the park. They perform the same manoeuvre on a girl in a phone booth. She keeps talking as she leans out of the box to see them skate on.

When I am near the phone I find myself looking at the girl. She's wearing a white midriff top and jeans, and chewing gum as she chats. I can't hear what she's saying, but she's completely absorbed in it, leaning one heel on her knee into the booth. She is probably sixteen, which means she was six years old when the Wall fell. She wouldn't remember a time without telephone boxes.

Before I know why I am stopped here, she sees me and nods to let me know she won't be much longer. I'm relieved for a moment to have found a purpose. But I'm stuck now. When she hangs up she waves and walks to her bicycle. I move to the booth. Sixteen, I think, sixteen was when she got on a train from here for Berlin and climbed the Wall. That's all I think, but I open my address book at her number and dial.

'Hello?'

'Miriam, Miriam, it's Anna Funder here. I'm—'

'Anna! Where are you calling from? Are you back in Berlin?'

'I'm—I'm actually in Leipzig,' I say. 'I thought of you, and thought I'd just call to say hi while I'm here. I didn't know if you still had the same number. I've been in Nuremberg, and I'm on my way back to Berlin. I just—'

'I'll come and get you,' she says. 'Where are you?'

'Near the station, I think.'

'OK. I'll be at the side entrance in ten minutes.'

I see her come towards me. She is dressed entirely in white: loose pants and a flowing top. She is my height, though finely built; when she hugs me I feel the wing-bones of her shoulder blades beneath my hands. She lifts her sunglasses and her eyes are the same blue. But the lines in her face are much more deeply drawn.

'I've moved house since you were last here,' she explains. We drive over cobbled streets from the station, under elms and plane trees and tram wires.

Miriam's is a corner building, beautifully restored. Hand-painted flowers curl up the walls of the grand stairway, and at the back a discreet steel-and-glass lift takes us up. Once more, her apartment is on the top level. The living room straddles the corner and all the windows are open. I move to the sill. Across the street there's another fine building with a glass atrium on its roof, and behind it a field of grass and trees, stretching as far as I can see.

'That's the Leipzig heath,' she says behind me. 'It's lovely for a walk. We can go there later, if you like. The Leipzig zoo is there too, which is worth a look.'

'What's that smell?' I ask.

'It could be the big cat enclosure,' she chuckles.

'No, it's sweet.'

'Oh, that's the acacias.' She joins me at the window and points to the top of the glorious trees right below us. Cream flowers dangle in bunches like grapes. 'It's a beautiful perfume, isn't it?' she says. 'More beautiful, at any rate, than the lions.' She laughs and touches my arm.

Miriam makes tea and we sit to talk. She doesn't seem surprised by my arrival, or not as surprised as I am to find myself with her. It is as if she always expected us to see one another again, almost like friends. What are a few missed phone calls between friends?

The scented air moves gently around us. The apartment has a parquetry floor, pale walls and a new kitchen at one end of this room. The adjoining room is a large space covered with a deep chalk-coloured carpet. It is lined with books and plants and there's a computer in the corner, the screensaver on clouds. Everything is white and light and comfortable.

I tell Miriam about my travels, about Stasi men and Julia's schoolgirl ordeal, about kidnappings and babies left on the wrong side of the Wall, about Renft and Professor Mushroom. I tell her I've just come from Nuremberg where I spoke with the puzzle women, who turned out to be men as well; a few dozen people doing something that will take a very long time. I find I can't say, 'Three hundred and seventy-five years.'

'Everything in this place,' she says, 'takes a very long time.' We are sitting at a glass-topped cane table. Miriam slips her sandals off and rests her feet on its supports. Her hair is still cropped short, but it is now dyed, a deep chestnut-brown. She wears the same small round eyeglasses and smiles the same kind and sudden smile, the shadows between her teeth overdefined by nicotine. 'A very…long…time,' she says again, lighting a cigarette. A breeze comes through, pushing her clothes against skin, revealing again for an instant how slight she is underneath—something I forget because of her magnificent voice.

Miriam works at a public radio station. Recently, she was asked to make a program on *Ostalgie* parties—where if you show an East German ID you get in for free, everyone calls one another 'Comrade' and the beer is only DM 1.30.

She says, 'Things like this feed into a crazy nostalgia for the GDR—as if it had been a harmless welfare state that looked after people's needs. Most of the people at these parties are too young to remember the GDR anyway. They are just looking for something to yearn for.'

Some of the men running the radio station are former Stasi informers, or, in one case, a former Stasi employee. This shocks me, but Miriam shrugs. 'The old cadre are back in power,' she says. She knows that one of them used to pass on listeners' letters of complaint and comments to the Stasi, and he knows she knows. 'He can't look at me,' she says. When she declined to make the *Ostalgie* program, he said to her, 'You know what your problem is? Your problem is you don't identify with the culture of the station.' Miriam rolls her eyes at the ridiculousness of the former Stasi man recycling Stasi threats, substituting 'station' for 'nation'. The program was made by someone else and broadcast anyway, feeding into the creeping nostalgia that, here, takes the place of a sense of belonging.

The put-put of Vespa motorbikes reaches us from below. The sound makes me think of beachy places, although we are landlocked deep in central Europe. I ask her what Charlie was like.

'Well,' she says, 'I haven't sorted all my pictures yet—they are still in that old suitcase.' She gets up and goes into her bedroom. I understand perfectly the impulse not to file him away under plastic in an album, or in a frame. And, suddenly, it is clear to me why the new museum was so irritating. Things have been put behind glass, but they are not yet over.

Miriam shows me a couple of old black and white photographs, and a Kodachrome colour snap like those from my childhood. I get a shock. 'This is you?' I ask. The photograph is of a young couple seated at a table. I recognise him from the last time: clear-faced, square-jawed Charlie. He's wearing a top hat but no shirt, larking around. I would not have recognised Miriam. The girl is exquisite, extraordinarily beautiful. She is thin and smooth-skinned, with a chiselled face and a breathtaking smile. She is utterly natural, but she could have come out of any magazine, then or now. 'That was after our wedding,' Miriam says. 'We went and had lunch.' I remember the torn photo. I'm glad she has let herself remain in existence in this one.

There's another picture of the two of them, she with her arms around him, looking at the camera. She is an apparition, a naughty angel caught flying over the Wall, put in a cage, and then let out, here with her beloved. In the third, a younger Miriam stares solemnly at the camera from under a fringe. She looks about twelve.

'That one was just when I got out of prison,' she says. 'My grandmother made me that dress.'

'But you look so young,' I say.

'I was, I guess,' she says. 'I was seventeen and a half.' I look at her. She has no vanity, she has expected no reaction to the beauty in the pictures. The sun slants in, painting half her face golden. I would never have seen this girl in her.

'There's this too,' she says. 'I thought of it last time you were here, and I found it afterwards.' She passes me a piece of paper folded into quarters. 'I don't think I'd looked through that stuff since Charlie died, actually.' She breathes in. 'It was hard for me to dig up.' The page is yellow with age and slightly torn. On one side there are rows of handwriting in pencil crossed out and started again, on the back a clean version. 'It's a poem of Charlie's,' she says.

'Can I make a copy?'

'Please, just take it,' she says, 'Send it back to me sometime.'

'What was he like?' I ask again.

She flicks a lighter for flame, and leans back in her chair. 'Well, he was a sensitive person,' she says. 'He was quite reserved—he noticed things. He had a good sense of humour, but underneath, I'd say, he took things to heart.' She looks out the window, at the sky moving past. 'He was individualistic—and an only child. That's why it is so hard for my parents-in-law.'

Miriam gets up and collects a bowl of cherries from the kitchen. 'Our friends thought our marriage was a catastrophe!' she laughs, sitting down again. 'But for us it was ideal.'

'Why did they think that?'

'Each of us did our own thing—to a certain extent, of course! It might be that one of us would want to go to the cinema and the other wouldn't, so one would just go alone. We thought that was quite normal. Or I remember coming back from being away in Gera, and running into Charlie in the corridor. I said, "Are you coming or going?" He said, "I'm going out for a bit, see you tomorrow then."'

Voices float up from the street, single notes of human music. 'Our friends said, "But that's no sort of marriage!" For us though, it was the only way we could be. That's why it worked so well.' She spits a cherry pip into her hand. 'I think it came, at least on my side, from my experience in prison. I reacted extremely when I got out of there. I just couldn't plan ahead. I couldn't say to someone, "I'll meet you on Sunday"—I found that sort of thing an unbearable obligation.' She laughs. 'I'm sure I was hard to get on with!'

I can't imagine her being hard to get on with, but I know she is hard to pin down. And I know all of a sudden that she really is pleased to see me; that this is the continuation of a conversation begun three years ago. She got my messages and my letter and, from an impulse I now understand, did not tie herself down with a response. Having had her every move anticipated by them for so long, these days she just wants to let things unroll. And my turning up here is part of the unrolling.

'After we wrote our applications to leave, things got pretty awful,' she says. 'They began to harass us on the street—we were constantly stopped. We were followed in the car quite a lot too—they really wanted to make life unpleasant for us. Eventually, Charlie was called in to the Department of the Interior for questioning. He said he just wanted an answer to his application: yes, or no? That was the first time they locked him up. After he was released the cards started appearing in the letterbox, calling him in to Room 111 at Dimitroffstrasse.'

Dimitroffstrasse was the police building, but Charlie Weber came to know that Room 111 meant an appointment with the Stasi. The complex had an internal yard, and 'You could walk in thinking you were going to clear up an administrative quirk and suddenly find yourself in a room being interrogated by the Stasi, or even locked up on remand in a cell out the back.' Miriam pauses. 'The last time Charlie went in there, he went to his appointment in Room 111 and ended up in one of those.'

'You wanted to exhume Charlie's coffin,' I ask. 'What happened?' She unwraps a new packet of cigarettes from its plastic. Her fingers are hard-looking and blue from lack of oxygen.

'The district attorney's office here just want to cover up everything that happened then, and most of all they don't want to pursue any of the Stasi. There are a lot of reasons for this I imagine, but in part it must be because they are still working with people who were with the Stasi— they are their colleagues! The judge, for instance, who signed the warrant for Charlie's arrest that last time he went into remand is still on the bench.'

But, it seems, there has been a development. The DA has found a witness to what happened in the cells the day Charlie died: another prisoner. 'According to that person's account,' Miriam says, 'there was a commotion in Charlie's cell early in the morning. Something happened, and the guard called others who came running. Then they all left. The witness says everything was quiet until midday, when they came to bring the meal. Then the guard had to call more guards again, and voices were raised in the cell. You'd think this new evidence would give some impetus to the inquiries, but no. The DA later informed me that he'd found another former prisoner who "credibly assured" him that he heard nothing from the other cells that day. Once more, he wanted to use that as a reason to close the matter.'

Miriam has lost faith in this investigation. About a month ago, she sent the file and all the correspondence over the years directly to the Minister for Justice. 'I haven't got an answer from him yet,' she says, 'but I'm waiting.' She has an elbow on the armrest and her chin in her palm. 'And of course there are still the puzzlers,' she says. 'I know for a fact that there were lots of pieces of paper that they didn't even put in the sacks, so they haven't been gathered up and sent to Nuremberg yet. Maybe there's something about Charlie in them.'

I don't say anything for a moment. Then I ask her what she thinks happened that day in the cell.

'Charlie was stubborn. I know from when he was in custody before, that he would refuse to co-operate—to speak or to go out into the exercise pen. I think maybe he wouldn't answer them or something when they came to his cell in the morning, and they roughed him up and he hit his head against the wall. Then they probably left him in the cell and when they came back at lunchtime they found him where he'd fallen. He was most likely dead, or dying, and that's why they called in the other guards then too.'

She stubs out a cigarette, and keeps stubbing the butt.

She is probably right about what happened. But will digging him up reveal anything? Perhaps it might prove whether he died by hanging or not, but at whose hands? Or, if they cremated him as the file indicates, there will be nothing in the coffin that can tell her what happened and she will still be here, with only the frail comfort of theories.

For now, though, this terrible game of waiting keeps her suspended from her life with Charlie, still in contact. And underneath the need to know, is the need for justice. The regime may be gone, but the world cannot be set to rights until Miriam has some kind of justice. Things have been put behind glass, but it is not yet over.

We talk into the evening, and eat tomato and basil, prosciutto and melon. Miriam speaks of friends, but she has no partner in life. 'Too hard,' she says sadly, 'to explain everything.' I ask her about her family. Her mother, she says, is a social climber—'you'd think that would have been hard under socialism, but she managed to give it a go!' She laughs. Her sister is a dentist. 'You would have seen her office downstairs in this building.' I am glad her sister is close.

'And your father?'

'My father was a doctor,' she says, 'a very kind man. He died in the early '70s, relatively young.' She taps the cigarette packet on the table. 'Of lung cancer.'

'Oh.'

'But the thing about that is,' she says as she exhales, 'it doesn't take very long at all.'

Through the double doors into the next room, my eyes catch a doll's china stare—it is an old puppet in a white silky suit, hanging limbs akimbo from its crucifix of strings on the corner of a bookshelf.

Miriam asks me to stay, and insists on giving me her bed. I wake in the night and need water and air. On the way from the bathroom to the window over the heath I see her in the moonlight and stop. She is asleep on the floor of the living room, in loose white pyjamas with a blindfold across her eyes. Her neck is bent and her arms and legs are spreadeagled over a round flat cushion. She's so slender and crumpled her whole body nearly fits onto it, strings cut, in the spotlight.

In the morning Miriam takes me to the station. To my relief I find a copy shop, so I can give Charlie's poem back to her. She comes to the platform and waits till the train moves out, silent and slow. The girl opposite me lip-smacks her puppy; on the platform an older dog huffs and rearranges itself in jealousy. Then Miriam waves and walks away, straightbacked into the sunlight.

I like trains. I like their rhythm, and I like the freedom of being suspended between two places, all anxieties of purpose taken care of: for this moment I know where I am going. We are quickly outside Leipzig, moving past maize and wheat and medieval-looking water towers near each station: Lutherstadt Wittenberg, Bitterfeld, Wannsee. In one field there's a scarecrow equipped for all comers in a black motorcycle helmet; behind him a parachutist looks for touchdown. Two boys in a dinghy sit among the reeds in this vast flat sea of improbable green, fishing.

I move back from the window and the puppy finds me suddenly fascinating. It has caught the rustle of paper in my pocket. I take out Charlie's poem.

> In this land
> I have made myself sick with silence
> In this land
> I have wandered, lost
> In this land
> I hunkered down to see
> What will become of me.
> In this land
> I held myself tight
> So as not to scream.

—But I did scream, so loud
That this land howled back at me
As hideously
As it builds its houses.
In this land
I have been sown
Only my head sticks
Defiant, out of the earth
But one day it too will be mown
Making me, finally
Of this land.

I fold it and think of Charlie Weber, now of this land. And I think of Miriam, a maiden blowing smoke in her tower. Sometimes she can hear and smell them, but for now the beasts are all in their cages.

I walk home to the apartment from Rosenthaler Platz station. The park is alive, the light so bright it picks out people and their shadows in exaggerated 3-D. Sunbathers loll on the grass, some in trunks and some bare-bottomed. There are teenagers removing gum from their mouths to kiss, a sheepdog with a single forelock dyed green, an adolescent cripple in a baby pusher being taken for a stroll. People shake infants up and down to make them calm, and children spin on swings and roundabouts I never noticed were there.

Some Notes on Sources

p. 5 Historian Dr Klaus-Dietmar Henke says the 'peaceful revolution' of 1989 was 'the only successful revolution in German history. The East Germans added one of the most splendid moments to the history of our country, to the very troubled way of our nation to find and to accept individual and political freedom as the main values.' He also states that the number of files generated by the Stasi is about 'the equivalent of all records produced in German history since the middle ages'.

'Lifting the Lid on Oppression—the Stasi Files' address to the International Bar Association, 26th Biennial Conference, Berlin 1996. Dr Henke was then head of the research department at the Stasi File Authority (*Der Bundesbeauftragte für die Unterlagen des Staatssicherheitsdienstes der ehemaligen Deutschen Demokratischen Republik* aka BstU).

p. 57 For figures on KGB agents in the Soviet Union, Gestapo personnel during the Nazi regime and Stasi employees and agents, see John O. Koehler, *Stasi: The Untold Story of the East German Secret Police*, Westview Press, Boulder CO, 1999, pp. 7–8.

pp. 57–58 On Erich Mielke's life, see Jochen von Lang, *Erich Mielke: Eine deutsche Karriere*, Rohwolt, Reinbek bei Hamburg, 1993; Koehler, pp. 33–72. For Mielke's famous speech in parliament see *Der Spiegel* 46/1999 (15 November 1999), '*Wende und Ende des SED-Staates* (8)', at http://www.spiegel.de/spiegel

This speech is also available at http://ddr-im-www.de/Geschichte/1989.htm Mielke's pronouncements on traitors and execution come from the television documentary *Die Stasi-Rolle: Geschichten aus dem MfS* by Stefan Aust, Katrin Klöcke, Gunther Latsch and Georg Mascolo, Spiegel TV, 1993.

p. 61 The GDR had the highest GDP per capita in the Eastern Bloc: Alexandra Ritchie, *Faust's Metropolis: A History of Berlin*, Carroll & Graf Publishers Inc., New York, 1998, p. 755.

The Russian publication *Sputnik*, for example, was banned by the GDR authorities in November 1988: *Informationen zur politischen Bildung*, 1, Quartal, 1996, '*Der Weg zur Einheit: Deutschland seit Mitte der Achtziger Jahre*', p. 15.

p. 62 The Stasi File Authority's report on Stasi preparations for the incarceration of citizens on 'Day X' is *Vorbereitung auf den Tag X—Die Geplanten
Isolierungslager des MfS*' by Thomas Auerbach and Wolf-Dieter Sailer, BstU,
1995.

p. 64 Honecker's words were, '*Den Sozialismus in seinem Lauf, wie man bei
uns zu sagen pflegt, hält weder Ochs noch Esel auf,*' Erfurt, 14 August 1989,
and again in his address to the parliament on 6 October 1989, the GDR's
fortieth anniversary: see '1989–40 Jahre DDR' at http://ddr-im-
www.de/Geschichte/1989.htm

See the same site for Gorbachev's famous admonishment. For Honecker's
order to 'nip the counter-revolutionaries in the bud' see *Der Spiegel* 40/1999
(4 October 1999), '*Wende und Ende des SED-Staates* (2)' at
http://www.spiegel.de/spiegel/0,1518,44895,00.html

For the Stasi taking notes on the protesters' cries against them, see *Der
Spiegel* 46/1999 (15 November 1999), '*Wende und Ende des SED-Staates* (8)',
at http://www.spiegel.de/druckversion/0,1588,52264,00.html

p. 65 Günter Schabowski's press conference speech of 9 November 1989
featured in the TV documentary *Die Stasi-Rolle: Geschichten aus dem MfS*,
Spiegel TV, 1993. The same program also has Stasi border guard Herr
Jäger admitting that passports were to be stamped in such a way as to refuse
certain people re-entry. Schabowski's speech is available at '1989–40 Jahre
DDR' at http://ddr-im-www.de/Geschichte/1989.htm

p. 69 On the numbers of Stasi informers participating in the *Runden Tisch*
negotiations, see *Der Spiegel* 49/1999 (6 December 1999), '*Wende und
Ende des SED-Staates* (11)' at http://www.spiegel.de/druckversion/
0,1588,52264,00.html

p. 84 Frau Neubert of the *Bürgerbüro e.V. Verein zur Aufarbeitung von
Folgeschäden der SED-Diktatur* told me of porn and ticking-package deliv-
eries; the Neuberts' car's brake leads had been cut; the writer Jürgen Fuchs
told the puppy story, and his daughter was detained after school. For the
threatened acid attack on the border guard, see Koehler, p. 29. Koehler also
quotes Manfred Kittlaus, director of Berlin's Government Crimes
Investigation Unit, calling the associations of former Communist
functionaries a 'classic form of organized crime', p. 30.

In 1998 a federal government parliamentary inquiry found that, in the weeks of the fall of the SED regime in 1989, somewhere between three and ten billion westmarks disappeared. See reference to *Untersuchungsausschuss 'DDR-Vermögen'* at *Der Spiegel* 50/1999 (14 December 1999), '*Wende und Ende des SED-Staates* (12)' at http://www.spiegel.de/druckversion/0,1588,52264,00.html

p. 100 Although most people were able to watch western television, the western signal could not penetrate a geographically inaccessible area that included Dresden. The region came to be known as the '*Tal der Ahnungslosen*', the Valley of the Clueless.

p. 119 Surveys conducted in the immediate postwar years showed that the Hitler period of German history (1933–45) was assessed positively by about 40 per cent of the German population: '*Umfrage des Instituts für Demoskopie Allensbach* 1951', in Alfred Grosser, *Die Bonner Demokratie: Deutschland von draußen gesehen*, Rauch, Düsseldorf 1960, p. 22.

In a 1971 survey of the German people, the majority still held that Nazism was a good idea, which had gone wrong in its implementation: Max Kaase, '*Demokratische Einstellungen in der Bundesrepublik Deutschland*' in Rudolf Wildenmann (ed.), *Sozialwissenschaftliches Jahrbuch für Politik*, vol. 2, Olzog, Munich, 1971, p. 325.

pp. 130–31 For Karl-Eduard von Schnitzler's own account of his life, see *Meine Schlösser oder Wie ich mein Vaterland fand*, Verlag Neues Leben, Berlin, 1989. For more of his views see *Provokation*, Edition Nautilus, Hamburg, 1993.

p. 191 The Stasi File Authority's report on the use of radiation against 'oppositional' elements is its *Bericht zum Projekt: Einsatz von Röntgenstrahlen und radioaktiven Stoffen durch das MfS gegen Oppositionelle—Fiktion oder Realität?'* by the Projektgruppe Strahlen: Bernd Eisenfeld (Leiter), Thomas Auerbach, Gudrun Weber and Dr Sebastian Pflugbeil. Published by BstU, 2000.

p. 200 I later found instructions to operatives on ways of crippling 'oppositional' people, which gave more detail than Herr Bock's little lecture. It comes from the Directive 'Perceptions' ('*Richtlinien, Stichpunkt Wahrnehmung*'). It aims:

To develop apathy (in the subject)…to achieve a situation in which his conflicts, whether of a social, personal, career, health or political kind are irresolvable…to give rise to fears in him…to develop/create disappointments…to restrict his talents or capabilities…to reduce his capacity to act and…to harness dissentions and contradictions around him for that purpose…

On 18 January 1989—long before anyone could foresee the October demonstrations of that year—the state issued a further refined Directive called 'Zersetzungsmassnahmen'. The German word Zersetzung is harsh, and has no direct English equivalent. Zersetzung, as a concept, involves the annihilation of the inner self. The Directive recommended these methods:

[the] targetted spreading of rumours about particular persons with the aid of anonymous and pseudo-anonymous letters…making compromising situations for them by creating confusion over the facts…[and] the engendering of hysterical and depressive behaviours in the target persons.

See Jürgen Fuchs, *Unter Nutzung der Angst* 2/1994, published by the BstU, and '*Politisch-operatives Zusammenwirken und aktive Maßnahmen*' in *Bearbeiten–Zersetzten–Liquidieren Analysen und Berichte* 3/93 of the BstU, pp. 13–24. For the Stasi's own definitions see also *Das Wörterbuch der Staatssicherheit: Definitionen des MfS zur 'politisch-operativen Arbeit'*, Siegfried Suckut (ed.), Christoph Links Verlag, Berlin, 1996.

p. 227 None of the torturers at Hohenschönhausen has been brought to justice. See Ritchie, p. 877.

pp. 237 and 242 Articles on Herr Bohnsack include *Der Spiegel* 29/1991 pp. 32–34 (in which Bohnsack confirms that West German politicians' votes were bought by the Stasi), and *Der Spiegel* 30/1991, pp. 57–58. On disinformation see also *Der Spiegel* 49/1991, pp. 127–30. Despite the Stasi vote-buying, Brandt's term as chancellor was short-lived. Two years later Brandt fell when it was revealed that one of his closest advisers, Günter Guillaume, was one of Wolf's agents.

Acknowledgments

My first debt of thanks is to the people who told me about their lives, most of all Miriam Weber, whose story was the impetus for finding the others. I am grateful too, to the people who spoke with me but whose stories are not in this book, in particular Herr Wolfgang Schellenberg, whose life deserves a book of its own.

I am indebted to many other people I spoke with in Germany. Frau Hollitzer at the *Museum in der Runden Ecke* in Leipzig was generous with her time and hospitality. The staff at the Federal Authority for the Files of the Former GDR (*Der Bundesbeauftragte für die Unterlagen des Staatssicherheitsdienstes der ehemaligen DDR*), in particular Regina Schild, Dr Klaus-Dietmar Henke, Thomas Auerbach, Roger Engelmann, Jens Gieseke and Bernd Eisenfeld were most helpful with their information and, sometimes, their own experiences. Frau Neubert at the *Bürgerbüro e.V. Verein zur Aufarbeitung von Folgeschäden der SED-Diktatur* provided invaluable insights, as did her colleague Uwe Bastian. Martin Gutzeit, the *Berliner Landesbeauftragte für die Stasi Unterlagen*, was helpful, as were staff at the *Antistalinistische Aktion Berlin—Normannenstraße e.V (ASTAK)*, the *Bürgerkomitee '15 Januar' e.V. zur Aufarbeitung der Stasi-Vergangenheit*, and the *Forschungs-und Gedenkstätte Normannenstraße, Berlin*. My thanks too, to Professor Manfred Görtemaker of the University of Potsdam.

This book would not have been written without the extraordinarily generous support at its inception of members of the Australian German Association. I thank the AGA for the award of the Educational Development Fellowship 1995, and most particularly its members BMW (Australia) Ltd, Dresdner Bank AG, Mercedes Benz (Australia) Pty Ltd and Deutsche Bank Group in Australia. I thank also Mr Andrew Grummet for his facilitation and friendship.

My heartfelt thanks to the Australia Centre, Potsdam, where I was writer-in-residence over 1996–97. Dr Ditta Bartels in Australia and Ruth Bader and Rico Janke in Potsdam provided invaluable encouragement and administrative support while the real work began.

I am grateful for the Felix Meyer Creative Writing Award, and a New Work grant from Arts Victoria which bought me time to write. A fellowship at Varuna—The Writers' House and the support there of Peter Bishop were terrific.

I thank the Australian Society of Authors and John Tranter for their assistance through the Mentorship Program. I am much indebted to Marion Campbell of the University of Melbourne for her insights and wisdom. I thank also Jenny Lee, whose early reading came at a crucial time and Gudruna Papak of the Goethe Institute, Sydney.

My great friends in Berlin provided a much needed sense of normal life while I explored Stasiland: Annette and Gerhard Pomp, Charlotte Smith and Markus Ickstadt, Harald and Marianne Meinhold, Lorenz and Monika Prell and Rainer Merkel. My father John and my late mother Kate were enormously supportive. I am especially grateful to my publisher Michael Heyward, whose unstinting enthusiasm kickstarted me many times whilst I was writing, and whose editing is magnificent. Most of all I am indebted to Craig Allchin, my constant inspiration, who asked all the right questions, without ever questioning whether this was worth four years of our lives.